Informal Labor, Formal Politics, and Dignified Discontent in India

Since the 1980s, the world's governments have decreased state welfare and increased the number of unprotected "informal" or "precarious" workers. As a result, more and more workers do not receive secure wages or benefits from either employers or the state. What are these workers doing to improve their livelihoods? *Informal Labor, Formal Politics, and Dignified Discontent in India* offers a fresh and provocative look into the alternative social movements informal workers in India are launching. It also offers a unique analysis of the conditions under which these movements succeed or fail. Drawing from 300 interviews with informal workers, government officials, and union leaders, Rina Agarwala argues that Indian informal workers are using their power as voters to demand welfare benefits (such as education, housing, and healthcare) from the state, rather than demanding traditional work benefits (such as minimum wages and job security) from employers. In addition, they are organizing at the neighborhood level, rather than on the shop floor, and appealing to "citizenship," rather than labor rights. Agarwala concludes that movements are most successful when operating under parties that compete for mass votes and support economic liberalization (even populist parties) and are least successful when operating under non-competitive electoral contexts (even those tied to communist parties).

Rina Agarwala is an assistant professor of sociology at Johns Hopkins University. She holds a BA in economics and government from Cornell University, an MPP in political and economic development from the Harvard Kennedy School of Government, and a PhD in sociology from Princeton University. Agarwala is the co-editor of *Whatever Happened to Class? Reflections from South Asia* (2008). She has published articles on informal work and gender in *International Labor Journal, Political Science, Research in the Sociology of Work, Theory and Society, Annals of the American Academy of Political and Social Science, Critical Asian Studies, Social Forces,* and *Indian Journal of Labour Economics.* She has worked on international development and gender issues at the United Nations Development Program in China, the Self-Employed Women's Association in India, and Women's World Banking in New York.

Cambridge Studies in Contentious Politics

Editors

Rina Agarwala, *Informal Labor, Formal Politics, and Dignified Discontent in India*

Ronald Aminzade et al., *Silence and Voice in the Study of Contentious Politics*

Javier Auyero, *Routine Politics and Violence in Argentina: The Gray Zone of State Power*

Clifford Bob, *The Marketing of Rebellion: Insurgents, Media, and International Activism*

Charles Brockett, *Political Movements and Violence in Central America*

Valerie Bunce and Sharon Wolchik, *Defeating Authoritarian Leaders in Postcommunist Countries*

Christian Davenport, *Media Bias, Perspective, and State Repression*

Gerald F. Davis, Doug McAdam, W. Richard Scott, and Mayer N. Zald, *Social Movements and Organization Theory*

Donatella della Porta, *Clandestine Political Violence*

Todd A. Eisenstadt, *Politics, Identity, and Mexico's Indigenous Rights Movements*

Daniel Q. Gillion, *The Political Power of Protest: Minority Activism and Shifts in Public Policy*

Jack A. Goldstone, editor, *States, Parties, and Social Movements*

Tamara Kay, *NAFTA and the Politics of Labor Transnationalism*

Joseph Luders, *The Civil Rights Movement and the Logic of Social Change*

Continued after the Index

Informal Labor, Formal Politics, and Dignified Discontent in India

RINA AGARWALA

Johns Hopkins University

CAMBRIDGE
UNIVERSITY PRESS

CAMBRIDGE UNIVERSITY PRESS
Cambridge, New York, Melbourne, Madrid, Cape Town,
Singapore, São Paulo, Delhi, Mexico City

Cambridge University Press
32 Avenue of the Americas, New York, NY 10013-2473, USA

www.cambridge.org
Information on this title: www.cambridge.org/9781107663084

© Rina Agarwala 2013

First published 2013

Printed in the United States of America

A catalog record for this publication is available from the British Library.

Library of Congress Cataloging in Publication data
Agarwala, Rina, 1973–
Informal Labor, Formal Politics, and dignified discontent in India / by Rina Agarwala.
    p. cm.
Includes bibliographical references and index.
ISBN 978-1-107-02572-1 (hbk.) – ISBN 978-1-107-66308-4 (pbk.)
 1. Labor movement – India. 2. Unskilled labor – Labor unions – India. 3. Informal
sector (Economics) – India. I. Title.
HD8686.5.A637   2013
331–dc23   2012038077

ISBN 978-1-107-02572-1 Hardback
ISBN 978-1-107-66308-4 Paperback

For Carsten

Contents

List of Tables

List of Figures

Acknowledgments

Nearly twenty years ago, I arrived on the front door of a women's organization in India, eager to begin my internship and oblivious to the journey I was about to begin. As I entered the office, a tall woman from Kutch stared at me with a perplexed expression. "Have you come for the march for rag pickers?" she asked. In response to my blank stare, she squatted next to me to explain the march and other activities of the trade union for informal women workers that I had unknowingly come to work for. The lesson continued for the next year and a half, where the members and staff of the Self-Employed Women's Association (SEWA) patiently introduced me to the informal workers I had seen but never noticed, challenged me to think beyond the development models I had so diligently learned, and inspired me to realize the voices that women workers were asserting every day. I thank SEWA, and especially Elaben, Reemaben, and Ushaben, for changing my worldview forever.

For changing the way I think, I owe my deepest thanks to Marta Tienda, Alejandro Portes, Atul Kohli, and Patricia Fernandez-Kelly. They set a standard for mentoring that will always inspire me. Marta Tienda introduced me to the discipline of sociology and was unrelenting in forcing me to write clearly. She repeatedly went beyond the call of duty – reading each of my countless drafts, humbling me with her red pen, and encouraging me when I was exhausted. Meeting with Alejandro Portes was like tapping into a river of new ideas that he generously shared with me. His insights on Latin American workers have been instrumental in shaping my thoughts on Indian workers. Atul Kohli's lectures provided me with an exemplar for passing on knowledge, and his questions pushed me to dispose of jargon and address the difficult substance of an issue. His work has been a constant guide for me as I try to understand the messy logic of India. Patricia Fernandez-Kelly's brilliance, irreverent sense of humor, and empathetic instruction sustained me through this project. Her rich fieldwork on women workers taught me the art of listening during an interview.

My move to Johns Hopkins University flooded me with new ideas, questions, and approaches to development – all of which considerably improved the manuscript. More importantly, this rich learning environment was coupled with the most supportive group of colleagues I could have wished for. I am especially grateful for the constant encouragement and feedback I received from Karl Alexander, Joel Andreas, Giovanni Arrighi, Mimi Keck, Kellee Tsai, and the students of the Seminar for Global Social Change. I owe a special debt to Beverly Silver for helping me navigate the world of teaching, for her suggestions on my manuscript, and for her book that gave me the confidence to assert my findings, not as an exception, but as part of a global and historical trend in labor organization.

To Ron Herring, I owe thanks for our countless conversations on class and the future of India's marginalized populations. His non-hierarchical style and his infinite enthusiasm for new ideas are traits that few can claim in academia. I thank him for going through each line of the manuscript with me, for being such an inspiring colleague, and for being such a gracious friend. Sharit Bhowmik taught me much of what I know about Mumbai and its informal workers. I remain in awe of his commitment to straddle the (unfortunately) large and difficult gap between scholarship and public service, and I thank him for our long discussions over multiple bowls of wonton soup. Jeemol Uni and Anup Karan kindly worked with me to analyze the National Sample Survey, sharing with me their expertise and answering each of my tiring questions. I thank Patrick Heller for his infectious passion for counter movements and his excitement over my findings. His work on labor in Kerala taught me how to examine India's democracy from below. I owe a special thanks to Irfan Nooruddin for his unending encouragement, for reading the entire manuscript, and for generously giving me his time and suggestions. Without him, this project would have remained an unpublished manuscript.

Several people read portions of the manuscript and provided me with invaluable ideas at all stages. For this, I thank David Bensman, Fred Block, Miguel Centeno, Vivek Chibber, Jennifer Chun, Dan Clawson, Mary Ann Clawson, Dorothy Sue Cobble, Peter Evans, Leela Fernandes, John Harriss, Devesh Kapur, Ching Kwan Lee, Ruth Milkman, Andrew Schrank,

Gay Seidman, Sid Tarrow, Emmanuel Teitlebaum. I thank Ken Bolton for his help with the index, and I thank my editors, Mark R. Beissinger, Deborah Yashar, and especially Lew Bateman, for their support of the project and their guidance in the process. I thank Nina Agopian, Jessie Albee, Anuj Antony, Wayne Appleton, Elana Broch, Linda Burkhardt, Nancy Cannuli, Elaine Keith, Diane Sacke, Barbara Sutton, Terri Thomas, Judith Tilton, and Shaun Vigil for making IT, library resources, financing, book production, last-minute FedEx packages, and grant applications somehow feel manageable.

Not one word of this project could have been written without the labor, expertise, and creativity of the 140 women workers and the hundreds of government officials, union leaders, and activists whom I interviewed. I thank them for their knowledge, their patience, and especially their time. My fieldwork would not have been possible without the generosity of those who housed me, fed me, and opened their Rolodexes to me. A million thanks to Asha Chatterjee, Sumit Choudhary, Aruti Dasgupta, Sudha and Lalit Deshpande, Rohini Hensman, Renana Jabhvala, K.P. Kannan, Arun Kumar, Lakshmi Lingam, Debashish Mazumdar, Kavita Panjabi, Krishna Raj, Alakh Sharma, R. N. Sharma, Praveen Sinha, and Shyam Sundar. The research for this project was made possible by the Fulbright-Hays Foundation, the Sasakawa Foundation, and the Center for Migration and Development at Princeton University.

I owe my deepest gratitude to my parents, Ramgopal and Bimala Agarwala, for inspiring me with their dedication to hard work and their openness to new ideas. Thank you for teaching me that the means are at least as important as the end. More than anyone, however, this work is for Carsten Stendevad, who reminded me in a tiny, crowded Italian restaurant in Boston about the genius and power of politics. For moving four times across three continents so I could undertake this project; for relieving my stress with so much deep laughter that I could keep going with this project; for providing sweet incentives, computer help, and child care relief so I could complete this project; and, most of all, for staying by my side from the beginning to the end of this very long project, I am forever indebted to him.

Abbreviations

ADMK	All India Anna Dravida Munnetra Kazhagam
AITUC	All-India Trade Union Congress (CPI-affiliated)
BJP	Bharatiya Janata Party
CII	Confederation of Indian Industry
CITU	Congress of Indian Trade Unions (CPM-affiliated)
CPI	Communist Party of India
CPI(ML)	Communist Party of India (Marxist-Leninist)
CPM	Communist Party of India (Marxist)
CSW	College of Social Work
DK	Dravidar Kazhagam
DMK	Dravida Munnetra Kazhagam
GDP	gross domestic product
GOI	Government of India
ICLS	International Conference of Labor Statisticians
ILO	International Labour Organisation
ILP	Independent Labor Party
INC	Indian National Congress Party
INTUC	Indian National Trade Union Congress (Congress-affiliated)
KMC	Kolkata Municipal Corporation
LPF	Labour Progressive Federation (DMK-affiliated)
MLA	Member of Legislative Assembly (state government)
MP	Member of Parliament (national government)
NCP	National Congress Party
NMPS	Nirman Mazdoor Panchayat Sangam
NSS	National Sample Survey on Employment and Unemployment

NSSO   National Sample Survey Organisation
OBC   Other Backward Caste
PWP   Peasants Workers Party
RPI   Republican Party of India
SDP   state domestic product
SEWA   Self-Employed Women's Association
TMC   All India Trinamool Congress
TMKTPS   Tamil Maanila Kattida Thozilalar Panchayat Sangham
UF   United Front
WBIDC   West Bengal Industrial Development Corporation

I

Introduction

Informal Labor and Formal Politics

"Listen sister, we are just poor folks who work to put bread in our stomachs. We can't do anything else. If we ask for more, we lose our jobs. If we lose our jobs, we will die," explained Basama, an unskilled construction worker in Mumbai, India.[1] Basama's statement reflects a sentiment of vulnerability often heard among poor, informal workers in India. Informal workers produce legal goods and services but engage in operations that are not legally registered. Therefore, unlike formal workers, informal workers are not officially recognized by their employers, and they are not regulated or protected by fiscal, health, and labor laws.[2] Although some work at home or in unregistered subcontractors' workshops, others operate openly on the employers' site or in a public space (such as the street). As a result of receiving decreased protection, informal workers usually work in harsh conditions, with low levels of technology and capital, and no labor rights.

In most developing countries, informal labor – labor that is not formally protected – represents the majority of the labor force. In India, informal workers comprise *93 percent* of the labor force or 82 percent

---

[1] Interview, August 21, 2003.

[2] In recent years, these workers have been variously called "informal," "precarious," "casual," "nonstandard," "Post-Fordist," and "flexible." I use the term "informal" throughout the book. This definition of informal workers was first offered by Portes et al. (1989). It has been accepted in much of the literature on informal work; see Cross (1998), De Soto (1989), and Portes (1994). To operationalize this definition, I use the worker-based definition of informal work that was endorsed by the 17th International Conference of Labor Statisticians (ICLS) in 2003 and used by the National Sample Survey of Employment and Unemployment (NSS) in India in 1999–2000.

of the nonagricultural labor force.[3] This informal labor is central to contemporary economies. Informal workers construct buildings, build roads, grow and sell fruits and vegetables, clean homes and streets, sew clothes, weld car parts, and make shoes – not to mention the boxes they come in. Despite early predictions of its eventual demise, informal labor has remained entrenched in poor countries and has even shown signs of growing in rich countries. During the 1980s and 1990s, the world's informal labor force grew as economies expanded and global employment increased by 30 percent (ILO 2008). After the 2008 financial crisis shook the world, the need for low-cost, flexible informal labor was predicted to increase even more (Koba 2009). The undeniable fact is that unregulated, unprotected workers can no longer be viewed as marginal or temporary. Yet, despite their significance, informal workers continue to live in dire poverty and insecurity.

To improve the lives of informal workers, activists from the left and the right have long tried to bring them into the fold of formal labor regulations. In India, and elsewhere, this approach has run into several obstacles and has largely failed. First, Indian labor regulations, which are relatively progressive, protect only a minority of the working class, and capital continues to avoid labor regulations by hiring workers informally. Second, even the minimal prospects for formalization have waned since the Indian government launched its version of neoliberal reforms in 1991.[4] At the center of the reforms has been an ideological shift from a belief in state regulation of capital, labor, and citizen welfare toward a new ideal of unfettered markets. This ideological shift has been credited for both the breathtaking speed of India's economic growth in recent years and its increasing income inequities across and within states (Deaton 2003; Deaton and Kozel 2005; Dreze and Sen 2002).

---

[3] Forty percent of the Indian population, or 400 million people, are in the labor force. More than 37 percent of the labor force, approximately 141 million people, work in the nonagricultural sectors. I calculated these figures based on the 1999–2000 NSS. For greater detail on the Indian labor force and the count of informal workers, see Appendix II.

[4] I define "neoliberalism" as the set of policies designed to decrease government control regimes and facilitate investment and capital formation. Such policies include delicensing industries, de-reserving the public sector, easing competition controls, decreasing import tariffs, deregulating interest rates, easing the interstate movement of goods, opening capital markets, and pulling back on protective labor laws. In India, these policies (known as "liberalization reforms") have been accompanied by privatization to decrease bureaucratic controls over industry. Although liberalization does not necessarily entail privatization, in India the two are often implemented together. Therefore, I use the terms "liberalization" and "privatization" interchangeably throughout this book.

The reduced tariffs, trade restrictions, and industry license quotas resulting from this ideological shift have flooded some Indian homes with Korean cell phones, Italian furniture, and Chinese toys. English-speaking youth are finding jobs servicing the back-office functions of American and European companies, and Indian business owners are freer to expand their operations and initiate new investments without many of the earlier constraints of government control. At the same time, this ideological shift has enabled the Indian state to overtly absolve employers of responsibility toward labor, which has increased workers' insecurities and poverty levels. In 2005, the World Bank, an important influence on Indian government policies, noted that the ability to "hire and fire" workers is a major factor in increasing a country's attractiveness to domestic and foreign investors and that "countries with rigid labor laws [protecting workers] tended to have higher unemployment rates" (Andrews 2005).[5]

Labor activists in India routinely decry this ideological shift away from state regulation of capital as a direct assault on the socialist experiment and the labor–capital compromise of social democracies, both of which tried to establish a working class that is formally protected against employer exploitation. Indeed the popularity and relevance of left-wing ideologies and institutions have plummeted in recent years. As Debashish Roy, a union organizer and senior member of the Communist Party of India-Marxist (CPM), explained as he served me a cup of tea with no milk, "This is red tea. It's the tea of our Party. Whether you are a peasant or a senior government official, our Party members drink the same tea. But people don't want red tea anymore. They are looking for cappuccinos."[6] Drawing from a familiar model of twentieth-century factory-based labor movements, Indian labor activists assume that unregulated workers are unable to organize because the structures of informal production prohibit organization. They, therefore, view the 1991 reforms that empowered footloose capital and overtly sanctioned informal work by cutting back on state labor regulations as a final nail in the labor movement's coffin. Throughout labor activists' discussions, informal workers appear just as Basama described herself – as commodified victims, shorn of agency.

Given this context, it is puzzling to see the recent evidence of informal workers' ability to organize and attain welfare benefits from the Indian

---

[5] The two exceptions that the World Bank makes for government interference in labor policy are for child labor and gender discrimination.

[6] Interview, November 18, 2003.

state. In 1999, the government's National Sample Survey on Employment and Unemployment (NSS) counted informal workers for the first time. In 2002, one of the two goals of the *Report of the Second National Commission on Labour* was to create new legislation that would ensure a minimum level of protection to all workers, even those in the informal economy (NCL 2002). In December 2008, the Indian Parliament passed the Unorganized Sector Workers' Social Security Bill to provide informal workers with life, disability, health, and old age insurance. Although informal and formal labor organizations have strongly criticized the bill, it stands as a testament to the government's perceived need to provide for informal workers' welfare. The largest program under this bill, the *Rashtriya Swasthya Bima Yojana* or "National Health Insurance Program" (RSBY) began in April 2008 (Range 2008; Special Correspondent 2008). Under this program, informal workers receive a credit card, known as a "smart card," of US$750 per family per year to cover medical expenses at participating hospitals.[7] The program is overseen by the national Ministry of Labor, implemented by state-level Labor Departments and participating insurance companies, and funded by the state and informal workers. The national government pays 75 percent of the premium, the state governments pay 25 percent of the premium and all administrative costs, and informal workers pay $0.75 per year as a registration or renewal fee. By December 4, 2008, nearly 950,000 cards had been issued in 46 districts, and by 2012, 60 million workers were expected to be covered.[8] At the state and industry levels, we find a plethora of additional laws designed to provide protections for informal workers. If the Indian state is pulling back on labor protections and the Indian labor movement is feeling increasingly neutered, who pushed forth these policies? And how effective are they?

This book addresses these questions by examining informal workers' organizing strategies and their interactions with the state in India. An increasingly neoliberal state, a rapidly growing economy, increasing inequalities, and an expanding informal workforce are typical features of many developing countries and even some industrialized countries today. In India, however, these features exist against a backdrop of a long history of social movements and a vibrant (albeit imperfect) democracy. This history, coupled with the Indian state's increasing attention to

---

[7] A family is defined as the head of the household, one spouse, and three dependents.
[8] Progress Report from Directorate of Labor Welfare, Ministry of Labor, Government of India.

informal workers, makes it an ideal location to study how the transformative forces of the contemporary era are being played out on the ground through informal workers' movements. Contrary to much of the labor and development literature, a portion of India's informal workers have been organizing since the 1980s.[9] Therefore, we can examine how recent alterations in state attention to labor have affected these movements by comparing the period before and after 1991. To begin this study, I ask: What collective action strategies do informal workers use? From where do they draw their structural power? Do their strategies vary across industry or state?

Underlying these questions is a recognition of the complex, dynamic relations tying state politics and structures to the origins, expressions, and outcomes of social movements (Goldstone 2003; Piven and Cloward 1979; Tarrow 1988; Tilly 1984; Yashar 2005). After all, it is these relations that shape the material realities of workers. In recent years, scholars and labor activists have highlighted one slice of the relationship between states and workers' movements when they argue that states' attempts to create unfettered markets have undermined workers' movements by eclipsing labor regulations and expanding the informal labor force. What is left unanswered is how workers respond to state actions. Just as states affect workers' lives, workers redefine the meaning of the state through social movements that resist or reify alterations in government rules and structures of production. After enduring the shock of reduced government intervention and increased market flexibility, how have informal workers responded?

Students of politics will not be surprised to find that there are virtually no data available on this vulnerable population in general or on their politics in particular. Therefore, to examine informal workers' movements, I conducted two sets of in-depth interviews (for greater detail, see Appendix III). For the first set, I interviewed 200 government officials, employers, and labor leaders of formal and informal workers' organizations. The second set of interviews consists of 140 interviews with informal workers who are members of an informal workers' organization. Drawing from these interviews, I offer in Chapter 2 an empirical snapshot of how the world's most vulnerable workers have reacted both to the failure of earlier state policies to protect them and to contemporary development prescriptions that avoid protecting them.

---

[9] See the later discussion for more detail on the scholarly literature that claims informal workers are unable to organize.

Informal workers in India have launched an innovative labor movement that has nudged an increasingly neoliberal state to open potentially new paths to state-based welfare. In the process, they are *re-embedding* the workers who have long been left out of labor's attempts to fight market commodification. A key trait of a capitalist market economy is that it treats human labor as a commodity. If there is no demand for labor power, there is no return to the living bearer of labor power and, therefore, no claim on subsistence. For nearly a century, formal workers have organized as a class to hold capital responsible for this dilemma. Capital, however, has always found ways to absolve itself of this responsibility. In India, the state has begun to overtly aid capital in this endeavor. In this context, it is striking that informal workers in India are now finding alternative ways to decommodify labor through the state. Even more striking is how they are addressing the dilemma of their work by claiming their rights as citizens. Ignoring these efforts undermines our understanding of contemporary efforts for social justice and the dynamic nature of labor movements.

However, questions remain about the effectiveness of informal workers' alternative movements. The first part of this book indicates that informal workers' movement strategies are consistent across states and industries, but that their effectiveness varies by state. Therefore, in the second part of the book, I compare three Indian states operating under three different political party contexts and ask: Under what state conditions do informal workers' collective action strategies succeed or fail? Underlying this question is the long-held understanding that social movement structures have a limited capacity to determine movement success in the absence of a conducive political and economic framework. In other words, even for those operating outside state jurisdiction, state structures matter. In Chapters 3–5, I examine the varying patterns of political mediation that result from different regime characteristics in India to explain why in some cases informal workers' new strategies have led to state-supported benefits for workers, despite neoliberal policy prescriptions to reduce welfare spending, and why in other cases they have failed. These findings lend important insights into the limits and contradictions of informal workers' movements, the future role of left-wing parties, the potential role of competitive populism, and the impact of contemporary class politics on the welfare state.

This study begins with the premise that informal workers *can* organize. This premise turns deeply entrenched assumptions about informal workers' inability to organize on their head. So let us begin by engaging this difference and exploring exactly how to study the massive, diverse group of organized informal workers.

1.1 INFORMAL LABOR ORGANIZES IN UNIQUE CLASSES

Scholars from the left and right of the political spectrum have long argued that the structural conditions of informal employment preclude informal workers from organizing as a class. Informality disperses the site of production through home-based work, complicates employer–employee relationships through complex subcontracting arrangements, atomizes labor relationships by eliminating the daily shop-floor gathering of workers, and undermines workers' bargaining power by denying them legally protected job security. Scholars of Latin American and African labor movements have shown how informal workers rely on local networks, rather than class-based organizations, to ensure their survival (Grasmuck and Espinal 2000; Gugler 1991; Macharia 1997). In India, the assumption that informal workers cannot organize is so entrenched that scholars and government officials use the terms "informal workers" and "unorganized workers" interchangeably.[10] Only once informal workers join the formal economy, so the argument goes, will they become an integral part of the workforce; only then can they use the power of their class location to join the labor struggle (Bairoch 1973; Geertz 1963).

This view of informal workers has dominated the labor movement literature since the early 1900s, thereby limiting most studies of class movements to urban formal workers and, in some cases, rural peasants (Herring and Hart 1977). In recent years, scholars have highlighted governments in traditional welfare states (Castells 1997; Held et al. 1999; Tilly 1995) and in formerly socialist states (Lee 1999; Stark and Bruszt 1998) that are promoting the informal economy as an alternative safety net for workers who no longer receive benefits from a welfare state or formal employer. Underlying this scholarship is an assertion that such trends are undermining labor's power, because informal workers are unable to make class-based demands. As Mihail Arandarenko (2001: 169) writes, "The informal economy is undoubtedly the most important buffer against class opposition in Serbia."

---

[10] As a result, scholars of India's informal economy focus almost exclusively on its definition and measurement. See Joshi (2000), Kulshreshta and Singh (1999), Kundu and Sharma (2001), Mahadevia (1998), Oberai and Chadha (2001), Sundaram (2001), Unni (1999), and Unni and Rani (2000).

Despite their continuing prevalence, these arguments about informal workers' inability to organize do not fit well with the empirical reality. According to the Indian government's own NSS, 8 percent of India's informal workers in the nonagricultural sectors *are unionized.*[11] In other words, more than 9 million informal workers participate in a union despite their informal working conditions. Although few scholars have examined these movements in depth, a handful of case studies in India indicate that informal workers' organizing activities are improving informal working conditions (Carr et al. 1996; Chowdhury 2003; Sanyal 1991; Sharma and Antony 2001). Recent scholarship on immigrant and service workers in the United States and South Korea and on street vendors in Mexico City indicates that Indian informal workers are not unique in their ability to organize as a class distinct from formal workers (Chun 2009; Cross 1998; Fine 2006; Gordon 2007; Milkman 2006).

Part of the discrepancy between scholarly claims about informal workers' inability to organize and the empirical reality of budding informal workers' organizations can be attributed to a problematic assumption ingrained in the labor and development literature – namely that informal workers are either an expression of a so-called reserve army of labor or a part of a precapitalist entity who perform odd jobs while waiting to be formally employed (for a more detailed discussion, see Agarwala 2009). In both cases, informal workers are viewed as invisible to the state and temporarily operating on the margins of the labor–capital relationship. To facilitate the transition to modernity, for example, development scholars in the 1950s and 1960s urged newly independent governments to accelerate migration, with the expectation that surplus informal, rural labor would move to cities in search of greater wealth, which in turn would spur economic growth in the formal economy and automatically eradicate the unprotected informal economy (Lewis 1954). Because informal workers (who remained vaguely defined as a remnant of a feudal, rural past) were not viewed as part of the modern proletariat, they were not counted in national labor force surveys, considered in state labor policies, or analyzed as a potential political class.

In reality, however, informal workers have long been and continue to be an integral part of capital–labor relations and a necessary subsidy

---

[11] I calculated these figures using the 1999–2000 NSS. They include only regular workers (in the case of formal workers) and regular and casual workers (in the case of informal workers). These figures change only marginally when self-employed own-account workers and employers are included (along with regular and casual workers).

to the growth of modern, formal capitalist economies. As Vladimir Lenin (1939) and Rosa Luxemburg (1951) showed, class struggles that increased European wages in the early 1900s forced European capitalists and workers to rely on their colonies' cheap, flexible, informal workforce for raw materials and for low-end manufactured goods and services. Imperialist power structures ensured that informal workers absorbed the formal economy's costs of low-end production and labor reproduction by not receiving benefits or minimum wages and by working in their homes to eliminate the need for overhead. By providing a cheap, flexible alternative, informal labor helps capital and states constrain the expansion of the more costly, formally protected working class (Bromley and Gerry 1979; De Janvry and Garramon 1977; Moser 1978). Lisa Peattie (1987) has detailed how formally regulated firms in Colombia's shoe-making industries rely on unregulated, unprotected subcontractors in Bogota to increase firm profits. In India, formal economy accumulation in most manufacturing industries relies on social networks to supply cheap informal labor that absorbs the costs of production and labor reproduction, even at the expense of efficiency (Breman 2003). Because market expansion in most developing countries still relies on external demand or a small, elite domestic consumer base, the mass labor force does not serve as the target consumer (Portes and Walton 1981). Wages can thus be pushed downward with little effect on consumption.

Recognizing informal workers' strategic role in the processes of accumulation helps explain the continued growth of the informal workforce even under modern capitalism. In addition, it helps us examine the diverse sources of bargaining power that informal workers can potentially tap. Informal workers hold unique and permanent positions in the class structure, and they therefore have unique interests and interactions with formal workers, capital, and the state. Whether or not they use their power in the class structure to organize, increase their visibility, and improve their well-being as a class is an empirical question. Evidence from India, South Korea, Mexico, and the United States suggests that some informal workers are organizing as a class (Carr et al. 1996; Chun 2009; Cross 1998; Fine 2006; Gordon 2007; Milkman 2006). In India, however, questions remain about the details of these efforts. Exactly how are these informal workers translating their position in the class structure into action?

To identify informal workers' unique interests and the sources of power they are using to organize, we must disaggregate the mass informal workforce by structure and type of work. The focus of my interviews reflects this disaggregation. First, I limited my interviews to poor women to expose the strategies that the most marginalized groups are using to express their political voices; women represent more than 90 percent of the lowest rung of contract workers in the two industries that I examine.[12] Second, I interviewed one class of informal workers – namely, contract workers. Third, I interviewed informal workers across two industries: tobacco and construction. Let us now examine these subdivisions in more detail.

Distinguishing Classes of Informal Workers

Informal workers can be disaggregated into two sub-classes – self-employed workers (such as street vendors, domestic servants, or owners of small, unregistered retail shops or restaurants) and contract workers who work through subcontractors for informal or formal enterprises (such as branded clothing, car, and shoe factories). Although both groups are unregulated and unprotected under state labor laws, they occupy distinct spaces in the class structure and are therefore likely to give rise to distinct political organizations. Before turning to the central focus of this book – contract workers – let me briefly discuss self-employed informal workers.

In recent years, self-employed workers (also called "petty bourgeoisie" or "micro-entrepreneurs") have received substantial attention from development scholars. In India, they comprise 45 percent of the nonagricultural labor force and 54 percent of the nonagricultural informal labor force (see Table 1). Keith Hart is often credited for first highlighting this subset of informal workers. Using data from Accra, Hart (1973) argued that urban migrants who could not attain jobs in the formal economy were not starving in unemployment lines; rather, they were creating new opportunities to generate income through self-employment. Following Hart, the International Labor Organization (ILO) incorporated urban self-employed workers into its poverty-alleviation programs in the 1970s (Mazumdar 1976; Sethuraman 1976; Weeks 1975). In the late 1980s, self-employed workers reemerged in the development literature as a beacon of hope for modern, unfettered markets. Using data on Lima's housing, transport, and petty trade sectors, Hernando De Soto (1989) argued that self-employment is a creative way for the majority of workers to use their entrepreneurial skills by acting outside the government's mercantilist

---

[12] Although I included some male informal workers, they were not randomly selected and served as a rough comparison to my 140 interviews with women workers.

TABLE 1: *Informal Workers and Class Structure in India*

Class	% of India's Non-agricultural Labor Force	% of India's Non-agricultural Informal Labor Force
Dominant Classes (capitalists, executives, professionals)	18	–
Petty Bourgeoisie/Micro-Entrepreneurs/Self-Employed	45	54
Formal Proletariat (skilled and unskilled workers with wage contracts)	18	–
Informal Proletariat (casual/contract workers and regular workers in informal enterprises)	38	46

Note: The structure of this table is drawn from Portes and Hoffman (2002). I calculated the figures using the NSS (1999–2000), which enables informal workers only to be calculated in the nonagricultural sectors and cannot distinguish between professionals in the dominant classes and those in the formal proletariat. Therefore, actual percentages for dominant classes and formal proletariat are a fraction of 18 (which is the total percentage of the two groups). This table has been reproduced from Agarwala 2006.

regulations. Government regulations, De Soto argued, were suboptimal because they enabled self-serving Latin America bureaucracies to secure support by disempowering the masses and granting privileges to ruling classes. During the late 1990s, the World Bank reversed its exclusive focus on formal workers and joined the ILO in promoting self-employment as a beneficial option for those squeezed out of the labor market (ILO 1999; World Bank 1995, 2003).

Although self-employed workers have been recognized in the development literature and in development projects, their relations with the state, capital, and the formal proletariat continue to be ignored. Scholars assume these workers cannot organize as a class, because they operate outside state regulation and they are their own employers. As Portes and Hoffman (2002: 45) note, however, in developing countries the self-employed class performs the critical "function of linking the modern capitalist economy, led by the three dominant classes, with the mass of informal workers at the bottom. Micro-entrepreneurs [or self-employed workers] organize labor to produce low-cost goods and services for consumers and low-cost inputs subcontracted by large firms." In other words, self-employed workers do hold structural power vis-à-vis capital and states that support capital accumulation. In India, the Self-Employed Women's Association has been organizing self-employed workers since the 1970s, and in recent years street vendors and domestic workers have begun to use their power in the class structure to organize alternative movements (Rose 1993). Jonathan Cross (1998) has analyzed how street vendors in Mexico City have organized. Although it is beyond the scope of this study to analyze self-employed workers' movements, it is essential to recognize from these studies that they do exist and can organize. Their organizations, however, are distinct from those of formal workers and of the second category of informal workers – contract workers.

Contract workers (also called "casual workers" or "informal proletariat") are located at the bottom of the class structure and include contract and regular workers in informal enterprises, as well as contract workers in formal enterprises. Unlike the self-employed, contract workers have received little attention in the development and labor literatures. Although scholars have disaggregated the two mega-classes of the "proletariat" and "bourgeoisie" to better fit a modern reality that includes the self-employed, middle classes, and even "contradictory classes," contract workers have not yet been incorporated into our understanding of social classes. It is this class of informal proletariats that forms the focus of this book. For the remainder of this book, I refer to this group as "informal workers." In India, this class makes up 38 percent of the nonagricultural labor force and 46 percent of the nonagricultural informal labor force (see Table 1). These workers lack control of capital and the means of production, and they are predominantly unskilled. That these workers lack formal contracts with an employer renders their work insecure and unregulated by definition; their insecurity makes them vulnerable to exploitation by the other groups that sit above them in the class structure. Because these workers have less access to economic or political resources than other classes, they have unique life chances and sources of power.

So how do contract workers draw from their vulnerable class position to exert power? Clearly, the move from structure to action is not an easy one and has been the subject of much discussion in sociology (Katznelson and Zolberg 1986; Wright 1997). As Jon Elster (1985: 326) writes, class membership predicts and explains endowment-necessitated behavior (i.e., that linked to tangible property, intangible skills, cultural traits); such behavior is shaped by what people *have* to do, not merely what they *want* to do. This conceptualization works best at the extremes: those who need to sell their labor power are driven to shared behaviors just as those who need to maximize return on capital squeeze labor to retain ownership of capital. In most cases, however, interests are difficult to deduce from structure (for more on this issue, see Herring and Agarwala 2006). Class interests are elusive because they are mediated by interpretive processes and are filtered through messy cognitive screens. For example, workers within the same structural location vary on whether they join a union or not. Moreover, political opportunity structures affect how interests are recognized, evaluated, given meaning, ordered, and rendered actionable. Women workers, for example, may interpret their interests in terms of class, gender, or a larger community defined by "the poor" depending on government programs that may be available at the time.

Examining why some informal workers make the leap to translate their position in the class structure into political organization and others do not is very important. However, it is a difficult question to address because of the practical challenge of locating and accessing unorganized informal workers. Therefore, this study focuses on the informal contract workers who are *already organized* to examine the variations in their strategies (within informal workers and compared to formal workers) and in their effectiveness. As with any examination of labor organization, my findings on organizational strategy may affect policies for all informal workers, but they are generalizable only to the subset of organized informal workers. Let us now turn to a further disaggregation of contract workers by industry.

Varying Industry Characteristics

Because unionization among informal workers (and formal workers) in India has been sector- or industry-based, it is possible that variations in the effectiveness of informal workers' movements could be related to industry factors, such as the circumstances of work and the socioeconomic characteristics of the labor force. To examine the potential effects of industry, I interviewed organized informal workers in two industries: (1) construction and (2) bidi. Bidi is a local Indian cigarette made of a rolled leaf and roasted tobacco; bidi workers comprise 98 percent of workers in the Indian tobacco industry (NSSO 2001a). The bidi and construction industries operate through private employers and long chains of informal subcontractors, and both are exploitative. Table 2 illustrates the salient characteristics of both industries' workers. Laws in several states protect the mass informal workforce in these two industries. According to official figures, more than 15 million people are informally employed in the construction industry, of whom nearly 3 percent are unionized;

TABLE 2: *Construction and Tobacco Industries in India*

	Construction	Manufacturing	Tobacco/Bidi[a]
Total Workforce	15,662,264	39,075,839	3,742,979
Employment[b] (% of nonagricultural workforce)	11	28	3
Informal Workers[c] (% of industry workers)	98	89	93
Share of total GDP[d] (%, 2003–04)	5	17	-
Female[e] (% of industry workers)	12	29	81
Illiteracy[f] (% of industry workers)	42	31	57
Union Density Among Informal Workers[g]	2.7		6.6

[a] Tobacco is a subsector of manufacturing.
[b, c, e, f, g] Calculated using the NSS 1999–2000. Union density is trade union members as a percentage of informal employees.
[d] From GOI (2004).

in tobacco, nearly 4 million people are informally employed, of whom nearly 7 percent are unionized (NSSO 2001a). These facts present an interesting puzzle: if informal workers are unable to organize, what do the subset of unionized informal workers do and how did the protective laws come into place?

Examining the nature of informal workers' unions in these two industries enables us to control for several important differences. First, the construction industry is among the fastest growing industries in India. In 2000, it employed more than 11 percent of India's nonagricultural labor force (NSSO 2001a).[13] During the last forty-five years, construction has accounted for 40 percent of India's development investment (NICMAR 1998). The tobacco/bidi industry, in contrast, is known in India as a "sunset" or a declining industry, especially in urban India. Since India agreed to sign the Framework Convention on Tobacco Control, launched by the World Health Organization (WHO) in 2003, much of India's bidi

---

[13] According to the International Standard of Industrial Classification of All Economic Activities (ISIC), the construction industry includes enterprises engaged in physical work on new or existing buildings; civil, mechanical, and electrical engineering works by contractors; public agencies; on-site fabrication of construction components; and some aspects of off-site manufacturing of construction materials and components (UNIDO 1968).

production has shifted to rural areas to reduce costs by avoiding municipal taxes and high fees.[14]

In addition to differences in growth structures, these industries differ in terms of type of work. Some construction workers have fixed homes in the city and wait at a local street corner for contractors to pick them up to do short-term jobs (lasting from a few hours to a few weeks). Others migrate to the city with a contractor to live on the construction site in temporary shacks constructed from materials that the builder provides (remaining on a site from a few months to several years). Bidi workers have fixed homes; those in urban areas congregate in particular slums. Because of the lack of mechanization involved in bidi-making, workers cut and roll bidis in their homes and take the finished product to a local contractor to get paid on a piece-rate basis. Contractors pass the finished products through subcontractors to a registered, retail manufacturing company. Only then do bidis get labeled, packaged, and sold to distributors.

Drawing from my interviews with 140 women contract workers in the bidi and construction industries, I describe in Chapter 2 how informal contract workers are organizing to meet their unique interests within the constraints of their unprotected work structure. I find that, rather than fighting flexible production structures and demanding traditional work benefits (such as minimum wages and job security) from employers, *Indian informal workers are using their power as voters to demand state responsibility for their social consumption or reproductive needs (such as education, housing, and health care)*. To operationalize their demands, informal workers have launched innovative tripartite institutions called "welfare boards" that are implemented by state governments and receive funds from employers, states, and informal workers. Welfare boards provide material benefits (such as health care clinics and education scholarships) to informal workers, who by definition are not entitled to such benefits from employers. As a result of this strategy, informal workers are ironically pulling the state into playing an even more central role in their daily lives than it has traditionally done for members of formal workers' movements. These strategies are consistent across industry and state.

---

[14] Despite promises to reduce production and consumption, India produced 13.5 percent of the world's manufactured cigarettes and bidi, and 7 percent of the world's unmanufactured tobacco products in 1992. In 2004, India was the world's third largest tobacco-growing country (CDC 2004).

In addition to tapping material benefits, informal workers are politicizing their unique class and gender identities to offer politicians a distinct vote bloc. Like formal workers, informal workers are addressing the sources of their exploitation in the class hierarchy. To join a welfare board, unions must certify workers' informal work status, and the boards' benefits are tailored to the specific needs of informal workers. Unlike formal workers, informal workers are forging a class identity that connects them to the state through their social consumption needs and forces the state to recognize their work, *even* in the absence of formal employer recognition. This recognition is provided through a state-certified informal workers' identity card. Given the mass numbers of informal workers, informal workers are using a rhetoric of *citizenship* – rather than labor – rights to frame their interests and attract the attention of elected state politicians. To mobilize the dispersed, unprotected workforce without disrupting production, informal workers are organizing at the neighborhood level, rather than on the shop floor.

Informal workers are also addressing issues arising from the intersection of class and gender. Women workers have long fought to expose the interdependence between reproductive and productive work, as well as between the private and public spheres. Informal work, which has until recently been considered "feminine," sits at these very intersections. Therefore, women are active members and leaders in informal workers' movements. Their efforts are finally establishing state responsibility for informal workers' reproductive work burdens and state recognition for productive work in the private sphere. Such support has empowered informal women workers to challenge patriarchal assumptions in the private and public spheres. Informal workers' efforts to present themselves as an organized vote bloc, distinct from formal labor and other identity groups, began in the 1980s. The informal worker identity does not necessarily alter individuals' other identity-based political allegiances. The workers I interviewed repeatedly reminded me that they simultaneously politicize multiple identities across multiple parties. In all cases, they offer *the promise* of identity-based votes in return for benefits salient to a specific group (such as caste-based employment quotas, education scholarships for children of informal workers, micro-loans for women). In the absence of costly monitoring mechanisms of actual voting patterns, influential organizational leaders have used targeted benefits and public pledges to fortify the promise of votes that informal workers offer politicians.

By using the power of their votes to reinstate their social rights, informal workers are framing themselves as citizens in a state that is constitutionally and electorally obligated to them. In the process they are "making" a new class, adding this new class to the panoply of claim-makers in India's democracy, and redrawing a contemporary version of a welfare state. Although informal workers in India have not yet secured guaranteed social rights for all citizens (as did formal workers in Western Europe), they have secured some welfare benefits and a voice for a previously invisible labor force in parts of India.

The next question then becomes: How feasible is it for informal workers to hold the state responsible in the era of neoliberalism?

1.2 INFORMAL LABOR ORGANIZES EVEN UNDER NEOLIBERALISM

In recent years, labor scholars have argued that the eclipsing role of the state in capital and labor regulation is a direct affront to labor organization. Indeed policies that eliminate industry subsidies, trade and quota regulations, and license restrictions have pushed firms to be more competitive. In the interest of lowering costs to ensure global competitiveness, states are strengthening capital's power relative to labor by sanctioning the spatial dispersion of capital. The increased ease with which investment and information can travel has enabled transnational corporations to avoid complying with existing labor laws designed to ensure that employers protect their employees (Castells 1997; Held et al. 1999; Sassen 1994; Teeple 2000; Tilly 1995). In addition, states are enabling firms to retrench their formal workers and hire more informal workers instead (Harvey 1990; Hyman 1992; Zolberg 1995). By definition, the state does not require employers to extend benefits, minimum wages, or job security to informal workers. In India, for example, the government has enabled firms to open company doors to new hires of unprotected, informal workers by initiating "voluntary retirement packages" in the manufacturing industry, in which formal workers are urged to retire early in return for a minor amount of compensation (Bhowmik and More 2001; Breman 2002; Uchikawa 2002).

In addition to pulling back on traditional labor protection policies, governments are privatizing their public welfare services as part of the expansion of market economies. As a result, the state's role is shifting to that of a facilitator, and workers who are no longer covered under state labor laws are also not receiving universal public service provisions for citizens. Between 1985 and 1990, government expenditure (as a percentage of gross domestic product [GDP]) in developing countries dropped for the first time since 1960 (World Bank 1997, 2003). Among the poorest countries, public expenditure on education as a percentage of gross national product (GNP) declined by nearly 30 percent between 1980 and 1997 (UNESCO 2000).

Scholars of Western Europe and the United States (Tilly 1995; Western 1995), Eastern Europe (Crowley and Ost 2001; Przeworski 1991), and the newly industrializing countries of East Asia (Deyo 1989) point to declining union density as evidence of a labor movement crisis resulting from these trends.[15] Some celebrate this trend as facilitating capital growth and undermining a class of protected workers perceived to be elitist and corrupt. For example, in response to organized workers' protests against economic reforms in France, Germany, Austria, Britain, India, and the United States in 2003, the editors of the *Economist* magazine (2003) wrote, "Do not be fooled by events in Europe this week ... Unions everywhere are in decline, and to a large extent they deserve to be." Others decry these trends for absolving employers of accountability and weakening a labor movement that is credited for ensuring minimal levels of safety, security, and fairness.

Despite the growing popularity of recent arguments that neoliberalism and globalization have weakened the labor movement, these arguments are flawed in several respects. First, although union density since the 1980s has decreased in some countries, between 1989 and 2005, union density increased by 1 percent in Brazil, 3 percent in India, 4 percent in China, 6 percent in Paraguay, and 8 percent in Singapore (ILO 2008). According to the Indian Ministry of Labor's verification of trade unions affiliated with central federations, union membership increased by 50 percent between 1996 and 2002 (GOI 1996b, 2008c). The reasons for this increase deserve to be systematically examined elsewhere, but for now, these numbers caution against sweeping claims of a global labor movement crisis.

Second, although in rich countries, such as the United States, Spain, and Italy, there has indeed been a striking and unpredicted growth in the informal workforce, the increase in developing countries has been minimal (Benton 1990; Kundu and Sharma 2001; Portes and Schauffler 1993). As already noted, informal workers have *always* comprised a majority of the labor force in developing economies. In the Latin American countries that experienced economic growth during the 1980s, the share of urban informal workers remained entrenched at 30 percent in 1980 and 31 percent in 1990 (Portes and Schauffler 1993). In India, the share

---

[15] Union density is defined as trade union members as a percentage of total paid employees.

of total informal workers is estimated to have grown from 91 to 93 percent between 1993 and 1999 (Kundu and Sharma 2001). This increase is, of course, significant because it represents millions of households, and it has been felt most dramatically in the public sector. As the Indian government sells its enterprises to the private sector, employees who earlier enjoyed the benefits of regulated employment are being fired and rehired (or replaced) on an informal basis.[16] Between 1991 and 2001, informal employment in the public sector increased by 2 percent, while formal employment decreased by the same amount (NSSO 2001a). Because public-sector employment in India covers only 6 percent of the labor force, however, we cannot accurately claim that the 1991 reforms have altered the lives of the majority of the workforce.

If neoliberal policies have not led to a uniform drop in union density or a mass increase in the informal labor force, why are labor scholars and activists so fixated on the impact of these policies on labor organization? In India, I argue that *the significance of liberalization policies lies in their impact on political actors and relations of power.* As Mr. Roy noted through his tea analogy, the pressures that globalization and liberalization policies have placed on labor protections have undermined the conventional collective bargaining structures of Indian labor parties and unions.

Since the early 1900s, when industrialization altered the structures of production, Indian workers have aspired to Walt Rostow's (1960) famous vision for a "final stage" of development, in which poor countries would follow rich ones in building governments that formally protect workers through legal contracts that hold employers responsible for their employees. Playing an instrumental role in the independence movement, Indian labor unions and left-wing parties demanded that the Indian constitution offer employee protection and benefits. Unlike in Brazil, Chile, South Africa, Singapore, and South Korea, where the state repressed radical workers' movements, the Indian state passed progressive legislation to benefit workers. Although the Indian state provides few direct welfare provisions to all citizens, it does guarantee a legal contract binding employers and employees to one another. In return for labor, employers are held responsible for their workers' wages, job security, and some

---

[16] Although privatization is not necessarily a part of liberalization, India's attempts to ease control regimes since 1991 (i.e., liberalization) have been tied to getting government bureaucracy out of the economy (i.e., disinvestment of government ownership and subsequent selling to the private sector).

health and retirement benefits. In addition to these collective benefits, the subset of workers who are covered under these laws receive individual recognition by the government and capital. Negotiations for workplace benefits, such as minimum wages, holidays, bonuses, and job security, take place between employers and formal workers organized into registered unions. When disputes arise between employers and unions, the Indian government serves as a mediator in compulsory arbitration procedures and enforces the legal contract, all the while promising to balance workers' livelihood interests against employers' demands for maximum accumulation and minimum social disruption.

These efforts to attain employer accountability for employees have faced mixed success. As evidenced by India's large informal workforce, they only cover a minority of the workforce. Although proponents of these conventional bargaining structures acknowledge that employers hire informal workers, they assume that informal workers cannot make demands, because employers are not required to recognize them under a legal work contract. Moreover, as in many Latin American countries, the minority of Indian formal workers who are covered have failed to institutionalize a secure class compromise at the state level, because the Indian state ultimately chose to partner with capital over labor.[17] Despite these deficiencies, however, Indian labor activists remain fiercely committed to this conventional labor movement strategy. Their victories, which were most pronounced in the public sector, are viewed as testimonies to India being a "modern" society. Indeed, India's official union density ranks higher than in the United States and is almost equal to that in Japan, Australia, and Germany.[18] These conventional labor movement strategies have also given rise to an empowered identity among formal workers, in which workers view themselves as being in perpetual conflict with the employer and a potential beneficiary of the state.

Today the Indian state is overtly pulling away from its earlier commitments to hold employers accountable for their employees. By freeing private market forces from state intervention, the reforms are expected

---

[17] For a detailed account of Indian labor's inability to hold the state responsible for labor in the post-independence period, see Chibber (2003).

[18] There is no internationally agreed-on definition of "paid employees." ILO calculations for India are based on India's Statistical Abstract. When using the 1999–2000 NSS data, union density figures are slightly lower. If "paid employees" are defined as formal wage workers and informal casual workers, union density in India is 10 percent among all workers and 21 percent among nonagricultural workers. If the self-employed are included (along with formal wage workers and informal casual workers), union density is 6.5 percent for all workers and 15 percent for nonagricultural workers.

to facilitate greater capital investment and employment. The type of new employment that has emerged to date, however, is not protected. Despite the increased publicity of workers' rapidly degrading work conditions, the Indian state's policy rhetoric on unprotected work has become favorable. The notion that workers ought to be entitled to benefits from employers and the state is decreasing in popularity, and informal workers, who are virtually invisible on national-level labor force surveys and are not eligible for state-supported labor benefits, are replacing formally protected workers as the *ideal* worker. In 1969, for example, the Indian government strove to ensure "secure, state-protected employment for all Indian men" (NCL 1969), but by 2002, it acknowledged and even promoted the growth of informal employment as the primary source of future work for all Indians (NCL 2002). Recent government reports also stress the important role that informal labor plays in ensuring the success of India's economic reforms (Ahluwalia 2002; Gupta 2002; NCL 2002).

By the end of the 1990s, the informal economy was estimated to account for more than 60 percent of GDP (Kulshreshtha and Singh 1999). In 2004, the central government appointed a high-profile committee, called the National Commission for Enterprises in the Unorganized Sector, to examine ways to increase productivity in the informal economy. In other words, the Indian state and capital are searching for new ways to resist workers' protective institutions and, once again, to change structures of production to protect capital over labor. After the conventional labor movement model collapses, then what will emerge to take its place? Where is Indian labor headed?

To answer these questions, we must make several changes in how we analyze the impact of neoliberal policies on workers' movements. First, rather than focusing on the declining state involvement in labor protection, we gain greater analytical leverage by examining the changing qualitative nature of the nexus between state and society. The state is still (and always will be) implicated in capitalist production relations, because it sets the ground rules within which business and labor contend for state attention. Moreover, the state must remain active in reproducing labor as a "fictitious commodity" for market economies (Block 2001). Therefore, rather than focusing on whether or not the state is involved in labor relations, we must examine how the state's role in labor relations is changing in the current global economy.

Second, we must recognize the diverse nature of state–labor relations over time and space. Recent arguments on the weakening relationship between state and labor in the current era assume a globally homogeneous past in which workers built institutions that forced the state to look out for labor. The reality, however, was much more complicated. The United States was notorious for being less active in containing capital than were the French and British states. As Kim Voss (1993: 204) writes, "The US state set the rules for industrial conflict and then generally absented itself from labor disputes"; when the United States did intervene, it was almost always against the strikers. Even in Sweden, the social democratic exemplar, Peter Swenson (2002) shows how the state designed welfare policies to benefit both labor and capital by limiting the realm in which capital had to compete for high-skilled labor.[19] The diverse models of state–labor relations reiterate the socially specific and historically contingent constraints under which organized labor and states have always intervened in industrial relations (Block and Evans 2005). Incorporating these insights into analyses of current state–labor relations is essential to unearthing new constellations of relations between state, labor, and capital that are being pushed by labor and states to accommodate today's economic pressures.

Finally, we must reconceive state–labor relations as being a two-way relationship. The existing literature posits that the direction of impact flows in only one direction: state actions harm labor. Yet, some scholars have demonstrated that the arrow of impact can also flow in the other direction: organized workers have played an instrumental role in reshaping state institutions. As Beverly Silver demonstrates in her study on the evolution of labor movements since 1870, labor movements have continually reinvented themselves to accommodate attempts by the state and capital to evade labor power through spatial, technological, product, and financial "fixes" (Silver 2003). Kim Voss (1993) has shown how state efforts to alter the structures of production during the 1800s in the United States and Europe not only altered the composition of the working class but also motivated the need to remake workers' movements in a way that redefined industrial relations. Charles Sabel and David Stark (1982: 440) argued that the planned economies of the Soviet Union in the 1980s, along with struggles within the party apparatus, inadvertently created "the precondition for shop-floor power" through tight labor markets; labor's increased bargaining position, in turn, helped determine state investment policy. Part of the reason for the perceived unidirectional impact from state to labor in the contemporary era can be attributed to the flawed

---

[19] As Peter Swenson (2002) argues, capital also supported these movements for compressed wages and universal, state-provided welfare policies, because they provided capital with a ceiling in labor market competition.

conceptualization of the state and of society as independent, static entities. Reconceptualizing the state and society as interdependent and dynamic entities that affect one another as they continually evolve can allow for a more accurate picture of state–labor relations.

Taking into account the qualitative, diverse, and dynamic nature of the state–capital–labor triad enables us to focus more on alternative labor movements (such as those among informal labor) that have emerged in India to address the deficiencies of conventional labor movements. Although for decades, informal workers fought to be included in labor's conventional bargaining structures, by the 1980s it became clear that the mass of informal workers would never be formalized and that informal workers had to form alternative bargaining structures to meet their unique interests and circumstances of work. The 1991 reforms have increased the salience of informal workers' alternative movements. Despite mounting pressures on formal labor, most Indian unions were slow to explore alternative strategies to the state-backed contract binding employers to employees. By the 1990s, therefore, the vast majority of India's workers faced not only a state that absolved employers of responsibility to protect their workers but also a weakened labor movement that still refused to address the unique interests of informal workers.

It is in this context that we should examine how the neoliberal reforms have affected Indian workers. The philosophical underpinnings of informal workers' movements (in which workers target the state to attain welfare benefits) are significant in that they fly against the neoliberal trend of reduced state responsibility toward workers. Informal workers' efforts may be thwarted in the contemporary era as state policies aim to decentralize structures of production, commodify labor by altering their choice set, and redefine labor to idealize unprotected informal workers. Yet state policies may also create conditions in which informal workers' movements attain social protection against market forces as they simultaneously redefine the state's role in society. This brings us to our second question: how do political conditions from above determine the varying levels of *effectiveness* among informal workers' contemporary movements?

1.3 STATES CONDITION INFORMAL LABOR MOVEMENT EFFECTIVENESS

Although Chapter 2 details how informal workers' movement strategies remain consistent across industries, as I illustrate in Chapters 3–5, their effectiveness varies by state. In some Indian states, informal workers have succeeded in ensuring their social rights in a context where the state and society have traditionally denied them the basic benefits of citizenship. In other states, they have been less successful. We must, therefore, ask how, when, and why some Indian states respond to pressures from India's most vulnerable workers, whereas others do not.

We know that most social movements have a limited capacity to be effective in the absence of a conducive political and economic framework from above. This argument has been shown to be relevant to Indian formal workers' movements. In his rich book on Mumbai's textile mill workers, Raj Chandavarkar (1994) argues that political solidarity among Mumbai's workers during the 1920s and 1930s emerged from the experience of the state as a repressive, antagonist force during industrialization, rather than from capitalist exploitation of labor. Lloyd and Suzanne Rudolph (1987: 23) call the post-independence Indian state "the most important determinant of the marginality of class politics," arguing that party fragmentation is the source of weak class compromises. Vivek Chibber (2003) argues that in the years just after independence, the Indian state enacted labor laws that undermined collective bargaining by making the state, rather than the unions, the arbiters of industrial conflict. Because informal workers' movements in India target the state, state characteristics likely condition informal workers' organizations' successes and failures. The question remains, however: Which political opportunity structures are significant for informal workers?

India's federalist legal structure provides an ideal opportunity to compare different political opportunity structures for informal workers. Although citizenship rights are managed at the national level, Indian labor laws are managed at the state level. Therefore, Indian state governments are responsible for either directly providing benefits to workers or indirectly ensuring their provision through a union or employer. States vary in how and why they interact with workers' organizations, the legislation they enact on state-level labor laws, and the level of enforcement they employ on national-level labor laws.

To identify the state characteristics that affect informal workers' movement effectiveness, I draw from my findings on informal workers' movement strategies. As I illustrate in Chapter 2, Indian informal workers attain state attention by framing themselves in two ways. First, they leverage their political power as voting citizens by asserting themselves as a mass vote bank; second, they assert their economic power by articulating themselves as key players in the state's liberalization project. On the

Economic Policy	Political Leadership	
	Pro-poor & competitive	**Not pro-poor & competitive**
Liberalizing	High Success (Tamil Nadu)	Moderate Success (Maharashtra)
Not Liberalizing	High Success (Kerala)	Low Success (West Bengal)

FIGURE 1: State theoretical framework.

basis of this, I argue in Chapters 3–5 that informal workers operating in states that engage in pro-poor competitive elections are most successful, because they can capitalize on politicians' desire for their votes to demand state-supported welfare benefits for poor, unprotected workers. Of secondary significance for informal workers' success is whether or not a state is liberalizing. Unlike the electoral context, liberalization is not necessary for the success of informal workers' movements. However, neoliberalism is prevalent, is undermining traditional collective bargaining structures, and is ironically providing informal workers with *some* political leverage. Therefore, in contexts where states are not engaging in pro-poor competitive elections but are liberalizing, informal workers experience medium levels of success in attaining state-supported benefits. In contexts where states are neither liberalizing nor competing for votes from the poor, informal workers do not have any leverage to make demands on the state and are least successful.

To examine this fourfold ideal typology, I interviewed informal workers and government officials across three city/states: Mumbai (Maharashtra), Chennai (Tamil Nadu), and Kolkata (West Bengal).[20] Figure 1 illustrates how each city/state was categorized in the typology (an explanation on Kerala is provided later). The columns represent two political party contexts – distinguishing between states where parties compete for votes from the poor versus those where they do not; the rows represent two forms of economic policy – distinguishing between states that are liberalizing versus those that are not (at least not rapidly). Tamil Nadu has been dominated by two opposing parties, All India Anna Dravida Munnetra

---

[20] The city of Madras was officially renamed "Chennai" in 1996, the city of Bombay was officially renamed "Mumbai" in 1998, and the city of Calcutta was officially renamed "Kolkata" in 1999. Although the old names are still commonly used in spoken form, I use the new, official names throughout the text for consistency.

Kazhagam (ADMK) and Dravida Munnetra Kazhagam (DMK), since the mid-1970s, and it has initiated liberalization reforms since the 1990s. To attain power, ADMK and DMK use populist measures to vie for votes from the poor. Maharashtra has embarked on a liberalization agenda, but its political leadership has been entrenched in the traditional Indian National Congress (INC) party. Since the mid-1990s, a right-wing, Hindu nationalist coalition of Shiv Sena and the Bharatiya Janata Party (BJP) has added some electoral competition, but the competing parties are dominated by middle castes, rather than class and pro-poor tendencies. Finally, West Bengal, which was dominated by CPM from 1977 to 2011, has been governed by a class-based leadership, but it has not been competitive and has resisted the nation's liberalization policies (until recently).[21]

The fourth category, pro-poor competitive parties that are not liberalizing, represents the important case of Kerala. Kerala's politics have been dominated by INC and CPM, which have competed for power through pro-poor policies and have resisted liberalization efforts. Kerala is not included in this study for two reasons. First, its experience has already been beautifully detailed elsewhere (see Heller 1999). Therefore, we can draw from the existing literature to offer Kerala as a comparative case for this study's other three states. Second, Kerala differs from this study's three states along nonstate characteristics that could have an impact on the effectiveness of workers' organizations and therefore may complicate the formal comparison.

Although Tamil Nadu, Maharashtra, and West Bengal represent the different combinations of political and economic characteristics that I wish to explore, they share similarities on nonstate characteristics that could also have an impact on the effectiveness of workers' organizations. The three state cases are not identical in nonstate-related terms, but their similarities allow us to hold nonstate characteristics relatively constant in accounting for the differences in effectiveness among workers' organizations. Moreover, because some nonstate characteristics are likely correlated with differences in economic policy and political leadership style, holding them constant helps deal with omitted variable bias. By selecting on these nonstate explanatory variables, I am unable to make assertions on their role in the effectiveness of informal workers' movements.

---

[21] For practical reasons, this study only included states with an organized informal workforce. The variation in the subset of informal workers who have already organized is sufficient to warrant an examination of effectiveness. This study cannot draw conclusions on political opportunity structures that block informal workers from organizing in the first place.

First, the effectiveness of informal workers' movements could be a function of the presence of formal workers' movements in the area. The three states examined in this study share a long labor history. Under colonial rule, the three capital cities (Mumbai, Kolkata, and Chennai) known as the "Presidencies," served as the key industrial centers and power bases of the British Empire. At the turn of the twentieth century, the three states of those capital cities became the sites of the first Indian labor movement, which was intricately tied with the Indian independence movement.[22] Eventually these states became the birthplaces of India's largest trade unions for formal workers. In 1951, when India launched its first Five-Year Plan, Mumbai (in present-day Maharashtra), Chennai (in present-day Tamil Nadu), and West Bengal represented the areas with the largest number of formal workers' unions and the largest number of registered labor strikes (GOI 1952). Today, union density among formal and informal workers is almost equal in the three states (see Table 3). Although their union densities are above the national average, they are far below the extremely high levels found in Kerala and Assam. Given this, we can be confident that differences between informal workers' effectiveness across these three states are not likely due to the presence or absence of a formal workers' movement.

Second, socioeconomic constraints could affect informal workers' ability to organize effectively. The states, and particularly the three cities, examined in this study are fairly similar in terms of socioeconomic indicators. As shown in Table 3, the Human Development Index (HDI) across the three states is similar and exceeds the national average but is lower than the extremely high case of Kerala (at 0.920).[23] The literacy rate in West Bengal is slightly lower than that of Maharashtra and Tamil Nadu. Because such a large proportion of informal workers are illiterate, especially among women, this difference is unlikely to affect the results. Moreover, if literacy was responsible for state differences in informal workers' effectiveness, we would expect to see the most success in Maharashtra. As outlined in the subsequent chapters, this is not the case.

Finally, in terms of net state domestic product per capita (NSDP), all three states are above the national average, although some differences can be seen between Maharashtra and West Bengal. Part of these

---

[22] For detailed histories of the early labor movements in these three regions, see Chandavarkar (1994), Fernandes (1997), and Gooptu (2001).

[23] The HDI is calculated as an index of per capita monthly expenditure adjusted for inequality, literacy rates and intensity of formal education, life expectancy at age 1, and infant mortality rates.

TABLE 3: *Socioeconomic Characteristics in Three States*

	Maharashtra	Tamil Nadu	West Bengal	India
Union Density (% among formal and informal workers)	8.3	8.4	8.9	6.3
Union Density (% among informal workers only)	7.9	8.8	8.9	6.3
HDI	.45	.47	.40	.38
Life Expectancy at Birth				
Males	67	67	66	64
Females	70	70	69	67
Birth Rate (per 1,000)	20	19	21	25
Infant Mortality Rate (per 1,000 births)	45	44	49	63
Death rate (per 1,000)	7	8	7	8
Population (millions)	97	62	80	1,029
Literacy Rate	76.9	73.5	68.6	64.8
NSDP/Capita (Rs.)	24,248	20,315	17,875	17,823
% of Workers in Agriculture	58.7	50.3	50.8	62.4

Note: I calculated union density using NSS 1999. Remaining statistics are drawn from GOI (2004), and HDI figures are drawn from (GOI 2001b). Rs. 50 = US$1.

differences is alleviated at the city level. As in the case of literacy, the differences in state wealth do not appear to be correlated with the differences we find in informal workers' ability to attain benefits from the state.

Historically strong labor movements, socioeconomic constraints on workers, or industry characteristics do not appear to explain the varying levels of effectiveness among organized informal workers. Rather, I find that the political and economic characteristics of state structures provide informal workers with the opportunity (or lack thereof) to put themselves on the state's agenda *as workers*. Indian informal workers' movements are most successful when operating within electoral contexts where parties must compete for mass votes from the poor, and they are less successful when operating under parties that do not need to compete through pro-poor policies, including those tied to left-wing, communist parties.

Pro-poor electoral competition gives informal workers an opportunity to *frame themselves as "the poor" and to appeal to politicians' desire to stay in power by offering their claimed access to a unified, mass vote bank.* This point is illustrated in Tamil Nadu and Kerala, where informal workers have enjoyed substantial successes. Unlike Kerala, which has been dominated by left-oriented parties, Tamil Nadu illustrates how even nonleftist, populist parties in a competitive context can provide informal workers with ideal structures for movement success. The comparison of Kerala and Tamil Nadu illustrates the primary importance of the patterns of political mediation that result from pro-poor competitive elections regardless of liberalization policies (which exist in Tamil Nadu and are absent in Kerala). In other words, liberalization alone cannot hurt informal workers' movements.

Among those operating in electoral contexts that are not pro-poor and/or competitive, however, a state's commitment to liberalization can ironically offer informal workers' movements some leverage to attain medium levels of success. Liberalization efforts from above give informal workers the opportunity to frame themselves as key pegs in the state's economic agenda of flexible production. In return for welfare benefits, informal workers offer the state industrial peace. Herein lies one of the many unintended consequences of neoliberalism.

Although some may argue that informal workers' movements could affect state economic policies and forms of leadership, this problem of reverse causality is not a factor in India. As detailed in Chapter 3, informal workers' movements emerged only after the rise of competitive populism in Tamil Nadu. These movements generally oppose liberalization efforts. Therefore, if reverse causality was a factor, we would expect to see effective movements in all states that are not liberalizing. In fact, as illustrated by West Bengal, we find no such correlation. Other commonly cited explanations for welfare benefits do not appear to fit the current scenario for informal workers in India. A correlation with economic wealth and growth, for example, would suggest that Maharashtra would provide more welfare benefits to its informal workers than Tamil Nadu does, because Maharashtra's state domestic product and growth rate exceed that of Tamil Nadu (see Chapter 5). Ideological commitment at the party level would suggest that West Bengal would provide more state benefits to informal workers than Tamil Nadu, because West Bengal's government was ruled by CPM for decades (see Chapter 4). The worker participation rate would suggest that West Bengal would be more successful than Tamil Nadu and that Maharashtra would be the least successful. Finally, Tamil Nadu's unique history of progressive caste and ethnicity-based movements would suggest material improvements for informal workers before the rise of mass-based populism. As shown in the following chapters, none of these outcomes are found to be true.

1.4 INFORMAL LABOR MOVEMENTS DIGNIFY WORKERS' DISCONTENT

This study illustrates how the deeply entrenched relationship between states and social movements is historically contingent, interactive (changes in state structures influence social movements and vice versa), and dynamic (its form and nature change across time and space). That these findings emerge from India lends important insights into how social movements in democratic contexts affect contemporary models of class politics and welfare states even in the face of the transformative changes taking place between state and labor.

As the limits of free-market ideologies and neoliberal policies become more evident the world over, scholars and political leaders are scrambling to articulate an alternative state model of development. In a larger sense, this story of informal workers' politics in India sheds light on at least one such model that is being formulated from below. Informal workers are dignifying their discontent with the limits of earlier modernization attempts to formalize all labor and with recent free-market policies to informalize all labor. They are doing so by creating new institutions and forging a new social contract between the state, informal workers, and employers. This emerging contract turns existing assumptions about the demise of contemporary workers' struggles on their head. Contrary to popular thought, informal workers are finding new ways to advance their humanity by holding the one actor that cannot escape (i.e., the state) responsible for their welfare. In return for their political support and unregulated labor, informal workers are demanding state recognition for their work and state provision for their reproductive needs. This emerging social contract bestows on informal workers a degree of social legitimacy, thereby bolstering their status as claim-makers in their society. That they are achieving legitimacy in an era of flexible labor markets warrants a rethinking of contemporary state–labor relations.

These findings also raise important questions about the limits and con-tradictions of democratic accountability in the modern era. The emerging contract between the state and informal workers does not, for example, alter the very structures that created workers' vulnerability and discontent in the first place. Rather, it enables the elected leaders of the world's largest democracy to meet social justice demands by employing populist tactics, while subsidizing capital accumulation under a veneer of liberal, free-market policies. This is a theme to which I return in the concluding chapter.

Let us now turn to our examination of informal workers' politics in India.

2

Struggling with Informality

The labor organization experience among India's informal workers since the 1980s challenges the existing labor literature, which asserts that informal workers cannot organize without an established employer, a single workplace, or a legal employment contract. Indeed, Indian informal workers have been organizing into unions and nongovernmental organizations (NGOs) since the 1970s and 80s. Of the seven organizations examined in this study, six are membership-based trade unions registered under the Trade Union Act (1926) and one is a NGO registered under the Trust and Societies Act. Whereas the construction organizations are independent of political parties, the bidi unions are affiliated with left-wing political parties. Although informal workers' unions are structured like formal workers' unions, their strategies differ from those of formal workers.

Drawing from both sets of interviews, I address my first set of research questions in this chapter. How does the informal nature of production affect workers' collective action strategies? From where do they draw their structural power? Do their strategies vary across industry or state? I argue that to accommodate their dispersed and insecure employment circumstances, informal workers have made three key changes to formal workers' struggles. These changes are consistent across industries and states, and they are significant to our understanding of workers' democratic participation in the current liberalization era. Moreover, they challenge conceptualizations of informal workers as delinked from the state (see also Agarwala 2006, 2008).

Portions of this chapter draw from Agarwala (2006, 2009).

First, informal workers' organizations target their demands to the state, not the employer. Traditionally, formal workers' movements in India held the employer (who in many cases was the state in pre-reform India) responsible for workers' well-being. They held the government responsible only for implementing labor laws, providing last resort conciliation services in industrial disputes, and passing protective legislation for certain industries. Because informal workers do not have a stable employer or the job security that backs the right to strike, informal workers prefer to hold the state responsible for their well-being, even as the state recedes from its role as an employer.

Second, to hold the state responsible, informal workers have shifted their primary demands from workers' rights at the workplace (such as minimum wages, work security, and the abolition of contract work) to welfare issues at the home (such as education scholarships; health care; social security; and subsidies for housing, funerals, and weddings). Formal workers' unions in India focus on what some scholars call "economistic" issues – wages and work security (Kothari 1989; Seidman 1994). Although informal workers do also struggle for these demands, their primary focus has shifted toward welfare issues. Welfare benefits can be distributed from the state to the workers, thereby bypassing the employer and avoiding what many workers feel is a losing battle to stop liberal reforms. Moreover, as state welfare programs diminish, workers are concerned about covering the reproduction costs of their families (who often assist in informal, home-based work). Welfare benefits ensure them minimal security at home.

Third, informal workers have defined their worker or class identity not as an antithesis to capital, but as a means to becoming a worthy citizen with basic rights. Early class literature argued that informal workers were not a part of the modern class structure, because they were not politically organized and did not work in the capitalist economy. In contrast, I find that informal workers' organizations have not only developed, but they have also provided their members with an identity that asserts their informal work as a distinct class that is a vital component of the modern economy. This class's members do not own their own means of production, they operate outside the state jurisdiction, and they build an identity that connects them to the state through their social consumption needs. This class identity provides informal workers with a degree of social legitimacy, despite their extralegal economic activities. It empowers them past their vulnerable individual status and traditional group identities (such as gender). It also gives them yet another political identity (in addition to those around ascriptive characteristics, such as caste) through which they can offer the promise of their group votes in return for group-based benefits. Finally, being a member of an organization helps workers focus and target their demands through a large, unified, and more powerful political voice.

As illustrated in the following section, these strategic alterations do not vary by industry or state. Rather, informal workers have made these alterations in both the bidi and construction industries, where structures of production have shifted from a formal to an informal one, and across the three states examined in this study. To inform Chapters 3–5, which examine the variation in effectiveness that does occur across states, first let us examine the nature of informal workers' strategies in more detail.

2.1 BUILDING A NEW CLASS STRUGGLE

The first change informal workers have made to fit the conditions of informal employment and retain their membership in a class is to target their demands to the state, rather than the employer; the second change is to make demands for welfare provision, rather than workers' rights. These strategic changes in target and demand have been accompanied by changes in the type of labor involved, the form of organization, and the tone of the struggles.

Beginning with the Traditional Workers' Struggle against an Employer

From the 1930s to the early 1970s, both the bidi and construction industries had significant labor movements, but they differed from those of today.[1] The early movements in both industries followed the conventional model of state–labor relations described in the Introduction. The primary axis of conflict and negotiation was located between the employer and the worker's union. The government served as a buffer between employees and employers and was responsible only for enacting and enforcing laws that held employers accountable to their employees. As shown in Figures 2 and 3, union presence and militant union action in both

---

[1] Construction and bidi workers' movements were tied to the national independence and trade union movements of the early 1900s. For more information on bidi workers' history, see Chauhan (2001) and Isaac et al. (1998). I could find no studies on the early history of India's construction workers. This section, therefore, draws from my interviews, labor union reports, and data on registered unions and disputes from the Ministry of Labor, Government of India.

Timing	1930s–1960s	1970–1979	1980–1989	Since 1990s
Union Presence	Trade unions and guild associations organize formally employed construction wks	Unions and guilds begin to fade as contract work increases	(1983) TN Construction Union forms for informal wks (1986) WB Communist Construction Union admits informal wks (1986) MH begins project with informal wks (1988) WB 1st independent union forms for informal wks	Maharashtra and West Bengal organizations expand membership
Union Action	Hold strikes against employers for minimum wages and holidays		(1979–81) TN Union initiates membership drive in slums; directs demands to state (1985) TN Union holds National Seminar to extend movement to other states and submit draft for National Construction Workers Act to Lower House of Parliament (proposal officially acknowledged by lower house in 1989)	(1995) Wks organize nation wide demonstration for state governments to enact Construction Workers Act WB Construction Union meets with top state officials. Holds rallies to pressure government to implement Welfare Board Bombay Union pressures state government to implement Welfare Board in MH
State Action		(1970) National Contract Labor Act enacted to forbid contract work and ensure decent work conditions when contract work was deemed essential	(1982) TN enacts Manual Workers Act to protect informal wks in construction. Provides ID cards to wks	(1996) National passage of Regulation of Employment Conditions Act & Welfare Cess and Fund Act (2002) WB enacts pension fund for informal wks in 20 industries (2003) MH drafts bill for Welfare Board for all informal sector wks (2006) WB implements Construction Welfare Board

FIGURE 2: Evolution of the construction movement.

	From Targeting Employers for Work Benefits		To Targeting State for Welfare Benefits	
Timing	**1930s–1960s**	**1970–1979**	**1980–1989**	**1990–2004**
Union Presence	Bidi trade unions tied to left-wing parties organize formally employed bidi workers		Bidi unions begin to fade as employers turn to informal workers, and unions are unable to hold employer accountable to laws	(1996) A new Mumbai Bidi Union forms to address needs of informal bidi workers
Union Action	Militant and leftist struggle. Hold strikes and violent takeovers of employers' offices. Demand minimum wages and improved working conditions	Unions pressure state governments to implement Conditions Act (1974) TN Union holds 22-day strike at High Court to implement Conditions Act (1979) MH Union holds 140-day strike for min. wage	Most unions not interested in Welfare Act until they can first ensure minimum wage TN, however, continues to fight for Welfare Act	(1990–1996) Bidi Unions demand state for industry protection Mumbai union marches in front of the State Parliament to demand Welfare Board identity cards for all Mumbai bidi workers Mumbai Union's main focus is to recruit workers and register them on Welfare Board
State Action	(1966) National Bidi Employment Conditions Act passes to ensure minimum wage and benefits to formally employed bidi workers	(1972) WB increases min. wage to Rs. 70 (1974) TN implements Conditions Act (1976) Bidi Welfare Fund Act passes to improve safety and health facilities through employer	(1980) TN implements Cess Act and Bidi Welfare Board. (1981) WB allows government to provide welfare card (1983) TN receives first dispensary for bidi workers. (1986) TN bidi workers receive	(1993) TN Labor Department appoints 9 labor inspectors in bidi-producing regions (1996) National Labor Minister agrees to provide Welfare cards to all Mumbai bidi workers (2007) WB implements state-level bidi workers scheme

FIGURE 3: Evolution of the bidi movement.

industries were strong during this period, whereas direct actions from the state were minimal.

It is important to note that not all workers in the bidi and construction industries during this period were formally employed. Since the late 1930s, bidi employers had tried to avoid being regulated by the 1926 Factories Act, which protected workers' wages and working conditions in establishments with more than twenty workers, by dispersing workers into smaller, unregulated units. Construction companies hired workers informally to complete short-term tasks, because the 1923 Workmen's Compensation Act, which compensated workers for employment-related accidents, did not apply to contract workers. In a report on labor conditions commissioned under British rule in 1929, officials of the South Indian Railway detail one construction project in which nearly 6,000 casual workers were employed on contract and were expected to be fired at the end of the project (GOI 1929).[2]

Despite the reality on the ground, the labor movement focused on striving for formal employment for all. The type of labor involved in the early movement was, therefore, exclusively formal – employed by private companies in the case of bidi and by government projects in the case of construction. Unions recruited members at the factory or employer level.[3] Additionally, formal workers tended to be men. By 1960, registered membership in the construction and bidi unions was 98 percent male (GOI 1960). Members also tended to be literate; in the case of construction, they were usually also skilled (Chakrabarti 1998; Girija, Ramakrishnan, and Ramakrishnan 1988). As Isaac et al (1998: 40) document, one of the primary union demands of the earliest bidi unions, the Durbar Bidi Union, in 1937 was that "while the workers are idle without work, they should be permitted to read newspapers or books."

Within unions, leaders focused on educating workers about class consciousness, teaching them that provisions from employers were to be viewed as "workers' rights." This traditional model implied a contract between capital and labor where employers formally recognized and provided for their employees and, in return, workers provided their labor for production. In a telling excerpt from a 1934 document written by the first bidi association in Kerala, union leaders write, "It is the duty of the

---

[2] For an excellent account of employers' use of informal labor in the textile industry during India's early industrial history, see Chandavarkar (1994).

[3] Although bidi manufacturing is not mechanized, the workshops in which workers sit to roll bidis are referred to as "factories."

employers to the human laborers to provide them with sufficient wages for subsistence and to limit the working time . . . It is because the employers do not give a return in proportion to their labor expended at the workplace that the workers are forced to sweat like bullocks."[4] Drawing directly from Karl Marx's labor theory of value, workers demanded that capital provide fair returns for their work.

Because the contract was between labor and capital, the fair returns that workers demanded centered on what employers could provide, such as a minimum wage, bonuses, and decent working hours. These provisions were considered sufficient to the broader goals of justice and human dignity. As Ram Ratnagar, general secretary of the All India Bidi and Cigar Workers Federation, recalled, "At that time, our main demand was a minimum wage from the employer. We thought everything else could only follow from that."[5] In the case of construction, early guild associations fought for employers to provide a minimum wage and an annual holiday. As illustrated in a report written by the Tamil Nadu construction union featured in this study, the holiday was viewed as an opportunity to visit the temple, which would "confer recognition of the services of construction workers . . . thus giving them social recognition."[6] By 1969, nearly 50 percent of all industrial disputes focused on minimum wages and bonuses (GOI 1970).

As part of their effort to ensure employer-provided rights to workers, unions sought to have all workers be formally recognized by employers. In 1962, Sundar Navelkar, one of the first female lawyers in India and a member of the revolutionary Maoist group of Naxalites, started the first construction workers' union for contract workers in Mumbai. Although the union's focus on informal workers was unique for the time, its organizing model and membership of literate men followed that of formal workers' unions (despite its female leadership). For example, the union fought to enact the National Contract Labor Act, which limited the use of contract labor and regulated working conditions in select cases where contract work was deemed essential. Contract labor was viewed as a second-best option to formal employment. Decent working conditions for contract labor were similar to those sought for formal workers, such as timely payment of wages and the provision of canteens, restrooms, drinking water, and first-aid kits at work sites. At the age of 83, Navelkar recalled this early movement: "The most important thing is struggle and

---

[4] Quoted in Isaac et al. (1998: 31).
[5] Interview, July 1, 2003.
[6] Quoted in Girija, G. Ramakrishnan, and S. Ramakrishnan (1988: 94).

changing public opinion. Workers learned they had a right to things. That was our greatest victory."[7]

Attaining these rights was framed as only possible through a necessary conflict that workers needed to engage in against capital. The tone of the early movements was militant and violent toward employers. As Isaac, Franke, and Raghavan (1998) document in their study of one of the few bidi cooperatives in India, by the 1930s, the labor supply was already in surplus, and earlier individual forms of protests, such as the threat of desertion, no longer proved effective. Instead, there was a call for collective action against employers. The first recorded strike in the bidi industry took place one month after the first bidi union was formed in Kerala in 1934. For the next three decades, the strike served as the most popular form of workers' resistance. In 1951 alone, the Government of India reported 120 registered strikes in the bidi industry; hundreds more were said to have taken place on a spontaneous basis (GOI 1952). Even when the strikes did not result in economic gains, they were heralded as a means to bolstering solidarity (Isaac et al. 1998). In the construction industry, workers held strikes on worksites to increase wages and bonuses; in the bidi industry, workers held several coordinated strikes within factories as well as *gheraos* (a form of protest in which workers prevent managers from leaving the workplace) to pressure employers to increase wages, bonuses, and holidays and, most significantly, to formally recognize the employer–employee relationship – whether production was dispersed or not (Chauhan 2001).

To enact protective laws, organized workers sought representation in the government through the election of left-oriented politicians. Therefore, the form of organization the early movements invariably took was as unions tied to left-wing political parties.[8] The bidi unions had formed close ties to the Communist Party of India (CPI) during the early independence movement. In 1966, bidi unions' efforts climaxed with the passing of the first national-level legislation to protect bidi workers. The Bidi and Cigar Workers Conditions of Employment Act mandated all employers to provide their workers with a minimum wage and work benefits (such as an annual bonus, maternity benefits, social security, and safe working

---

[7] Interview, August 4, 2003.

[8] Each of the two primary left-wing political parties in India has its own federation of trade unions. The Communist Party of India's, (CPI's) federation is the All India Trade Union Congress (AITUC), and the Communist Party of India-Marxist (CPM)'s federation is the Center for Indian Trade Unions (CITU). Although unions affiliated with right-wing and center parties also existed, their strategies were less revolutionary, and they did not make major gains in the bidi or construction industries.

conditions). The passing of this act was largely due to the collaboration between bidi unions tied to left-wing political parties and A. K. Gopalan, then Member of Parliament (MP) from Kerala's Communist Party of India-Marxist (CPM), leader of the opposition in Parliament, and leader of the movement to pass the Bidi Act in Parliament. Construction unions operated more independently than bidi unions during this period; guild associations engaged in efforts to organize skilled workers, and the Maoist movement of Naxalites recruited unskilled workers. Toward the end of the 1960s, CPM tried to enter the construction industry by recruiting workers into the General Workers Union. However, this recruitment effort was not as successful as it had been in the bidi industry (Chakrabarti 1998).

By the early 1970s, these movements had succeeded in attaining some protective legislation at the national level. In 1970, the Minimum Wages Act of 1948 was extended to include the construction industry. In 1972, the Contract Labor Regulation and Abolition Act was passed to hold principal employers and contractors responsible for providing casual labor with minimum wages and decent working conditions; this act was to be applied to construction workers. Finally, by the early 1970s, almost all states had passed the 1966 Bidi Act (Samant 1998).

However, these apparent victories soon boomeranged against the unionized workers. To avoid complying with the new regulations, employers in both industries hired informal workers who fell outside the jurisdiction of the laws. In construction, the Contract Labor Act applied only to contractors with more than twenty workers. Given the lack of enforcement, it was easy for contractors to claim they had fewer than twenty workers. Moreover, the demand for unskilled manual labor had grown during the mid-1970s with the increased use of cement. Unskilled women were targeted to perform menial tasks, such as carrying bricks and cleaning and mixing cement (Vaid 1997). This population of unskilled women workers had not been involved in the labor movement, they were desperate for employment, and they were willing to work informally, outside the jurisdiction of the laws (Vaid 1999). Moreover, alongside women workers were their children, who were also available to perform small tasks for low wages.

Today the most unskilled construction workers make US$1 to 2 per day (women make $1, whereas men make $2); on-site workers are paid partly in kind with materials provided for their housing and electricity. Seventy-one percent of workers in construction have only a primary education or less, and 42 percent are illiterate.

Similarly, bidi workers suffered after the Bidi Act was passed. In 1968, Kerala became the first state to implement the Bidi Act after CPM had won the state elections based on promises to protect the massive bidi workforce. On October 15, just months after CPM implemented the Bidi Act, Kerala's largest bidi company (Mangalore Ganesh Bidi) shut down all its factories in the state, immediately laying off 12,000 workers (Isaac et al. 1998). By the mid-1970s, almost all bidi factories in the three cities covered in this study had closed. Once bidi labor was dispersed through households, subcontractors were used to veil the employer–employee relationship, and employers were no longer held responsible for their workers. Because bidi manufacturing did not require skills or technology, shifting to home-based work suited employers' production and financial needs. Home-based work, in turn, enabled women workers to avoid going out in public and to combine income-generation activity with family care duties. As with construction, these changes produced a change in the sex composition of bidi employment from male to female, while eroding the base of the previous workers' movement.

Today the bidi labor force is 81 percent female. Most family members of bidi workers are employed in non–tobacco-related work, although children are often used to help women workers increase their bidi output.[9] Nearly 60 percent of bidi workers are illiterate, and 87 percent have only a primary education or less. Government reports have long highlighted the disproportionate incidence of tuberculosis, asthma, and bronchitis among bidi workers (GOI 1981). On average, workers get paid approximately US$1 per 1,000 bidis; depending on their skill, workers roll 500 to 2,000 bidis a day. Some contractors provide workers with the raw materials, whereas others require workers to buy their own (from a locally based distributor). Contractors often refuse to pay for pieces citing their poor quality, but then keep them nonetheless; insufficient raw material is often delivered, forcing the worker to pay for the remaining amount needed to finish the order; and contractors often demand sexual favors in return for payment on delivery.[10]

As predicted by conventional labor movement models, both the construction and bidi movements became dormant once the labor force shifted from a formal to an informal one. As shown in Figure 4, the

---

[9] This practice has been spotlighted by ILO's recent focus on the elimination of child labor.

[10] Incidents of sexual harassment were widely and openly reported to me by the interviewees.

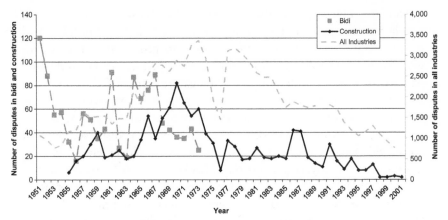

FIGURE 4: Number of disputes in bidi, construction, and all industries.
Note: Data drawn from *Indian Labour Year Book*, Ministry of Labor, Government of India (multiple issues). Reproduced from Agarwala 2008 with kind permission from Springer Science+Business Media B.V.

number of bidi disputes declined markedly after 1967, and from 1973 onward, the National Ministry of Labor no longer even reported that number. The incidence of registered disputes in construction showed a rising trend until 1970, after which it steadily declined. These trends mirror the aggregate picture of all industries at the national level.

The circumstances of informal employment, such as changing employers and unregistered workers, made it impossible for unions to hold employers accountable to complying with the labor acts. As Sundar Navelkar lamented in an interview, "My attempt to bring workers' rights to informal workers failed." Unions' time and resources were spent handling costly, drawn-out court cases against employers each time a new site was built.[11] As the employer–employee relationships became divided into chains of subcontracters, guilds and unions were unable to apply their usual strategies. Bidi unions did not have the bargaining power to force employers to apply the labor acts to informal workers, and with the exception of Tamil Nadu, bidi union action faded during the early 1980s.

Launching an Alternative Struggle against the State

The setback in workers' organization efforts in these two industries appears to have been temporary, however, because both movements were

---

[11] Interviews with the heads of former Mumbai construction workers trade unions, Sundar Navelkar (August 4, 2003) and G. S. Madukant (May 25, 2003).

revived by the mid-1980s, although in new forms. By the end of the 1970s it became clear that informal workers' stark vulnerability was unsustainable. In 1979, Tamil Nadu experienced a severe shortage in cement and steel, and the price of raw materials rose rapidly in the unregulated market. As a result, the middle-class housing construction market weakened, and millions of construction workers lost their jobs. Skilled and unskilled workers joined forces to agitate for fair prices of construction materials and job security for workers. However, the government did little to ensure that employers applied the existing labor legislation mandating job protection to informal construction workers. These experiences led informal construction workers in Tamil Nadu to begin organizing. In 1982, workers formed a union for informal construction workers called, the Tamil Maanila Kattida Thozilalar Panchayat Sangham (TMKTPS). Today, TMKTPS is the largest, most active construction workers' unions in the state, and it has been heralded in the media as the forerunner of a new informal workers' movement (Manchanda 1993; Staff Reporter 1994, 1999).

This new movement has shifted its target and demands to address the unique needs of informal workers. Because informal workers operate through subcontractors and often do not know who their employer is, and most workers are too frightened to risk losing their jobs by making demands on an employer, the new movement directs its demands to the state. The state is viewed as a target that affects all workers. To make demands on the state, informal workers' unions appeal to state responsibilities to citizens, rather than to workers' rights alone.

Alamele, a 60-year-old construction worker in Chennai, explains, "We need to fight with the government for a pension or we will be alone one day. Nobody cares for old women. Employers don't want to hire us and children leave us."[12] Alamele has been the sole income earner in her family since she got married. Her husband had numerous health problems and was unable to work. Ten years after their marriage, he passed away. As a migrant to the city from the countryside, she had no family members nearby to lean on. To Alamele, the government is the only source of protection left. The construction union for informal workers, TMKTPS, was established just after ADMK,[13] a newly formed political party, had won the state government elections, and as TMKTPS founder and

[12] Interview, August 13, 2003.
[13] The Anna Dravida Munnetra Kazhagam (ADMK) is a local party in the state of Tamil Nadu, and it is one of the two major parties that have ruled the state since the early 1960s. The other party is the DMK (Dravida Munnetra Kazhagam).

General Secretary Geeta Ramakrishnan said, "There was an element of hope that the newly elected government would look into our demands more sympathetically."[14]

This model of a welfare-oriented movement targeting the state spread across construction and bidi workers' organizations throughout the country in the 1980s and 1990s. As Aran Pande, founder and general secretary of West Bengal's Independent Construction Union, explains, "Our state [West Bengal] has so many laws for labor, but they are useless and corrupt, even with my good connections. Now, we don't even fight for a minimum wage, because it created so much unemployment here. Instead we fight for our workers to live."[15] In Maharashtra, Vayjanta, general secretary of NIRMAN, the Mumbai's Construction Workers NGO, explains, "Laborers are not interested in fighting for wages anymore. They are more concerned about human rights issues, such as education, malaria, safe child delivery, and isolation. They don't want to rebel anymore, they want a job."[16]

As the following testimony eloquently illustrates, even bidi organizations that remain tied to left-wing political parties have altered their movement frame from worker versus employer to citizen versus the state. Vajeshwari Bital Iravati, a 55-year-old member of the Mumbai Bidi Union, has a typical background for women bidi workers in the area. She is a member of the weaver caste. Her family migrated to Maharashtra from the southern state of Andhra Pradesh. Although Vajeshwari grew up in rural Maharashtra, she moved to Mumbai with her husband and in-laws shortly after her marriage thirty-five years ago. In Mumbai, the men in the family got jobs in the textile mills, whereas the women continued to roll bidis at home. Although the mill work sustained the family for some years, after her husband died, Vajeshwari was responsible for raising their two sons and caring for her elderly in-laws. The mill did not provide any pension.

Vajeshwari joined the bidi union shortly after arriving in Mumbai. She learned about the union from the women with whom she rolled bidis. As a member of the Mumbai Bidi Union, which is affiliated with CPM, Vajeshwari was steeped in the traditional class struggle philosophy. She recalled the early days of the bidi struggle: "One time we wanted a

---

[14] Interview, July 9, 2004.
[15] Interview, November 16, 2003.
[16] Interview, April 16, 2003.

bonus like they got in the village. We quickly spread the word to fight the employers, so when the union told us to strike, 2,000 of us stopped working! Another time they locked us in jail until late at night for striking without permission. The police had sticks in their hands, so we picked up rocks and hit them. We had to do it for our stomachs! What else could we do?" she exclaimed.

Despite her traditional labor politics background, Vajeshwari now directs her efforts to targeting the state for her demands: "We always sit outside some parliament building to make sure those fat government officials give us what we need. There is no use in going to the employers. They are all thieves. They don't even admit we work for them. They will just kick us out of our jobs if we ask them for anything. But the government cannot kick us out of the country for making demands!"[17]

Workers' Welfare Boards: Operationalizing the New Struggle

Informal workers' appeals to the state for welfare benefits have been operationalized in the form of tripartite workers' welfare boards or committees.[18] These boards are funded by workers, employers, and the government and implemented by state governments. Workers pay to become members, and in return they receive welfare benefits. The government checks against union rolls to verify that all members are indeed workers.[19] Benefits are thus extended to workers, regardless of who their employer is. Rather than factory-based strikes and violent threats toward employers, the new movement holds demonstrations and hunger strikes in front of politicians (not judges), demanding them to implement the welfare boards – hence the decline in registered employer disputes shown in Figure 4. Geeta Ramakrishnan, founder and general secretary of TMKTPS, recalled informal workers' efforts with pride: "We gathered thousands of angry workers outside his [the Labor Minister's] door. We were immediately arrested and spent twelve days in jail. But we were so

---

[17] Interview, May 27, 2003.

[18] Differences between the institutional structure of welfare boards and welfare funds/committees are minimal, and they are thus examined together in this study. The construction industry operates through state-level "welfare boards," whereas the bidi industry operates through a national-level "welfare committee" and nine regional "welfare committees," which are overseen by the central government's Ministry of Labor. The bidi committees are funded by the Bidi Welfare Fund. For simplicity, I use the term "welfare board" when referring to both construction workers' welfare boards and bidi workers' welfare funds/committees.

[19] Manohar Lal, director general of Labor Welfare Organization, interview, June 2, 2003.

happy we had made him scared and angry."[20] Since the mid-1990s, both construction and bidi workers' struggles in India have focused on pressuring the government to create and implement welfare boards/committees.[21]

Labor welfare has been one of the pillars of Indian labor legislation since the early 1950s. As the Indian Ministry of Labor reiterated in its 1960 *Labour Year Book* (GOI 1960: 134), the role of the welfare state is to "bring matters connected with workers' welfare within the purview of legislation." To this end, several laws were enacted to ensure the welfare of Indian workers. According to the Indian government in 1952 (GOI 1952: 275), "After independence, welfare became a central part of the Indian Republic, because it [the Indian state] was wedded to the idea of a welfare state." In addition to enabling the government's ideological commitment to justice, labor welfare was viewed as a means to increase productivity. In the same 1952 report, the Ministry of Labor went on to recount (GOI 1952: 275), "During WWII the Government of India became interested in welfare schemes for industrial workers when they introduced such schemes in ammunition factories to increase the morale and productivity of workers." Thirty years later, the Ministry of Labor (GOI 1980: 119) reiterated the same sentiment: "In India, labor welfare is important because it creates a healthy atmosphere in the workplace, keeps labor force stable, and contented, helps in maintaining industrial peace, thereby improving productive efficiency of workers."

In these early years, labor welfare laws aimed to protect formal workers in areas to which labor legislation had not yet extended. Drawing from the International Labor Organization (ILO), the Indian government in 1952 defined labor welfare as "services, facilities, and amenities which may be established in, or in the vicinity of, undertakings to enable persons employed in them to perform their work in healthy, congenial surroundings, good health and high morale" (GOI 1952). Such facilities and amenities, which included canteens, rest and recreational facilities, sanitation and medical facilities, travel costs to and from work (if there is no public transportation), and housing (if the place of work is far from home), were provided to formally employed workers at the workplace. As noted by the Ministry of Labor in its 1960 labor report (GOI 1960: 136), welfare provisions were "very slim" among informal workers tied to contractors.

---

[20] Interview, July 9, 2004.
[21] Although many are also fighting for a minimum wage, welfare demands comprise the bulk of activity.

India's welfare laws have never been universalized; rather, they have remained specific to a state or an industry.[22] State-level welfare acts were pushed by social workers and thus reflect the social work approach. The first state-level Labor Welfare Fund Act was passed in Mumbai in 1953 (and later extended to all of Maharashtra when the state was formed in 1960). This act provides community centers for formal workers covered under the Factory Act of 1928. The majority of community center members in Mumbai were textile mill workers. With an attitude of proud paternalism, Mohand Dhotre, commissioner of the Maharashtra Labor Welfare Board, explained to me, "When the textile mills were growing rapidly in the 1930s, rural migrants were streaming into the city for economic reasons. However, with the increased incomes, many of them were turning to gambling and drinking and red light districts." The welfare activities of the community centers, therefore, have focused on recreational programs that could "distract" the workers.[23] Today the Mumbai Center has a gym, a pool, drama classes, sports competitions, handicraft classes for the "wives of the workers," and day care centers for workers' children. From the mid-1960s to the mid-1970s, several states followed Mumbai's example by enacting similar state-level welfare fund acts.[24] Such state-level welfare acts did not serve as a model for contemporary welfare boards among bidi and construction workers.

In contrast, the early industry-level welfare acts, pushed forward by organized workers, did serve as a blueprint for contemporary welfare boards in the bidi and construction industries.[25] The first industry-level labor welfare act was passed in 1934 for dock workers. This act, which was conceptualized by a coalition between the Dock Workers Union and the ILO, was designed to compensate workers if they were injured by an accident during work; it was not implemented until 1948.[26] Shortly

---

[22] The lack of universalized welfare benefits in India may, in part, be attributed to the fragmented, group-based nature of Indian social movements that often demand group-specific benefits.

[23] Interview, May 7, 2003.

[24] Mysore Labor Welfare Fund Act (1965), Punjab Labor Welfare Fund Act (1965), Uttar Pradesh Labor Welfare Fund Act (1965), Tamil Nadu Labor Welfare Fund Act (1972), and West Bengal Labor Welfare Fund Act (1974).

[25] This was clear from numerous interviews with union leaders in both industries across all three states. It was unclear, however, what was the exact history of the struggles designed to attain these acts. I could find no written reports on this subject, and union leaders were not involved in these early struggles.

[26] The Indian Dock Laborer's Act (1934).

after independence, three additional industry-level labor welfare fund acts were passed for mica and coal mine workers and for dock workers (in Kerala).[27] These acts broadened the scope of the 1934 Dock Workers Act to provide workers with medical facilities, toilets and baths (for mine workers), housing, and educational/recreational facilities for workers' families.[28]

These acts created an institutional structure – a tripartite welfare board that collects contributions from employers, workers, and the state government – that connected workers to welfare provisions. In addition to annual contributions, the boards were funded through the sale of food in canteens and fees from community events, such as films and dance competitions. In subsequent years, several states enacted similar acts in additional industries.[29] The acts were effective for many years, but their relevance diminished during the 1970s, because many of the provisions specified as welfare benefits (such as canteens, baths, and toilet facilities) had been turned into legal obligations under the Conditions of Employment Acts for factories, plantations, and mines.[30] The national government also passed social security provisions to cover pensions and medical care for employees.[31] The fact that welfare acts lost importance in the face of mainstream labor legislation reflected their focus on formal workers.

In recent years, informal workers have reignited the demand for state-provided welfare; the target and purpose of their advocacy efforts, however, have changed. In 2008, the Indian Parliament passed the Unorganized Sector Workers' Social Security Bill to provide informal workers with life, disability, health, and old age insurance. Following the model of earlier industry-level welfare struggles, the Social Security Bill calls for the creation of a National Welfare Board to formulate and monitor

---

[27] Mica Mines Labor Welfare Fund Act (1946), Coal Mines Labor Welfare Fund Act (1947), and Kerala's Dock Workers (Regulation of Employment) Act (1948).

[28] The Mica and Coal Mine Workers Welfare Funds were initiated as a pilot project to finance welfare activities in industries owned by the government. Although the pilot was slated to end in 1952, it was extended indefinitely.

[29] Uttar Pradesh Sugar and Power Alcohol Industries Labor Welfare and Development Fund Act (1950), Assam Tea Plantation Employees Welfare Fund Act (1959), Maharashtra Mathadi, Hamal (railway porters), and other Manual Workers (Regulation of Employment and Welfare Act) (1969).

[30] Factory Act (1948), Plant Labor Act (1951), and Mines Act (1952).

[31] Employees' State Insurance Act (1948), Employees' Provident Fund and Miscellaneous Provisions Act (1952), Maternity Benefit Act (1961), and Payment of Gratuity Act (1972).

welfare programs for informal workers. The Board has not yet been set up, because the bill is still under debate. Some criticize it for being limited to workers below the poverty line and to nonagricultural workers, whereas others view it as an important catalyst to implementation of welfare for informal workers. Past governments had instituted welfare programs that applied to informal workers, but they were poorly implemented and often ended once there was a change in government. As K. P. Kannan, senior member of the Indian government's National Commission for Enterprises in the Unorganized Sector, explained, "Yes, the bill is a watered-down version of what we wanted. But at least we now have something. The bill is key, because it ensures that welfare for the informal sector is an *entitlement.*"[32]

Additionally, the Ministry of Labor's reduced focus on industrial disputes and resolutions is being replaced with a focus on welfare for poor, informal workers. "This is essentially a welfare ministry now," exclaimed, Directorate General of Labor Welfare (DGLW) Anil Swarup in the Ministry of Labor.[33] Indeed, the Health Insurance Program for Unorganized Sector Workers (RSBY), which is administered by the DGLW and comes under the National Social Security Bill, was the largest line item in the Ministry of Labor's 2008–09 budget. Labor training programs received the next largest share of the budget, whereas allocations for industrial relations and working conditions and safety were at the bottom of the list. As then Minister of Labor Oscar Fernades confirmed, "Our top priorities now are providing technical training to the masses and passing a realistic social security bill for unorganized workers." Fernandes linked the government's interest in labor welfare to development and modernity: "The Prime Minister is very keen on passing this Bill. She asks me daily what I am doing about it. There is a lot of controversy around it, but we must at least take this first step to climb Everest. You see, the difference between the West and us is that the West has a social security system. And it is time we have one too now."[34] How did this shift take place? As I detail later through an examination of the bidi and construction industries, informal workers' organizations had been pushing from below for this shift since the mid-1980s.

Drawing from the model laid out by the early industry-level struggles for labor welfare, TMKTPS, the Tamil Nadu construction union, held a

---

[32] Interview, December 13, 2008. Emphasis in original.
[33] Interview, December 11, 2008.
[34] Interview, December 16, 2008.

national seminar in 1985 to discuss how to extend into other states its movement for a Construction Workers Welfare Board targeting informal workers. As a result of this seminar, the movement began in the states of Kerala, Maharashtra, Delhi, Gujarat, and Karnataka.[35] In addition, the National Campaign Committee for Central Legislation on Construction Labor (NCC-CL) was formed under the chairmanship of Dr. Krishna Iyer, a member of CPM and a former Supreme Court Justice. The committee's role was to pressure the central government to require all states to implement a Construction Workers Welfare Board. On December 5, 1986, the NCC-CL submitted a draft bill to the Petitions Committee in the Lok Sabha, the lower house of the Indian Parliament. For the next ten years, organized construction workers fought against builders' associations to lobby chief ministers, MPs, and the prime ministers of India to pass this bill. In 1989, NCC-CL submitted a petition with 400,000 signatures of construction workers from across the nation demanding the protective legislation.

Unlike earlier union movements that were tied to left-wing political parties, the revived national construction workers' campaign transcended political and ideological affiliations to hold the state, regardless of the party in power, responsible for workers' well-being.[36] During the 1989 national elections, for example, NCC-CL lobbied all major political parties to support their demands in their election manifestos. Later that year, the Lok Sabha accepted the NCC-CL proposal and recommended that a "comprehensive bill be introduced so as to cater to the long-felt demands of a hitherto neglected segment of the working class." On August 21, 1995, construction workers held a nationwide rally in front of state legislatures demanding that state representatives enact the legislation. NCC-CL received letters of support from then National Labor Minister Shri. G. Venkatasamy, the chief ministers of Gujarat and Karnataka, and several MPs. From the mid-1990s onward, NCC-CL efforts received substantial media attention (Staff Correspondent 2001a; Staff Reporter 1994, 1995, 1996).

Finally, on August 19, 1996, then Prime Minister H. D. Deve Gowda enacted the Building and Other Construction Workers' Welfare Cess Act, which called on each state to create and implement its own Construction

---

[35] Construction workers in Kerala were active during the 1970s, and the Tamil Nadu movement was inspired by Kerala's experiences. Kerala organizations, however, have not been as involved in the national-level campaign as have Tamil Nadu organizations.

[36] Various interviews with activists in the construction workers movement (2002–08).

Workers' Welfare Fund and Board.[37] The fund is financed through state funds, contributions from workers, and the construction workers' welfare tax. The tax is 1 percent of the building cost applied to all building projects that employ ten or more workers and cost more than Rs. 1 million (US$2,000). The announcement received substantial media coverage, because it was the first of its kind (Gopinath 1997).

In West Bengal, the independent Construction Union held biweekly "reading circles," where two literate workers taught fellow workers about welfare boards, so they could pressure the state government to implement it. From 2001 to 2004, the union met with the governor of West Bengal; the central, regional, and state labor ministers; and several district magistrates; it wrote to West Bengal's chief minister; and it held three large public rallies on the lawns outside the state legislature. In 2004, the West Bengal government began formulating the rules on implementation of the welfare board.

In Mumbai, the construction NGO provided its own welfare benefits, such as on-site child care centers, as a way to interact with workers and teach them their welfare rights, while simultaneously fighting for welfare boards at the policy level. The child care centers have been funded by grants and contributions from some employers.

To date, eighteen state governments have constituted their Construction Workers' Welfare Boards. Only Tamil Nadu and Kerala have fully implemented their boards, whereas the remaining states have only begun the process (GOI 2008a; Staff Reporter 2001). Table 4 summarizes the contributions required for the Construction Workers Welfare Boards and the benefits promised to informal construction workers.

In the bidi industry, organized workers tried to enact a bidi welfare fund during the 1960s. At that time, the labor struggle mirrored those in the coal and mica mines, docks, railway loading, sugar, and tea plantations – it aimed to provide formal workers with welfare provisions not yet covered under the law. In 1976, the Government of India passed the Bidi Workers Welfare Cess and Fund Act. Under this act, the Indian government collects a tax of Rs. 5 (US$1) per 1,000 bidis to build a fund for bidi workers' welfare.[38] The Labor Welfare Organization,

---

[37] On the same day, the government also enacted the Building and Other Construction Workers' Regulation of Employment and Conditions of Service Act, which catered to the requests of the builders' association to apply minimal protections of work conditions.

[38] Unbranded bidi manufacturers that produce fewer than two million bidis per year are exempt from the tax. The tax amount has been periodically increased over time from Rs. 2 to Rs. 4 to Rs. 5.

TABLE 4: *Construction Workers Welfare Board*

Contributions

Employers: 0.3% of cost of building. Required for approval from municipal corporation
Workers: Rs. 25 for registration and Rs. 10 every two years for renewal
Government: Contribution for start-up and continuation (varies by government)

Benefits to Workers (Rs.)	
Accident compensation for worker	
Death of worker	100,000 paid to beneficiary
Loss of limbs, eyes	up to 100,000
Education scholarship for worker's children	
10th grade	1,000
12th grade	1,500
BA, BS, B Law	1,500; 1,750 if in hostel
English, medicine, veterinarian	2,000; 4,000 if in hostel
Industrial and technical course	1,000; 1,200 if in hostel
Postgraduate	2,000; 3,000 if in hostel
Professional postgraduate training	4,000; 6,000 if in hostel
Marriage	2,000 to child or worker
Maternity leave, abortion, or miscarriage	2,000 to woman worker
Natural death of worker	10,000 to family
Worker's funeral	2,000
Eyeglasses	250–1,000
Pension	Under consideration

Note: These benefits are promised under the law. Not all have been received in the cities under study. Rs. 50 = US$1.
Source: Reproduced from Agarwala 2008 with kind permission from Springer Science+Business Media B.V.

which is headed by the DGLW in the central government's Ministry of Labor, is responsible for administering the Bidi Fund and for overseeing the tripartite Central Advisory Committee and the nine tripartite State Advisory Committees. The State Advisory Committees, each of which is headed by a regional welfare commissioner, are responsible for approving the fund's annual budget and for working with a regional group of state governments to implement the Bidi Fund at the local level. In addition to the Bidi Fund, the DGLW administers four additional welfare funds.[39]

The Bidi Welfare Act was not implemented immediately. During the mid-1970s when it was enacted, the power of bidi unions was fading

---

[39] These are the Mica Mines Labor Welfare Fund Act (1946); Limestone and Dolomite Mines Labor Welfare Fund Act (1972); Iron Ore, Manganese Ore and Chrome Ore Mines Labor Welfare Fund Act (1976); and Cine Workers Welfare Fund Act (1981).

as employers dispersed production to avoid abiding by the provisions of the recently passed Bidi Conditions Act. If the Conditions Act, which was designed to formally recognize and protect bidi workers, was unenforceable, bidi unions did not see much purpose in fighting to implement the Welfare Act. They had envisioned the Welfare Act as an extension of employer-based protection for formal workers.[40] As shown by the Bidi Welfare Fund's annual financial profile (see Table 5), it remained relatively inactive from the mid-1970s to the mid-1980s. As a result of bidi unions' lack of interest in the Welfare Act, the collection of the tax designed to fund the Bidi Welfare Board was stopped in 1979.

During the mid-1980s and 1990s, however, bidi unions revived their struggle to pressure state governments to implement the Welfare Fund for informal bidi workers. The unions held well-publicized rallies in front of the offices of the national Labor Ministry and state-level Labor Departments, as well as marches through city centers (Staff Reporter 2002). As a result, tax collection was resumed on May 22, 1987. In addition, the Bidi Welfare Fund Act was amended to make the failure to issue worker identity cards to bidi workers a punishable offense. Finally the revised act made family welfare one of its primary objectives (GOI 1990). Between 1981 and 1991, the number of bidi workers covered under the Welfare Act increased from 1.6 million to 3.7 million workers. The number of identity cards distributed under the act increased from 4.4 million in 2002 to 4.74 million in 2007 (GOI 2008b). Table 6 summarizes the contributions required for the Bidi Welfare Board and the benefits promised to informal bidi workers.

The area in which the Bidi Fund has made the greatest progress since the 1980s is health. By 2007, the Bidi Welfare Fund had built 6 new hospitals and 204 dispensaries designed especially for bidi workers.[41] These hospitals and dispensaries are located in those slums and villages where more than 5,000 bidi workers live (GOI 2002a, 2008b). In 2002, nearly 40 percent of the Bidi Fund was allocated to sustain the bidi hospitals and clinics (Rehman 2007). In that year, more than 600 bidi workers were treated for tuberculosis, cancer, mental diseases, leprosy, or heart and kidney disease; nearly 2,000 bidi workers received assistance to purchase eyeglasses; and nearly 4,000 workers received maternity benefits

[40] Interviews with Ram Ratnagar, general secretary of the All India Bidi and Cigar Workers Federation, and Rajangam, general secretary of CITU Bidi Federation for Tamil Nadu.
[41] A seventh hospital was under construction at the time of writing in Bihar. The six existing hospitals are located in West Bengal, Bihar, Karnataka, Madhya Pradesh, Uttar Pradesh, and Tamil Nadu.

TABLE 5: *Bidi Welfare Fund Financial Profile*

	Income (Rs. '000s)	Income (US$ '000s)	Expenditure (Rs. '000s)	Expenditure (US$ '000s)	No. of Bidi Workers
1976	69,682	1,394			
1977	22,350	447	36,800	736	
1978	21,655	433	3,182	64	
1979	7,773	155	7,729	155	
1980	90	2	9,196	184	
1981	5,550	111	11,045	221	1,562,100
1982	20,100	402	11,455	229	
1983	41,725	835	18,036	361	
1984	40,607	812	21,014	420	
1985	31,113	622	26,660	533	
1986	41,698	834	32,382	648	
1987	110,205	2,204	41,946	839	
1988	119,890	2,398	65,986	1,320	
1989	122,622	2,452	83,189	1,664	
1990	120,540	2,411	58,228	1,165	
1991	121,410	2,428	109,119	2,182	3,731,000
1992	97,257	1,945	120,475	2,410	
1993	132,820	2,656	166,182	3,324	
1994	124,609	2,492	215,949	4,319	
1995	147,027	2,941	253,387	5,068	
1996	212,070	4,241	237,631	4,753	
1997	214,200	4,284	261,498	5,230	
1998	250,700	5,014	314,100	6,282	
1999	400,000	8,000	378,400	7,568	
2000	530,000	10,600	520,629	10,413	
2001	811,400	16,228	533,100	10,662	4,411,000
2002	844,800	16,896	658,200	13,164	
2003	858,400	17,168	813,100	16,262	
2004	–				
2005	1,257,900	25,158	1,325,800	26,516	
2006	1,275,100	25,502	1,345,100	26,902	
2007	1,846,200	36,924	2,329,400	46,588	

Note: Figures from 1976 to 2003 are from Rehman (2007: 6). Figures from 2004 were not available. I obtained the figures for 2005–07 from the Ministry of Labor. All figures are nominal.

(Rehman 2007). By 2007, nearly eight million patients had been treated in the bidi hospitals; 1,040 bidi workers had received direct assistance for the treatment of tuberculosis, cancer, or heart and kidney disease; more than 5,000 workers had received assistance to purchase eyeglasses; and nearly 9,500 workers had received maternity benefits (GOI 2008b).

TABLE 6: *Bidi Workers Welfare Board*

Contributions
Employers: Rs. 5/1,000 bidis produced. Collected by Department of Custom & Excise Worker: Rs. 100 for registration, Rs. 25/year renewal Government: By item (e.g., housing, pension)

Benefits to workers (Rs.)	
Health	
Tuberculosis and cancer	100%
Kidney failure	200,000
Eyeglasses	200
Childbirth	Two child deliveries per woman worker
Basic treatments	Free dispensaries
Education scholarship for worker's children	
1–8th grade	250–500/year
9–12th grade	700–2,000/year
College	3,000/year
University	100,000. Must score >70% on exams (Girls receive double after 5th grade)
Housing – 250 square feet	
From central government	25,000
From state government	25,000 (Worker pays remaining costs)
Worker's funeral (natural death/ accidental death)	10,000/25,000
Disability	12,500

Note: These benefits are promised under the law. Not all have yet been received in the cities under study. Rs. 50 = US$1.
Source: Reproduced from Agarwala 2008 with kind permission from Springer Science+Business Media B.V.

The most publicly lauded success of the Bidi Welfare Fund has been the housing projects for bidi workers. State governments and the national government contribute Rs. 40,000 toward a one-room tenement with kitchen plus a courtyard for each bidi worker, toward which each worker must contribute Rs. 5,000. Each home is leased in the woman worker's name. In 2002, nearly 15 percent of the Bidi Fund was used for bidi workers' housing, and 5,742 new houses were sanctioned to be built (Rehman 2007). In March 2004, then president of India, A. P. J. Abdul Kalam, inaugurated the largest housing project of 10,000 homes in Sholapur, Maharashtra. Since 2000, a Maharashtrian workers' organization had partnered with Narsayya Adam, a CPM Member of the Legislative Assembly (MLA), to pressure the government to approve the project.[42] Since the housing project was completed in 2004, it has been promoted as a model for public–private partnerships (Pandhe 2002). Chief executive officer of the Maharashtra State Housing and Area Development Authority, Uttam Khobragade, wrote, "[This] is a wonderful experiment executed by the collective efforts of the poor" (Singh 2004: 9). By 2007, nearly 40,000 bidi workers had benefited from the Bidi Welfare Fund's housing projects (GOI 2008b).

The area in which the bidi welfare boards are most active today is providing education scholarships for workers' children. In 1993, 93,581 children received scholarships, and by 2002, the number had increased to 329,714 beneficiaries (Rehman 2007). By 2007, 845,219 children had received the bidi scholarships (GOI 2008b).

Recasting the Type of Worker, Form of Organization, and Tone of Struggle

This new movement includes the new labor force of illiterate men and women, working for both public and private employers. It aims to protect workers within their informal employment status, rather than trying to transform them into formal workers. The movement is expressed through a variety of organizational entities; in addition to left-wing unions, the new movement also organizes through independent unions and NGOs. Because employees' workplaces can change daily, it identifies and recruits members by going through slums, rather than work sites. Finally, the tone of the new movement is nonviolent, framed as a bargain between the citizen and the state.

Leaders of earlier labor movements often view the new welfare-oriented struggle as a second-best option to the earlier struggle. When asked what she thinks of today's construction unions, Sundar Navelkar, founder of the first construction union, replied, "Nowadays the unions are fighting for these welfare boards and compensation for fatal accidents. But none of this provides permanent work for labor like we had tried for. That is a must!" Chandrashekhar, general secretary of Tamil Nadu's Bidi Union, views the strategic changes as a retreat from the stronger movement of the past: "They [the government] are just taking money from the poor and paying them back part of it in the name of welfare. What workers need is a minimum wage and secure employment, not these games."[43]

---

[42] The Legislative Assembly is the state parliament in India.
[43] Interview with Sundar Navelkar, August 4, 2003. Interview with Chandrashekhar, July 10, 2004.

To the members and leaders of the new movements, however, the welfare-oriented struggle is as important as the struggles of the past. Many pride themselves for being less violent toward employers, and therefore more appealing to workers, than the traditional movements. Others emphasize the empowering quality of the new movements in contrast to the earlier movements' failure to meet the needs of informal workers. Ramakant Patkar, general secretary of the Mumbai Bidi Union, recalled with great pride a rally he led of 3,500 bidi workers in front of the Parliament: "We rolled our bidis outside all day. Finally, the Labor Minister and the Housing Minister came out to speak with us. This gave the ladies a lot of confidence. They offered to get us tea, but I warned them not to make these ladies' heads hotter than they already were!"[44]

As this incident illustrates, workers in the new struggle do not express their power through violence toward employers. In fact, workers ensure that production is not disrupted during their rallies. Leaders of earlier movements who critique the new movements view this lack of willingness to fight the employer as a tacit approval of employer exploitation. Leaders and participants in the new movement, however, view this shift in attitude as their only alternative, given the state's approval of new structures of production. They argue that, if they stop production to protest, they will not only forfeit their already low incomes but also risk being fired.

Rather than taking these risks and losing members, new movement participants prefer to express their class power toward the state. In September 2001, a leading English-language newspaper, *The Hindu*, reported that social activists in Tamil Nadu were seeking cooperation directly from MLAs. Informal workers' organizations asked MLAs to match workers' contributions to the welfare boards, increase the amount of benefits provided, expand the number of industries covered, and "to raise questions on [informal workers'] demands to draft better policies and amendments" to regulations on informal work (Staff Reporter 2001). In other words, informal workers wanted to engage state representatives in the dialogue for increased state benefits. Most notably, informal workers expressed themselves in this interaction as equal negotiators, on par with state officials.

These alterations in movements among informal workers reflect adjustments in the traditional labor movement model on which India's early unions relied. As outlined in Figure 5, the new model provides a parallel structure to the traditional formal workers' labor movement in which

[44] Interview, March 31, 2003.

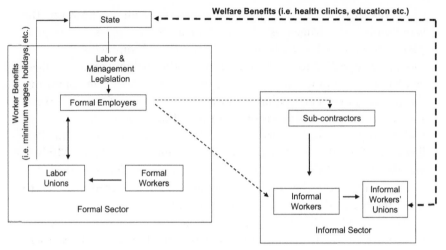

FIGURE 5: Reformulated model of state–labor relations.

informal workers are also organizing into class-based entities. Although they continue to engage in economic activities outside the jurisdiction of the state (just as they did under the traditional model), informal workers negotiate demands directly with the state. Whereas the employer continues to serve as the primary target of formal-sector workers' movements, the employer remains outside the direct interaction of informal workers' movements. To accomodate the shift in target, the nature of demands among informal workers has shifted from workers' rights to welfare demands at home and for the family.

2.2 CREATING A NEW CLASS IDENTITY

The strategic changes that informal workers' organizations have made to survive have had an important impact on organization members' class identities. As Patrick Heller (1999: 506) writes, "Struggles affect class formation only in as much as they come to define new identities." In this section, I examine the third major change informal workers organizations have made to traditional workers' struggles: the creation of a new identity for informal workers.

This identity underscores informal workers as an integral part of the working class. Unlike formal workers, however, informal workers view membership in the working class as a way to legitimate them as worthy citizens, not as antitheses to capital. The informal worker identity also integrates labor into identity-based options for political attention. Although the informal worker identity is never addressed in identity-based scholarship, Indian citizens on the ground are using it to attain state benefits for unprotected workers (a group that the state is said to be shunning). The political identity of "the informal worker" exists alongside informal workers' other political identities (such as those around caste), but it yields a different set of benefits.

As noted in the Introduction, informal workers are not just a leftover product of a pre-capitalist era, but rather are a vital component of modern, capitalist economies. Capital accumulation relies on informal workers (both self-employed and contract workers), because they absorb the reproductive costs of formal and informal labor. In addition, informal labor provides an attractive alternative that enables employers to constrain the expansion of the costly, protected formal working class. Despite informal workers' integral role in capitalist accumulation, trade unions in India virtually ignored them when recruiting new members, because the unions did not view informal workers as part of the "proletariat." Informal workers, in turn, organized along several identities simultaneously, including gender, caste, and neighborhood. To the extent they organized as workers, they fought to "join" the ranks of the formal proletariat by muting their informality in order to attain the same benefits as their formal-sector counterparts (i.e., minimum wages and secure work).

Recently, however, organized informal workers in India have begun to redefine their worker identity as one that simultaneously asserts their informality and their position within the working class. The informal worker's identity is based on work status, not income or occupation. To be a member of any of the seven organizations examined in this study, one must prove one's status as an informal, subcontracted worker. To attain benefits from the welfare boards, organization members must prove their line of work and then attain a worker identity card, which is given after informal workers' organizations confirm a member's work status to the government.[45] Because state governments lack the capacity to reach the dispersed mass of informal workers, informal workers' organizations verify work status by visiting each member (at home or at the workplace)

---

[45] Although the welfare boards were designed to reach all workers (not just those in an organization), the government has turned to organizations for assistance in finding and reaching workers. As a result, almost all recipients of the board benefits are members of an organization.

and confirming his or her employment. Almost all the respondents in my interviews expressed one or more of the following benefits of being a member of the working class: as a means to social legitimacy, empowering women past traditional groupings, and attaining a focused collective identity.

Today, the effectiveness of the informal workers' movement has encouraged traditional left-wing unions, which earlier shunned informal workers, to acknowledge the connections between informal and formal work and incorporate informal workers into a broader workers' movement. For example, M. K. Pandhe, general secretary of CITU, made a surprising suggestion that was echoed by other formal workers' union leaders: "We have to remember, current conditions are bad in the informal sector, because of the concessions and benefits the government gave to the formal sector. Therefore, I believe the government should tax the formal workers to provide for informal workers. There is no doubt that informal sector workers must be organized for the future of the left!"[46]

Toward Social Legitimacy

Forty percent of the respondents in this study who had received a worker identity card said it was one of the most important benefits they had received from the organization, even when they had not yet received any material benefits from the card. On February 10, 2000, only one month after the Tamil Nadu government implemented an expanded welfare board for fifty-four unorganized occupations, *The Hindu* reported that activists and trade union leaders expressed "a general agreement that the most important aspect of the scheme [Board] was that it provided an opportunity for the unorganized sector workers to acquire an identity as toilers/workers" (Special Correspondent 2000). Workers see an official acknowledgment of their work status as a means to social legitimacy, especially when their other identities (such as caste and gender) tend to demote them in the social hierarchy.

Take Jyotsna Bhoya, a member of the CPM-affiliated Kolkata Construction Union, for example. Jyotsna's mother and father were construction workers and migrated to West Bengal from the neighboring state of Bihar before she was born. Because her family moved from site to site and she is a member of the lowest caste in Hindu society, Jyotsna did not attend school and is illiterate. At the age of 13, she was married to a family of sweepers. She is now 28 years old and the mother of four girls; she has no sons. At the age of 17 years, Jyotsna began working as a construction worker because her husband's income was not enough to sustain the growing family. Each day, Jyotsna commutes four hours on the train by herself to find work in the city. To complete a full work shift, she must board the train to the city before dawn and return after sunset. As a young, lower-caste, illiterate Bihari migrant woman, traveling alone at odd hours, Jyotsna is vulnerable to abuse. Four years ago, a fellow worker convinced her to join the union, because it promised to "empower" her.[47] The most empowering benefit Jyotsna felt she had received from the union to date has been the identity card: "With this card, I don't feel scared walking home from work at night. If the police stop me, I can show them that I am a construction worker, and not a prostitute or some wasted woman," says Jyotsna.[48]

For Badhrunisa, a member of the Chennai Bidi Union, the worker identity card legitimates her as a vital part of modern, urban society. Badhrunisa is 32 years old, illiterate, and Muslim – a minority group in India that is not officially included in the Hindu caste system. Badhrunisa was born into a bidi-making family and began rolling bidis by her mother's side when she was 7 years old. When she was 20, she was married, and she gave birth to a daughter the following year. Shortly after her daughter's birth, her husband left her. Today she lives with her mother and her 12-year-old daughter. Like many of her neighbors, Badhrunisa's most important goal in life is to educate her daughter. Still, she needs to rely on her daughter's help in rolling bidis as soon as her daughter returns home from school. Living in an all-female home, Badhrunisa constantly faces charges that she was a "bad wife" because she could not keep her husband happy or bear any sons, a "bad daughter" because she could not keep her father alive, and a "bad mother" because her daughter is still working in "the dirty bidi profession." In 1998, Badhrunisa joined the union because it helped connect her to a new bidi contractor. Badhrunisa was adamant that she "did not join the union to fight." "I don't want to fight," she told me. The biggest benefit of the union for Badhrunisa has been the identity card: "This card proves that I am a good worker. I show it at the municipal office, when I have to ask for water. I show it when I register my daughter at the school. I show it at the bidi workers' hospital, so I can get help faster than at the corporation hospital. With this card, everyone knows I work."[49] To Badhurnisa, a government-issued card that

---

[47] Jyotsna used the word "empower" in English, although she does not speak English.
[48] Interview, December 16, 2003.
[49] Interview, July 14, 2003.

proves she is a worker arms her with an identity of legitimacy that she would otherwise have lost by joining the informal sector. Being a "legitimate" member of society allows her to meet her basic consumption needs.

Although, by ensuring state recognition for informal work, the informal worker identity card undermines the state's attempt to avoid regulating workers, it still does not prevent employers from avoiding their responsibility. Yet, unlike other identity cards given in India, such as those for voter registration and the Public Distribution System (PDS), the informal worker identity card ties individuals to an organized group. Although non-union members are entitled to receive cards, it is the informal workers' unions and NGOs that facilitate the attainment of cards. Being viewed as part of an organized group, rather than a vulnerable individual, is especially helpful when informal workers are interacting with people of authority (including employers and state officials).

Empowering Women

In addition to facilitating informal workers' access to social legitimacy and basic needs, the informal worker identity has empowered women past their traditional social groupings, especially those based on gender. More than 80 percent of the 140 respondents spoke to this point. Within the organizations and at meetings women spoke on par with men, and caste delineations were rarely mentioned. Bidi organizations, for example, are still predominantly led by men who belong to a different caste from the members. Yet women spoke forcefully toward male members and leaders when they felt they were being belittled.

Anamabai Dararat Yamool, a 90-year-old bidi worker in Mumbai, explained, "All I got after all these years of fighting was the title of being a daring person. But I would not be alive today without this title. One time a union member was making fun of ladies for going to the rallies. I grabbed his collar and hit him so hard; he wouldn't walk down my street for three months. He was so frightened of me!"[50]

Anamabai was married at the age of 9 years, and at the age of 11 years, she moved with her new husband and in-laws from rural Maharashtra to the city of Mumbai, where the men could work in the textile mills. As was common for most male textile workers at the time, their wives stayed at home rolling bidis. Anamabai learned the trade from her mother-in-law and rolled bidis for the rest of her life. No one in her family was

[50] Interview, May 27, 2003.

literate. "At that time, you didn't need schooling to get the jobs. All the men were illiterate. There was just a lot of hard work, drinking [alcohol] and eating," she explained. Although they had enough money to eat and drink for some years, Anamabai had no security of her own. She had no children, so when her husband died, her in-laws kicked her out of the house. She moved to a one-room home and lived by herself. As a widow with no family, Anamabai was particularly vulnerable. However, she had been an active union member for several years, which she said has helped her survive.

In another interview, Bappu, the general secretary of the Chennai Bidi Union, began chiding women for being uneducated and inactive in the struggles: "Now these women members just want free scholarships. They don't want to fight." Tajunisha, a 38-year-old Muslim bidi roller and member of the union, immediately yelled back in front of all the bystanders, "We were there with you fighting for housing, for cards, against the anti-smoking ban! You just don't notice us, and then you tell others you did all the work! You think we are dogs that can't think. We are the ones rolling the bidis and cooking and cleaning. You just come in and eat and leave."[51]

Tajunisha wears a burkha (a Muslim head scarf) and a gown to cover her whenever she is outside. Inside the union office, however, her burkha slips from her head, and she does not bother to fix it, despite the presence of men in the room. Although Tajunisha does not want to participate in the violent fights that the union leaders engaged in during the 1970s, she views her actions as a "strong fight" nonetheless. Tajunisha's mother and husband used to forbid her to roll bidis because they felt it demoted the family. Her husband has a part-time job in a bakery, but "he rarely goes to work. He just drinks and sleeps all day." Therefore, Tajunisha rolled bidis and collected her own income in stealth. "My bidi has been my Laxmi [Hindu goddess of wealth]. If it wasn't for my bidi, my family would not be alive today," she explained.

Tajunisha went to school until the fifth grade and can only sign her name. She regrets that she is not more educated, but she is proud of what she has done despite this "weakness." In great detail she described to me the marches that she participated in and the newspapers and television cameras that came to cover her. Tajunisha's greatest reward for her struggles is that none of her three children "even know how to roll bidis!" She exclaimed with pride, "I made sure they are all in school." When she

[51] Interview, July 12, 2003.

joined the union five years ago, she received an identity card; as a result, her children received scholarships for the past two years, she qualified for a pension account, and she was able to use the specialized bidi hospital in her slum. Tajunisha's work and membership in a workers' organization assure her the ability to take care of her children, regardless of her sex or caste.

In addition to attaining welfare benefits from her union membership, Tajunisha uses the union as a support system that she relies on for new information and for increased power with which to make demands, regardless of her sex. For example, after my interview with Tajunisha, she overheard me asking another interviewee about bonuses. Tajunisha was not aware that she was eligible for a bonus. As soon as she heard me asking about it, she grabbed a fellow union member and neighbor and approached their contractor about bonuses. The contractor denied her the bonus, so she returned to the union office the next day to request the union leader's help in getting the bonus. Information becomes a powerful resource to union members; it is a medium of exchange to strengthen the tangible benefits represented by the card.

Other women spoke of how the unions had given them autonomy in their household decision making. Hajira, for example, is a 29-year-old bidi roller in Chennai. Both she and her mother are members of the bidi union. However, because Hajira's husband does not let her leave the house, she is not able to attend most meetings. Instead she learns about the union announcements through her mother. Like many of the members, she and her husband are illiterate, and she is determined to educate her children. To Hajira, her work and her membership in the organization are a means to educating her children. Hajira said, "My husband does not let me out of the house, so I make bidis in the house. If I work, I can get scholarships for my children's studies. When it is time, I leave the house without telling my husband and pick up the forms at the union office. I cannot read, so my children fill them out, and the union submits them. We don't tell my husband."[52]

In the construction organizations, leaders are both male and female, and men and women participate equally in meetings. In Tamil Nadu, TMKTPS provides a space for members to gather after work and relax. In this space (the office that is run out of the general secretary's home), members vent their frustrations about their employers and their spouses, gossip, and even nap. Most importantly, they bond over their common

[52] Interview, July 16, 2003.

work experiences and vulnerabilities, although they span an array of castes and communities. Muniyama expressed similar sentiments to many of the bidi workers: "I have not gotten any monetary benefits from the union. But emotionally, I am more confident, I know my rights. I like coming to meetings here. In this house, I feel like I belong to a group." Although this "group" includes men and women of various castes, as a member, Muniyama feels she is equal to the others. When a policeman once asked her why she is bold enough to participate in a strike, she answered, "I am in the union. The men are striking, so I must too."[53] The collective identity that comes from the union through increased information and the identity card is a source of strength.

As a new bride, Muniyama moved from rural Tamil Nadu to the city of Chennai. Her husband was a construction worker and was told that he could get more work in the city. At the time Muniyama was not employed. Shortly after their second daughter was born thirty years ago, however, Muniyama's husband died, forcing her to start working. Since then, she has been a construction worker, and she joined the union twenty years ago. The union provides Muniyama, a woman living alone, with the support she needs to manage her daily struggles. For example, Muniyama's most important experience with the union occurred when her daughter was kicked out of her husband's home with none of her personal belongings. Muniyama cried to her fellow union members, and the union, along with the union leader, filed a case with the police. "I don't yet know what will happen, but it made me and my daughter very happy."[54] As a member of the union, Muniyama gains visibility in society.

Krishnaveni is a 45-year-old construction worker in Chennai. Unlike most other workers, she is literate. She has been the primary income earner in the family since she married, because her husband has an illness and cannot work. "He does the cooking, and I don't give him any money for drinking," she explained to me. Despite her education and her control over the family income, however, she attributes her strength to the union. "I have received no benefits since I joined this union, just frustration. My body still aches and I am still not able to pay rent. But the union has given me strength. I know my rights, and no one can take that away from me," she asserted. Krishnaveni proudly listed all the meetings she has attended and the fast she participated in the previous year, as well as the list of demands she personally handed to the chief minister's office. "Before I couldn't even look at my husband in the eye, and now I will yell at the big men in government without being scared," she proclaimed. As if reciting directly from theories of social disarticulation, she said, "I tell them [government officials] we need a house. We build all these houses all our lives for other people, and we don't even have one for ourselves! That is not right, and I tell them."[55]

Like TMKTPS, the Mumbai Construction NGO uses its child care centers as a space for workers to bond over their common needs. Although it is registered as an NGO and has not yet attained worker identity cards, it provides services to construction workers only. Sheila, a schoolteacher in one of the child care centers, said, "The mothers love to pick up their children after work, so they can ask me questions about their gynecological problems." Sheila recalled the numerous occasions on which she has had to explain women's health problems to the mothers or had to teach the younger girls to avoid eye contact with the contractors, so the contractors would stop harassing them.[56] In this case, caste fades to the background as women workers bond over their daily experiences working and living on the construction sites.

Focusing a Collective Identity through Selection and a Target

The final area in which women expressed the benefits of their class identity was in terms of their activism. Class-based collective action focuses workers' demands and identifies a target for their demands, which in turn strengthens activism. As poor women who are members of lower castes or religious minorities, the workers I interviewed faced multiple and varying problems each day, ranging from sexual abuse at the work site, to depression, and to fear of starvation. As members of informal workers' organizations, however, many expressed their demands in surprisingly similar and limited ways. They demanded certain welfare benefits (almost always those benefits they were entitled to under the welfare board, but had not yet received), and their target was, very clearly, the state.

In virtually all of the interviews, workers narrowed their demands to one or two issues, despite the fact that they lacked basic needs in several areas. Seventy-two percent of the expressed demands dealt with issues of welfare, whereas 28 percent concerned traditional workers' rights issues.

---

[55]   Interview, July 17, 2003.
[56]   Interview, March 28, 2003.

In six of the seven organizations, members' demands were consistent within their organization and reflected a campaign that it was waging against the government.[57] For example, in the Mumbai Bidi Union, nearly all the interviewees said their primary need is home ownership. At the time of my interviews, the union was in the midst of a massive campaign to hold the state government accountable for its promise to provide all bidi workers with housing subsidies under the Bidi Welfare Act. Similarly, more than half the interviewees in the Tamil Nadu construction union, TMKTPS, said their primary need is support for the education and marriage of their children. Again, that union was in the midst of a massive campaign to force the government to implement these benefits promised by the Construction Welfare Board.

This congruence between the organizations' advocacy campaigns and members' individual responses showed that those campaigns were being waged by members, not just organizational leaders. Members often contrasted their involvement in the new movements to their exclusion from earlier ones. For example, Laxmi Panday Nakka has been a member of the Mumbai Bidi Union for fifteen years. Like most other bidi workers in Mumbai, she is illiterate, a member of the weaver caste, and a migrant. She explained,

Nowadays, I understand what is happening in the rallies. Before, the big men [union leaders] went inside to talk with employers, and we didn't know what was said. They never taught us how to speak. But now we make Ministers come out and talk to all of us. We speak very softly to them and explain our situation.[58]

Workers also viewed their membership in a union as a way to protect themselves. Although the identity card is designed to simply certify an individual's membership in a welfare board, in practice it also indicates a worker's connection to a union, because unions are so instrumental in connecting workers to welfare boards. Therefore, many workers waved their identity cards in the faces of officials to indicate that they are not isolated, vulnerable individuals, but members of organizations that hold political power. As states overtly absolve employers of responsibility toward their workers, it is significant that most informal workers' organizations are unions, and not identity-based civil society organizations.

[57] In the case of the Kolkata Bidi Union, union leaders stated they were fighting for the implementation of the Bidi Welfare Board, but most members did not know what the board was and stated that they needed "everything," when asked what their primary needs were. The reasons for this lack of knowledge and organization may be located in leadership style, although a detailed exploration is beyond the scope of this study.

[58] Interview, May 30, 2003.

2.3 CONCLUSIONS

As I argued in the Introduction, informal workers occupy their own position in the class structure and therefore have unique interests. Despite scholars' claims to the contrary, the findings in this chapter show that informal workers in India identify, articulate, and demand these unique interests. Class remains an organizing and mobilizing principle for these workers, because their access to resources, their relationship with other classes, and the structures of production within which they operate influence how they identify and organize as a class.

The alternative labor movement model presented in this chapter illuminates the dynamic nature of the relations between capital, labor, and the state. In India, the victorious formal workers' struggles that followed the traditional labor movement model resulted in increased legislation on labor protection; formal workers ensured that employers were held responsible for workers' rights. Not surprisingly, capital worked hard to recommodify labor; to avoid costly labor protection laws, employers turned to unprotected informal workers. Recently, the Indian government has increased its support for capital's reliance on informal labor. Although these trends have no doubt hurt labor, they do not bring about an end to the relationship between the state and labor.

Informal workers in India's bidi and construction industries have been forcing the state, rather than the employer, to "decommodify" their labor power since the 1980s. Even in the face of the great economic transformation of the twenty-first century, informal workers are holding the state responsible for meeting their basic social consumption needs, regardless of their informal labor status, by demanding welfare benefits. Informal workers have operationalized this strategy through tripartite welfare boards that are implemented at the state level. In contrast to traditional labor struggles, informal workers' movements today include the mass of illiterate men and women and employees in public and private enterprises. They organize by neighborhoods, register as NGOs and trade unions, and use nonviolent tactics.

Finally, although informal workers in the past mobilized to become formal workers, since the 1980s, they have fought for state recognition of their informal work status and their specific interests. Therefore, in addition to fighting for material welfare benefits, informal workers are building a unique class identity that connects them to the state through their social consumption needs, rather than pitting them as antitheses to capital. Workers view this identity as a means to attaining social legitimacy, empowering women by trumping traditional groupings, and strengthening their own social status by connecting them to a focused collective.

These findings force us to refine our conventional definitions of informal workers. Informal workers are not delinked from the state or capital, and they are able to organize to demand state benefits. The difference between informal and formal workers, however, is that informal workers do not receive any protection from employer exploitation. Why would the state government agree to recognize informal workers when employers refuse to do so? Why would the state agree to be held responsible for these vulnerable workers' welfare needs? How effective are these movements? In the next three chapters, I examine these questions and explore the conditions under which informal workers' recent struggle has been more or less successful.

3

The Success of Competitive Populism

The previous chapter analyzed how changes in the structures of production in India have given rise to a social movement that has spurred innovative institutions and a new class consciousness among informal workers. The type of workers involved in the new informal workers' movement, the strategies used, and the demands made are consistent across states and industries. *The movements' ability to secure material benefits for their members, however, varies by state.*[1] As outlined in Table 7, material benefits include work-based benefits (such as job security, wage increases, and bonuses) and welfare benefits. Welfare benefits can be further differentiated into those provided by the union (such as leadership training, child care, and provision of school supplies) and those provided by the state (such as scholarships, health care, loans, and social security).

Table 8 shows how the amount and type of material benefits received by the informal workers in this sample differ by state. Tamil Nadu had the largest number of interviewees who received material benefits, Maharashtra had the second most interviewees, and West Bengal had the least. Consistent with the findings in Chapter 2 – namely that informal workers'

[1] As shown in Chapter 2, Indian informal workers' organizations have secured material and nonmaterial benefits for their members. Nonmaterial benefits include group support, education on rights, expanded networks, dignity, and significantly, an identity card. Although the identity card is an important means through which informal workers attain material benefits, it is not defined here as a direct material benefit. Nonmaterial benefits are important in terms of class-based organization. They, however, cannot be expected to vary by state, because state governments cannot directly provide them (with the exception of the identity card). Rather, they vary by organization characteristics, such as quality of leadership or organizational structure. A more detailed examination of this variation is beyond the scope of this study.

TABLE 7: *Material Benefits (Worker vs. Welfare)*

Benefit Type	Examples
Worker Benefits	Job protection, timely payment, wage increase, bonus
Welfare Benefits	
From the union	Leadership training, child care, school supplies
From the state	Education scholarships, health care, loans (marriage and other), social security (including widow benefits)

recent movements focus more on attaining welfare benefits than work-based benefits – I find that nearly all interviewees who received a benefit in Tamil Nadu and Maharashtra received welfare benefits. Many workers in Tamil Nadu also reported receiving work-based benefits, whereas very few in Maharashtra received any such benefits. Interestingly, the state provided nearly all welfare benefits received in Tamil Nadu, in contrast to less than half of those received in Maharashtra and to only one received in West Bengal.

In this and the next two chapters, I examine how the political and economic characteristics of state governments affect the amount and type of material benefits that informal workers receive. Drawing from the

TABLE 8: *Type of Benefit Received by City/State*

	Chennai/ Tamil Nadu	Mumbai/ Maharashtra	Kolkata/ West Bengal
Received a benefit (as % of members interviewed)	75 (30/40)	58 (23/40)	35 (21/60)
Received a worker benefit (as % of members who received benefit)	30 (9/30)	9 (2/23)	81 (17/21)
Received a Welfare Benefit (as % of members who received benefit)	100 (30/30)	91 (21/23)	24 (5/21)
Received a Welfare Benefit from the Union (as % of those who received a Welfare Benefit)	20 (6/30)	62 (13/21)	80 (4/5)
Received a Welfare Benefit from the State (as % of those who received a Welfare Benefit)	90 (27/30)	48 (10/21)	20 (1/5)

Note: Members may receive more than one benefit. For more detail on benefit type, see Table 7; for more detail on interviews, see Appendix III.

state theoretical framework outlined in the Introduction, I argue that the social base and electoral context of party politics, as well as the economic policies of the government in power, interact with informal workers' movements from below to explain why informal workers in some states have been more successful than those in other states in ensuring their social rights. That such successes are occurring in a context where the state and society have repeatedly denied informal workers the basic benefits of citizenship is significant. These findings illustrate how social movement structures have a limited capacity to predict informal workers' movement success in the absence of a conducive political and economic framework from above.

In this chapter, I show that political parties that compete for votes from the poor have given informal workers' organizations a unique opportunity to attain state-supported welfare benefits for their members. The states of Tamil Nadu and Kerala exemplify this claim. Yet unlike Kerala, Tamil Nadu illustrates how (1) competitive, pro-poor electoral contexts can enable a range of parties – *even those unrelated to traditional leftist parties* – to assist informal workers and how (2) such electoral contexts interact with liberal economic reforms to provide informal workers with additional leverage in the contemporary era.

The particular form of pro-poor politics that characterizes Tamil Nadu has become well known and extensively analyzed for its populist tendencies (de Wit 1996; Harriss 2000; Kohli 1990a; Rudolph 1961; Subramanian 1999; Swamy 1996b; Washbrook 1989; Wyatt 2008). I argue that these populist tendencies have given Tamil informal workers an ideal opportunity to convince the state's politicians that informal workers comprise a large, organized percentage of the plebian support base that parties must please to get votes. Informal workers focus on the *promise* of their votes.

To lend credibility to their promises, Tamil informal workers use influential leaders to make the promises publically, and they demand benefits targeted only to informal workers. These strategies are similar to those used in other poor patron-client settings where costly mechanisms to monitor how clients actually vote, such as official exit poll data, are unavailable (see Kitschelt and Wilkinson 2007b). In addition to promising votes, Tamil informal workers frame themselves as distinct from the traditional, formal working class. Unlike formal workers' labor movements, organized informal labor in Tamil Nadu is not attached to a particular party or does not espouse a specific political or economic ideology. Rather, it appeals to every politician's desire to retain or attain power.

In addition, it frames its interests within the context of an increasingly liberalized economy that relies on cheap, flexible labor.

In return for their votes and their labor, informal workers demand basic social rights and civic goods from the state, such as access to drinking water, education, health care, and housing. Because of the lack of employer accountability, employers still fail to cover workers' production costs. But informal workers in Tamil Nadu are convincing the state to at least cover their *reproduction costs*. They make their claims using a universalistic rhetoric of citizenship (such as "the masses"), but they institutionalize the receipt of their citizenship rights through a system specific to informal workers. In turn, Tamil Nadu's politicians have attained political and economic benefits from informal workers' support.

Let us now examine the state-provided benefits that informal workers in Tamil Nadu have received.

3.1 TAMIL NADU: SUBSTANTIAL STATE BENEFITS FOR INFORMAL LABOR

Tamil Nadu is one of the most progressive states in India in terms of protecting informal workers. In 2005, then-State Labor Minister P. Annavi began his *2005–06 Labour Policy Note* by emphasizing both the importance of the informal economy to economic growth and the government's commitment to protecting the welfare of informal workers:

One of the most important contributors to economic activity is labour...The Policy recognizes that harmonious relations between labour and management are needed to maximize production and speed up economic growth. The Policy takes note of the fact that the workers in the unorganized [or informal] sector constitute the majority of the work force and they play a major role in the economic development of the country. The problems faced by them are many, complex and peculiar. The Policy also aims at strengthening of institutional arrangements for welfare and social security of this labour force. (Tamil Nadu Government 2006a)

Similarly, in my interview with then-State Labor Minister Anabarasan, in December 2008, he said unequivocally, "Our government's top priority is supporting unorganized [i.e., informal] workers. We want to give them full security."[2]

In terms of conventional workers' rights, the Tamil Nadu government has fixed minimum wages in ninety employment categories, making it the state with the largest number of protected employment categories. As

---

[2] Interview, December 17, 2008.

TABLE 9: *Official and Reported Minimum Wage by State and Industry (Rs.)*

		West Bengal	Tamil Nadu	Maharashtra[a]
Construction	Official Wage	67.17	56	12
(wage/day)	VDA[b]	28.38	45.57	101.65
	Total Wage	95.55	101.57	113.65
	Reported Wage[c]	40–80	80–90	50
Bidi	Official Wage	79.14	31	29
(wage/1,000	VDA	-	21.91	11
bidis)	Total Wage	79.14	52.91	40
	Reported Wage	30	45–50	30

Note: Official minimum wages are based on 2002 figures. Although some states revised their minimum wages in 2004, the new levels were not implemented at the time of interviews. Rs. 50 = US$1.
[a] Maharashtra's official minimum wages vary within the state by zones. The difference between zones is Rs. 1–2. Official wages in table represent the state average.
[b] VDA is the "variable dearness allowance." VDAs were implemented in 1991 to ensure that minimum wages accounted for inflation by being linked to the Consumer Price Index.
[c] Reported wages are based on my interviews in the three states.
Sources: Ministry of Labor and Employment (2002) and interviews with workers.

shown in Table 9, Tamil Nadu's official minimum wages in construction and bidi are in between those in Maharashtra and West Bengal: they are Rs. 101.57/day for construction and Rs. 52.91/1,000 for bidi (GOI 2002b). Effective minimum wages vary widely in India, depending on the nature of the job and worker characteristics (such as gender, ethnicity, and caste). They vary even more in the informal sector because there is no record of payment. Still, of the three states examined in this study, union leaders and members in Tamil Nadu were the only ones to say that they are *basically* receiving their minimum wages, although women in construction consistently reported receiving only Rs. 80–90 per day. General Secretary Geeta Ramakrishnan of Tamil Maanila Kattida Thozilalar Panchayat Sangham (TMKTPS), the Tamil Nadu construction union, said that members have been receiving minimum wages for the past decade and compensation for work-related accidents and natural death for five years.[3] Recently, the Tamil Nadu government also instituted pensions for

[3] Interview, July 9, 2003.

construction workers (Tamil Nadu Government 2004b, 2005). Bappu, the general secretary of the Chennai Bidi Union, said that members have been receiving minimum wages and pensions for nearly fifteen years.[4] Bidi workers reported receiving Rs. 45–50 per day.[5]

As argued in Chapter 2, the increasing flexibility in structures of production is threatening the provision of employer-provided workers' benefits in India. It is significant, therefore, that in addition to conventional work-based benefits, Tamil Nadu's government has also delivered more welfare benefits to informal workers than other states. Kerala has been lauded for its early intervention for informal workers, and indeed its policies have served as a role model for the government of Tamil Nadu. Yet Tamil Nadu was, in fact, the first state to legally protect informal workers, and as I detail later, it is Tamil Nadu's movement that has pushed its demands at the national level in India. State-provided welfare benefits in Tamil Nadu reflect informal workers' demand for some social justice, even in the face of state support for declining employer responsibility.[6]

Although the Bidi Workers Welfare Fund is under the jurisdiction of the national government, state governments are responsible for advising the national government and overseeing its implementation.[7] Tamil Nadu's government has been particularly active in this regard. Throughout the 1980s, Tamil Nadu was the only state in India to provide welfare benefits to bidi workers. In July 1999, in a much-publicized move, the

---

[4] Interview, July 15, 2003.

[5] Although the effective wages in Tamil Nadu were higher and more consistent than those in Maharashtra and West Bengal, members in both industries in Tamil Nadu did report that employers often manipulated their wages. Bidi employers have been providing increasingly low-quality inputs, forcing workers to spend their wages on purchasing better inputs. Construction employers discriminate between male and female employees, paying women nearly half the wage of men. Most often, women complained that they could not find enough work. Finally, the Minimum Wage Act of 1948 does not specify a time frame in which minimum wages must be reviewed; therefore, they often remain static.

[6] Note this differs from policies such as the 1974 Kerala Agricultural Workers Act (KAWA), which aimed to protect agricultural workers. KAWA mirrored conventional labor movement approaches in that it aimed to provide permanent work for attached labor, social security, conciliation mechanisms at the district level, reduced work hours, breaks, an employment register to keep on the farm, and a minimum wage. Workers even referred to KAWA as the "factory acts." For an insightful analysis of KAWA, see Herring (1989).

[7] Welfare boards are the primary institutional mechanism through which informal workers in India are implementing their new class movement. They are implemented by state governments and are funded by taxes placed on employers, state and national government contributions, and membership fees from informal workers. In return for becoming members of the board, informal workers receive welfare benefits. At present, welfare boards are industry specific. For greater detail on the history, operation, and structure of bidi and construction workers' welfare boards in India, see Chapter 2.

Tamil Nadu government compelled the national government to form Tamil Nadu's State Advisory Committee earlier than scheduled. In addition, the state labor minister personally met with the Bidi Manufacturers Association of Tamil Nadu to force them to pay their dues to the Bidi Workers Welfare Fund (Special Correspondent 1999).

On March 11, 2003, the Tamil Nadu government passed the Integrated Bidi Workers Housing Scheme. Under this project, the state government agreed to provide subsidies (along with the national government) toward the construction of 10,000 houses for bidi workers (Tamil Nadu Government 2003a), with each home to be owned by an informally employed woman bidi worker.[8] By May 19, 2003, the state government had released its subsidies for the construction of 499 homes (Tamil Nadu Government 2003b). By the end of 2008, the government had released its subsidies for the construction of 4,169 homes; more than half of these homes (2,222) had roofs, and 817 were completed by that time.[9]

At the state level, the Tamil Nadu government passed the Manual Workers Act in 1982, making Tamil Nadu the first state to legally protect informal workers. This act regulates the conditions of informal work, ensures welfare provision for informal workers, and enables the establishment of welfare boards for informal workers. By 2008, the state government had specified sixty-eight categories of informal workers to be protected under this act.

In 1994, the state government established the Construction Workers Welfare Board, making Tamil Nadu the second state to protect informal construction workers.[10] In 2003, the Construction Board purchased its own four-story building, and by 2008, it had 110 staff. In January 2005, 630,812 construction workers had become members of the Construction Welfare Board; by December 2008, this figure had more than tripled to 1,927,779 members (Tamil Nadu Government 2006a, 2008a). Since the Welfare Board's inception, the Tamil Nadu government has periodically expanded its benefits. In 2005, the state government increased the

---

[8] The state government is providing Rs. 5,000/house and the national government is providing Rs. 20,000/house. The remainder of the costs will be borne by the worker.

[9] Figures attained on December 19, 2008, from monitoring reports provided by M. Ravichandran, deputy commissioner of labor, Department of Labor, Tamil Nadu government. Ravichandran is responsible for bidi housing in Tamil Nadu.

[10] Kerala was the first to implement a state-level Construction Workers Welfare Board in 1990. In November 1995, Kerala transformed its state-level board to fit the national requirements for a Construction Workers Welfare Board. To date, Tamil Nadu's Construction Welfare Board remains at the state level.

TABLE 10: *Welfare Benefits from Tamil Nadu Construction Board (1995–2008)*

Assistance Type	No. of Workers	Amount (Rs.)
Accident Death and Funeral Assistance	825	84,158,000
Disability due to Accident	165	4,393,050
Natural Death and Funeral Assistance	16,185	235,877,300
Marriage Assistance	43,897	87,794,000
Maternity Assistance	4,014	16,801,585
Education Assistance		
10th Studying (only for girls)	12,687	12,687,000
11th Studying (only for girls)	9,158	9,158,000
12th Studying (only for girls)	9,626	14,439,000
10th pass	40,419	40,419,000
12th pass	23,820	35,730,000
Higher education	23,938	38,919,939
Eyeglasses	3,178	1,359,733
Pension and Pension Arrears	4,681	47,212,981
TOTAL	192,593	628,949,588

Source: Tamil Nadu Construction Workers Welfare Board Monitoring Reports (Tamil Nadu Government 2008a). Rs. 50 = US$1.

education scholarship amounts and added pensions to the Construction Welfare Board (Tamil Nadu Government 2004b, 2005). In 2006 and 2007, the state government increased the monthly pension and maternity assistance amounts, eliminated workers' registration fees, increased the number of staff, formed district-level monitoring committees, and offered training services to registered members (Tamil Nadu Government 2006b, 2007a, 2007c, 2007d). As of December 2008, 192,593 members had received direct welfare benefits from the Construction Welfare Board, totaling Rs. 628,949,588 (US$12.8 million; Tamil Nadu Government 2008a). Table 10 details the types and amount of welfare benefits that have been sanctioned by the Construction Board since it began.

In addition to the Construction Welfare Board, the Tamil Nadu government has established several other informal workers' welfare boards. In 2000, the state government became the first state in the country to launch nine new welfare boards for nine categories of informal workers.[11] By January 2005, 701,841 informal workers had become members of

---

[11] These include auto-rickshaw and taxi drivers, tailors, hairdressers, washermen, palm-tree workers, handicraft workers, handloom and silk weavers, footwear and leather goods workers, and artists.

these new boards. In 2007, the state government added three more welfare boards for three new categories of informal workers: goldsmiths, potters, and domestic workers. That same year, the state government sanctioned Rs. 139,843,000 (US$2.85 million) for these boards, and in 2008, it sanctioned Rs. 200 million (US$4 million) for them (Tamil Nadu Government 2008b).[12]

Today, the management and implementation of the welfare boards for informal sector workers are among the top-three priorities of the state government's Labor Department (along with enforcing labor laws in the formal sector and managing conciliation between formal workers and employers) (Tamil Nadu Government 2006a). In 2005, the State Department of Labor dedicated an entire section in its main office in Chennai and equipped fifteen regional offices with personnel and resources to administer the state's welfare boards for informal workers (Tamil Nadu Government 2006a). In August 2007, the state government created fifteen additional regional offices and increased the number of staff in existing offices (Tamil Nadu Government 2007a). Claims submissions and welfare provisions were decentralized to take place in the thirty district-level offices (Tamil Nadu Government 2007b).

Of the twenty bidi members in Tamil Nadu whom I interviewed, nearly 75 percent have received pensions, and just under half have received education scholarships. Just above half of the respondents frequent the dispensary designed specifically for bidi workers, which is located in the heart of the slum where almost all the bidi workers and union members reside. Two-thirds of the twenty construction workers in Tamil Nadu reported receiving a state-provided welfare benefit. Although the construction members have received fewer benefits than the state's bidi workers, they received more benefits from the state government than have construction members interviewed in Maharashtra and West Bengal.

Why have Tamil Nadu's informal workers been so successful (relative to other states) in procuring state-conferred benefits? As a primary explanation, I explore Tamil Nadu's competitive, pro-poor populist political parties, and as a secondary explanation I explore its pro-liberalization agenda. Together, these state characteristics have given informal workers an opportunity to capitalize on the interests of their political leaders

---

[12] Government funds are used for all the welfare boards except for the Construction Board, which is financed through a tax on builders of 3% of the building cost, and for the Auto-rickshaw and Taxi Drivers Board, which is financed through a motor vehicle tax of 1% on employers of motor transport carrying passengers or goods by road.

by framing themselves within politicians' interests. Before exploring this argument, a brief discussion of the concept of populism is in order.

3.2 POPULISM: A SURVIVING PHENOMENON

The variation in politician–citizen linkages across countries has gained increased attention in recent years (Kitschelt and Wilkinson 2007b). Populism represents one of these linkages. The term "populism" has been variously defined, and not surprisingly, some have questioned the use of the term as a result.[13] The increasing salience of populist leadership throughout the world, however, has forced a reexamination of the phenomenon.

In broad terms, most uses of the term "populism" share the following theme expressed by the *Oxford Companion to the Politics of the World*:

> Populist movements claim to represent the people as a whole: sometimes the entire nation, sometimes the majority of the people. They often begin as movements of protest against parties which they see as entrenched defenders of the existing social order; if successful, they themselves end as parties. Radical versions of populism, sometimes right-wing, sometimes left, seek to represent and mobilize the poor or the underprivileged masses. (Worsley 2001)

Although populism has not yet been translated into a programmatic text as has "nationalism," "liberalism," or "socialism," it does occupy a distinct political space representing a common linkage between politicians and voters. Unlike nationalist regimes or movements, populist ones tend to define their support base as the mass of "common" or "ordinary" people (Wiles 1969). Unlike liberalism, populist regimes promise to secure the benefits of the market economy for ordinary people while simultaneously protecting them from the downsides of competition. Unlike socialism or communism, populist leaders promise to improve ordinary people's access to privilege but do not offer to change the structures

---

[13] For a detailed review of the populist literature, see Roberts (1995). Roberts outlines four perspectives on populism from Latin America: (1) the historical/sociological perspective, which emphasizes the multiclass sociopolitical coalitions that arise during the early stages of industrialization; (2) the economic perspective, which reduces populism to a lack of fiscal discipline and redistributive policies in response to pressures of mass consumption; (3) the ideological perspective, which associates populism with a discourse that articulates a contradiction between "the people" and a "power bloc"; and (4) the political perspective, which equates populism with a pattern of top-down mobilization by personalist leaders that bypasses institutional forms of political mediation (pp. 84–85).

and systems that generated the exclusion in the first place (Subramanian 1999). To unify the large (often heterogeneous) group of "ordinary people," populist leaders rely on notions of unjustified oppression and exclusion from privilege by the elite, who are specifically defined as distinct from the ordinary masses. Populist leaders, who as Peter Wiles (1969: 167) writes, "are in mystical contact with the masses," promise to reverse this discrimination and usually relay their promises using direct communication, rather than operating through institutional intermediaries.

Scholars have argued that populism arises when politicians take advantage of the mass backlash that occurs during transitions to capitalism. Empirical evidence for this claim has come from Russian peasant and American farmer movements against urban lawyers in the nineteenth and early twentieth centuries, as well as the lower- and intermediate-class movements that rose during the early phases of industrialization from the 1930s to the 1960s in urban Latin America (Collier and Collier 1991; Ionescu and Gellner 1969). In Latin America, for example, the government's ability to impose import-substitution policies was said to follow from mass support for populist leaders' redistributive efforts (Kaufman and Stallings 1991; Vilas 1992). Once capitalism developed, so the argument goes, organized, educated social classes emerged that no longer found broad populist promises appealing. Scholars have also claimed that the rise of neoliberal policies that preached fiscal austerity undermined populist rulers' ability to engage in fiscally irresponsible actions. As the money available for rulers to give handouts decreased and redistribution of wealth failed to take place, populist regimes became unpopular and eventually disappeared. In other words, populism and modern-day neoliberalism are viewed as mutually exclusive.

The static definition of populism underscoring these arguments undermines our ability to understand its persistence in the contemporary era. Recently scholars have instead highlighted populism's dynamic political adaptability, thereby decoupling it from specific economic policies. In Peru, for example, Kenneth Roberts (1995: 88, 114) shows how Fujimori redefined the contemporary populist support base to one that *coexists* with neoliberalism and is concentrated in "the informal sectors, rather than [formal-sector] organized labor." The burgeoning informal workforce serves as a crucial peg in neoliberal agendas. Similarly, as Pereira, Maravall, and Przeworski (1993) show, Fernando Collor de Mello in Brazil implemented welfare schemes targeting lower class workers while simultaneously implementing neoliberal reforms.

Tamil Nadu provides further evidence of populism's ability to adapt to the economic policies of liberalization. It also lends support to the ability of populist parties to exist even in competitive party contexts.[14] Since the late 1960s, two populist parties have competed for power in Tamil Nadu. Unlike conventional portrayals of populism that predict its downward spiral into authoritarianism or fascism (as in Germany and Italy in the 1930s or in Latin America after the 1950s), I find that populism in Tamil Nadu has *strengthened* democratic participation by enabling representation among new groups. Which groups emerge depends fundamentally on how a particular populist leader defines his or her support base of "underprivileged masses" and how groups frame themselves to fit into that definition.[15] Until the mid-1980s, one party in Tamil Nadu relied on a narrow band of middle strata supporters, whereas the other relied on the mass base of poor workers (similar to Fujimori and Collor de Mello).

As I illustrate in the following pages, it was the latter form of a subaltern or mass populism in Tamil Nadu that created an opportunity for informal workers to frame their needs in a way that appealed to politicians. The competitive party context not only gave rise to mass-based populism but also set the stage for subsequent populist politicians (whether mass based or not) to respond to informal worker demands by providing state benefits. During the 1990s, Tamil leaders from both parties added a liberalization agenda to their populist political tactics. Contrary to what might be expected from scholarship on liberalization's negative effect on workers, Tamil Nadu's commitment to liberalization did not suffocate informal workers' movement success; in fact, it expanded it.

As a result of the state's response, an increasing number of previously unrepresented informal workers are joining informal workers' organizations and attaining group-based power as well as welfare benefits. At the same time, because informal workers are relying on populist politicians, the structural changes needed to reverse the exploitation they face are not necessarily being made. Why political parties in other states did not follow the lead of Tamil Nadu's populist parties and garner electoral support from informal workers is explored in the following chapters. Before examining the details of Tamil Nadu's populism and its impact on informal

---

[14] For a detailed discussion of competitiveness and clientelist/populist politics, see Kitschelt and Wilkinson (2007a).

[15] It should be noted that Tamil Nadu's populist regimes have provided growth opportunities not only for progressive organizations fighting for social justice but also for right-wing Hindu fundamentalist organizations.

workers, let us first explore why informal workers in Tamil Nadu did not organize to attain state protection before the rise of mass-based populism.

3.3 CASTE AND ETHNIC NATIONALISM OVERLOOKS INFORMAL LABOR (1800–1977)

As summarized in Table 11, the gains that informal workers' movements achieved in Tamil Nadu coincided with the establishment of mass-based populism in the 1980s. Before this, Tamil Nadu was led by a series of social movement leaders who fought for social equality by focusing on caste and ethnic identities. Although a populist political party arose out of these movements, its leader focused on a narrow, middle stratum of the population. This focus failed to legitimate the class-based needs or identities of poor, informal workers and thus created a vacuum that was successfully filled by the mass-based populism of a competing party founded by M. G. Ramachandran (popularly known as MGR) in the 1980s.[16] The mass-based populism that emerged in the 1980s was a direct result of Tamil Nadu's competitive party context.

Programmatic Caste and Ethnic Movements (1800–1947)

Among scholars of South Asia, Tamil Nadu is well known for its progressive social movements that arose to fight caste-based inequalities during the nineteenth century,[17] specifically the entrenched social position of the uppermost caste of Brahmins.[18] During the 1800s, Brahmins' already-privileged stature in the Tamil Nadu economy increased even more under British rule.[19] The growth in public administration and higher education required to manage the transition to modern capitalism created space for some Indian citizens to advance within the colonial economic structure. Because of British policy, nearly all professional jobs opened to Indians were given to Brahmins.

At the turn of the twentieth century, modern factories emerged in the growing industries of cotton, sugar, and cement, and people flocked to

---

[16] Exploring the reasons behind early leaders' unwillingness to see informal workers as a large, unified vote bank, although important, is beyond the scope of this study.

[17] For a detailed analysis of the impact of caste structures on caste-based movements in Indian northern and southern states, see Jaffrelot (2003).

[18] Brahmin is the highest of the four major castes of the Hindu social hierarchy. Traditionally, Brahmins were similar to a "priestly caste" – responsible for officiating religious rites and studying and teaching the sacred Hindu texts, the *Vedas*.

[19] Under British rule, the region that most closely shares borders with modern-day Tamil Nadu was called the "Chennai Presidency."

TABLE 11: *Gains for Informal Workers in Tamil Nadu*

Time	Leader (Party)	Movement Claim	Movement Strategy	Legislation for Informal Workers
1800–1947	Justice Party	Caste equality	Uniting under mega-caste identity	NONE
	Periyar (Self-Respect League)		(non-Brahmin)	
	DK			
1947–67	Kamaraj (INC)	Employment equality	Patron–client	NONE
1967–1977	Annadurai (DMK) Karunanidhi (DMK)	Ethnic equality	Uniting under mega-ethnic identity (Dravidian)	NONE
1977–87	MGR (ADMK)	Justice for plebian masses	Populism	1980: Implemented Bidi Cess Act and Bidi Welfare Board
				1981: Enacted Handloom Workers Act
				1982: Enacted Manual Workers Act
				1983: Built first health clinic for bidi workers; increased minimum wage for construction workers
				1984: Enacted Tamil Nadu Construction Workers Act
				1986: Provided pensions to *bidi* workers

(continued)

TABLE II *(continued)*

Time	Leader (Party)	Movement Claim	Movement Strategy	Legislation for Informal Workers
1987–89	Jayalalitha (ADMK) and Karunanidhi DMK fighting			NONE
1989–91	Karunanidhi (DMK)		Uniting under mega-ethnic identity (Dravidian)	NONE
1991–96	Jayalatha (ADMK)	Justice for plebian masses	Populism	1993: Expanded State Labor Department to implement Bidi Workers Welfare Act 1994: Enacted Tamil Nadu Construction Workers Welfare Board
1996–2001	Karunanidhi (DMK)	Justice for plebian masses	Populism	1999: Enacted Tamil Nadu Manual Workers Social Security and Welfare Board 2000: Implemented 9 new welfare boards for informal workers
2001–06	Jayaltha (ADMK)	Justice for plebian masses	Populism	2002: Launched Bidi Workers Integrated Housing Scheme 2004: Combined nine welfare boards into one

Time	Leader (Party)	Movement Claim	Movement Strategy	Legislation for Informal Workers
				Manual Workers Board
				2005: Increased education scholarship and added pension to Construction Welfare Board
2006– present	Karunanidhi (DMK)	Justice for plebian masses	Populism	2006: Separated nine welfare boards and added three new boards (total of twelve)
				2006: Increased pension and maternity assistance and waived registration fee to Construction Welfare Board
				2006: Increased staff and computerization of Construction Welfare Board, and created district-level monitoring offices
				2008: Budgeted for the creation of a free Construction Workers University

the urban areas to provide a ready workforce.[20] In Tamil Nadu, British favoritism toward Brahmins led to significant resentment among the

---

[20] Nonfactory, home-based, and small-scale industries (such as cotton handlooms, unrefined sugar, pottery, bidi, and weaving) still provided the bulk of the state's employment, especially in rural areas. A third source of nonagricultural employment was in

growing group of urban, educated non-Brahmins, in large part because Brahmins represented less than 3 percent of the state's population. Moreover, unlike most states that had a sizable population of upper-caste non-Brahmins, nearly all non-Brahmins in Tamil Nadu were members of the middle and lower castes. This unique caste structure enabled middle- and lower-caste Tamils to mobilize together around a mega-caste identity of "non-Brahmins" – all of whom were seen to be deprived by the Brahmin monopoly on power.[21] In the late 1920s, E. V. Ramaswamy Naicker (popularly known as "Periyar" or Great Man), led the Self-Respect Movement, which merged the mega-caste identity of "non-Brahmins" with a mega-ethnic identity of "Dravidian," the supposed indigenous people of south India.[22] Dravidians were said to have been oppressed for centuries by Aryans, the supposed indigenous people of north India *and* of Tamil Brahmins. To unite the majority of south Indians by simultaneously distinguishing them from north Indians and from Tamil Brahmins, the Self-Respect Movement focused on articulating and promoting Dravidian history, culture, and language.[23]

The early anti-Brahmin movements in Tamil Nadu, along with the later Self-Respect Movement, were not populist in that they tried to alter the structures that created Brahmin power in the first place. Movement leaders forced a change in hiring policies away from an exclusive preference for Brahmins, and in the 1880s, they worked with the British government to make "non-Brahmin" an administrative category under the British policy of giving preference to lower castes in educational institutions. Although these movements did not transform into a distinct political

---

subsidiaries to agriculture, such as extracting oil from seeds and nuts and crushing sugar cane.

[21] These initial movements were known as the South Indian Liberal Federation, which later became the Justice Party.

[22] This new overlapping ethnic and caste identity emerged from Periyar's experiences as a member of INC. In its effort to mobilize against the British, INC promoted a single Indian consciousness that transcended ethnic, religious, gender, class, and caste differences. Periyar argued that the "Indian" identity was dominated by a north Indian Aryan culture, Sanskrit language, and Brahmin ideology and that it ignored the deep ethnic, caste, and social inequalities that remained in India. The incompatibility of his views with that of INC came to a head in 1925, when INC failed to pass a resolution on social justice. Seeing this as a sign that equality could not be achieved from within INC, Periyar left the party to build the Self-Respect Movement. For the next two decades the movement fought for Tamil linguistic nationalism and against caste and other social inequalities.

[23] Eventually the Justice Party and the Self-Respect Movement merged to form the Dravidar Kazhagam (DK) or "Dravidian Party."

party before independence, they succeeded in resisting north Indian dominance in the independence movement and in the budding national Indian political parties.

However, in their efforts to unite the majority of south Indians (minus the 3 percent of south Indian Brahmins), movement leaders downplayed the class cleavages among non-Brahmins.[24] Movement leaders tended to be educated, middle-caste landlords and mercantile capitalists, whereas most movement members were poor, low-caste workers in the informal economy. By subsuming lower classes under the mega-caste identity of non-Brahmins, movement leaders not only gained considerable leverage in numbers but they were also able to tailor movement efforts to meet their own interests. Informal workers, in turn, had little space to distinguish themselves, promote their own identity, make unique demands, or create distinct organizations.

Politicizing Anti-Brahmin Dravidians (1947–77)

After independence, Tamil Nadu was ruled by the Indian National Congress (INC), the party that led India's independence movement and ruled the state until the late 1960s. K. Kamaraj, a Tamil Brahmin freedom fighter and a popular leader, was the INC chief minister in Tamil Nadu from 1954 to 1963. As a national party, INC steered clear of ethnic, religious, and caste-based identities, which tended to be localized. Instead, Kamaraj expressed a strong commitment to social welfare and equality across classes. INC leaders in Tamil Nadu passed progressive laws designed to protect workers. Although the mass group of informal workers remained outside the jurisdictions of these laws, INC leaders expressed a commitment to attaining formal employment for *all* workers. As detailed in Chapter 2, informal workers did not identify as a separate class from formal workers during this period. Rather they fought to be recognized and protected with the same rights as formal workers. Despite

[24] On occasion, the Justice Party even cooperated with the British to oppose the Indian independence movement, because the independence movement was led by the Brahmin-dominated INC. In 1919, INC boycotted the first elections held in the Chennai Legislature under a limited franchise as part of its Non-Cooperation Movement against British rule. The Justice Party, however, refused to boycott the elections. It won the elections, and by 1926 it had an independent ministry. The Justice Party ruled Chennai Presidency under the authority of the British government until 1937. For an excellent account of Tamil Nadu's early mega-caste movements, see Barnett (1976b). It should also be noted that several Tamil leaders, such as V. O. Chidramaram Pillai and Subramaniam Siva, played an active role in the national movements for Indian independence (MIDS 1998).

its expressed commitment to class-based equality, however, INC failed to enact the policy changes necessary to reverse persistent social inequalities. The reasons for this failure have been detailed elsewhere (Chibber 2003; Kohli 1987, 1990a). For our purposes, it is important to note that INC's failure to improve the material realities of Tamil masses provided a window of opportunity for the anti-Brahmin Dravidian movement to form an opposition party in the 1960s, thereby planting the seeds for Tamil Nadu's early phase of populism.

In 1949, C. N. Annadurai, a protégé of Periyar, formed a Dravidian political party, Dravida Munnetra Kazhagam (DMK), to compete in local elections against INC. DMK politicized the caste-based inequalities that Periyar's Dravidian movement had articulated and that INC had ignored. To focus attention toward all non-Brahmins, DMK minimized class distinctions among Tamils in its early years. Annadurai called for a revival of Tamil culture, glorifying the past Dravidan kingdoms of Chera, Chola, and Pandya and offering to right the wrongs done to non-Brahmin Tamils. All Tamils were identified as "the common men," as opposed to upper class, Aryan Brahmins from the North. This rhetoric offered *anyone* in Tamil Nadu (including upper-, middle-, and lower-class members) an attractive alternative to INC. INC was portrayed as the oppressive "ethnic outsider" and DMK as the "ethnic local." INC's push to make Hindi the primary language of India made DMK's rhetoric on INC's cultural oppression all the more salient. To publicize its ethnic message, DMK relied heavily on Tamil films, replete with heroes of social justice. Many of the actors and screenwriters later left their artistic careers to lead DMK and subsequent Dravidian political parties.

DMK's early rhetoric of ethnic supremacy resonated well among upper-class, urban non-Brahmins, particularly students. This support secured DMK an electoral victory in the Chennai Municipal Corporation as early as 1957. However, to attain political support at the state level, DMK needed to expand its base to include the lower classes. Its use of film attracted attention from some members of the middle and lower classes, many of whom were illiterate. But to attract more support, DMK focused on material needs. Most Tamils had not fared well in economic terms under INC, and during the 1960s, DMK was able to capitalize on two national trends that were hitting the poor especially hard. First, the food production crisis that hit India in 1964 was deeply felt in Tamil Nadu. Second, the rate of industrial growth in Tamil Nadu was declining, because the state was unable to generate sufficient hydroelectric power (a necessity for factories at the time), and industries were shifting to other states (Barnett 1976a). In this context, DMK complemented its ethnic criticisms of INC with promises of material benefits that appealed to the working poor, such as subsidies for rice and cheap public housing. In addition, DMK allied itself with the Communist Party of India (CPI). The promise of some material benefits guaranteed support from the lower classes without threatening DMK's support from the upper classes.[25] In 1967, DMK defeated INC in the State Assembly elections, making Tamil Nadu the first Indian state to be ruled by a regional party.[26]

It was in this context, in which DMK began to rely on the lower classes for votes, that informal workers had an opportunity to advance their unique interests as a part of the proletariat *and* "the poor." Unfortunately for informal workers, however, Annadurai died two years after gaining power. Karunanidhi, who had been a screenwriter in the Tamil film industry, assumed party leadership and remains the leader of the party to this day. Under Karunanidhi the party became less radical, shifting away from appeals to the lower classes and returning to an exclusive focus on a mega-caste and ethnic identity. Part of this shift was due to budgetary constraints, which led Karunanidhi to drop DMK's earlier promises to alleviate the material needs of the lowest classes. For example, Karunanidhi failed to initiate land reform, in 1970 he reduced rice subsidies, and in 1971 he repealed the dry laws (which were supported by poor women) to attain taxes from the sale of liquor (Subramanian 1999).

In addition to turning attention away from the poor masses, Karunanidhi viewed all organized workers as a threat to his ethnic nationalist party, despite the important role that property relations and economic factors played in attaining mass support for DMK's rise to power. Class issues featured in DMK's rhetoric only to the extent that they overlapped with its anti-Brahmin stance. For example, the Bidi Workers Conditions Act had been passed in 1966 to protect working conditions among formal bidi workers. Although the neighboring states of Kerala and Karnataka implemented the act immediately, Tamil Nadu's DMK government had still not implemented it by the mid-1970s. Rather than addressing working-class interests, DMK tried to undermine the strength of communist trade unions (thereby breaking its earlier collaboration

[25] During this period, DMK also moderated its ethnic militancy to lure Brahmin professionals into the party by abandoning its demand for a separate Dravidian homeland in 1963 and even accepting Brahmins as fellow Tamils.

[26] Since then, INC has not returned to power at the state level. At the national level, it has retained power among Tamil representatives by forming coalitions with state-level Dravidian parties.

with CPI) by forming new DMK-affiliated unions that promoted class compromise. DMK unions targeted all factories that had any communist strength, and worker militancy was severely repressed (Subramanian 1999).

Because informal workers were focused on attaining formal employment, they organized along the lines of traditional formal workers' unions at the time. As a result, organized informal workers were suppressed along with formal workers during DMK rule. For example, in 1975, the DMK government conducted a study to examine the living conditions of the state's informal workers (Tamil Nadu Government 1975). The report focused only on informal workers who were *not* members of any union or organization (Tamil Nadu Government 1975: 26). This focus is in sharp contrast to present-day state programs for informal workers that rely heavily on unions to connect the state with the scattered informal workforce. Moreover, the report admitted to an "inadequate understanding of the real problem at issue due to scanty evidence" (Tamil Nadu Government 1975: 120).

The only concrete recommendation made was to extend existing labor laws designed to provide work-based benefits, such as the 1948 Minimum Wage Act, to informal workers. This focus on work-based benefits, rather than welfare, reflected informal workers' efforts to formalize themselves at the time. The report acknowledged that union attention to informal workers to date had been "mainly concerned with improvements to [their] working conditions," which were "miserably unprotected." But it also critiqued union efforts to date, noting that they had "hardly touched the living conditions of those workers," which were "generally deplorable" (Tamil Nadu Government 1975: 42–43).

The report went on to note that extending existing laws did not require the creation of more unions or disputes with employers. Rather, "workers can easily secure relief with the assistance of the enforcement machinery provided by the Government" (Tamil Nadu Government 1975: 120). Having recognized the failures to improve informal working conditions to date, the report concluded with recommendations for extended welfare facilities for informal workers, such as housing, medical care, education, and death benefits. It recommended that programs be designed along the lines of the national government's Bidi Welfare Board. Despite the authors' intentions, however, the report did not result in any changes for informal labor.

DMK's failure to address formal and informal workers' class interests in unions, work-based benefits, and welfare protections ensured support for the party from middle and upper strata groups. In return for their electoral support, DMK enabled middle strata groups to assert themselves against discrimination by the entrenched elite (Subramanian 1999; Swamy 1996a). For example, DMK rationed entitlements to government jobs and education to give access to privilege to non-Brahmins who had been denied benefits under INC rule. However, because these entitlements were so substantive, they were also limited in number. Groups that had what Subramanian (1999) calls "some social capability, but little political influence" were most successful in claiming the entitlements. As a result, DMK's largest support base came to be urban, literate middle castes and classes, such as small shopkeepers and small to middle property holders (Frontline 2002).[27] These groups were marginal to INC (which mobilized support through local rural elites) and the Communist Party of India-Marxist (CPM), which identified primarily with the landless. Poor, informal workers in the lowest strata remained an untapped electoral resource sitting on the margins of all three parties: INC, DMK, and CPM. Although individual informal workers no doubt voted, they did not organize en masse as a single bloc. It was this resource that a new populist party embraced in the mid-1970s.[28]

3.4 NEW SHADES OF POPULISM PROTECT INFORMAL LABOR (1977–PRESENT)

DMK's lack of attention to the lowest strata opened the door for the rise of a new competing Dravidian party, the All India Anna Dravida Munnetra Kazhagam (ADMK).[29] In 1973, hit film actor MGR split from the then-ruling DMK to start the ADMK party. ADMK won the state government in 1977 and ruled the state until MGR's death in 1987. It was under MGR that Tamil Nadu began to exhibit its strongest strain of mass populism, and an informal workers' movement was finally born (in and for itself) and legitimized as a force by the state.

Like DMK, ADMK displays typical traits of populism. Although both parties use a rhetoric of exclusive ethnicity that transcends class to highlight Dravidian cohesion, culture, and glory, they both also emphasize (at

[27] Although the middle strata comprised DMK's largest support base, DMK also relied on some support from upper and lower strata.
[28] CPM did appeal to rural informal workers in Kerala. Why this happened in Kerala and not in Tamil Nadu has not yet been explored and is beyond the scope of this study. In Chapter 5, I do explore why CPM did not appeal to informal workers in West Bengal.
[29] Also known as AIADMK.

least in rhetoric) the "common Tamil" to ensure mass electoral support (Barnett 1976a; Subramanian 1999).[30] Both parties channel their benefits directly to the common Tamil in the name of social justice, so party leaders receive credit for any benefits received and beneficiaries are bound to the party benefactor. Yet neither party alters the structures that generated the common Tamil's exclusion in the first place.[31]

The subtle difference between DMK's and ADMK's populism can be found in how each party defined the common Tamil, at least until the late 1980s. As outlined in the previous section, under Karunanidhi DMK focused on the middle and upper strata. In contrast, MGR claimed to represent the original mandate of DMK under its founder, Annadurai, who targeted the lowest strata. To stress the point, MGR placed "Anna" in the party's name and a picture of Annadurai in the AMDK party flag. Substantively, a return to the original mandate meant a revival of the anti-Brahmin, redistributive rhetoric that Annadurai's DMK had originally used to attract urban slum dwellers and members of the lowest castes in rural areas. Just like the characters he played in his popular films, MGR catered to the needs of the lower castes and classes that were not being met under the current system. As a party leader, MGR assumed the responsibility of a benevolent leader who protected the lowest strata by providing targeted state benefits, such as subsidized welfare goods. Doing so bound members of the lowest strata to the elite members of ADMK.

MGR's supporters were predominantly poor, illiterate women with little or no property. In return for their support, MGR offered them direct welfare benefits, such as food, housing grants, pensions, unemployment doles, agricultural loan forgiveness, agrarian subsidies, and the popular mid-day meal scheme that provided one free meal to all school-aged children. Total subsidies increased from Rs. 283 million between 1965 and 1970, to Rs. 3,875 million between 1980 and 1985 (de Wit 1996). These benefits were smaller than the entitlements attained under DMK and could thus be spread across a larger group. As an illustration, the incidence of poverty measured by the Headcount Index fell by 17 percent during the decade of MGR's rule (1977–87), whereas it fell by only 12 percent during the previous decade of DMK's rule (1967–77).[32] The urban poverty gap fell by 35 percent during MGR's rule, compared to

---

[30] This rhetoric was ironic because MGR was not a native Tamil, and his successor, Jayalalitha, is a Brahmin.

[31] This strategy contrasted with that of INC, whose party leaders channeled political patronage to the public through local elites, who then received the credit for benefits.

[32] Headcount Index is the percentage of the population living below the poverty line.

only 15 percent during DMK's rule.[33] The support base that MGR built among the very poor and among women remained strong long after he died. As shown by the exit polls taken during the 1999 and 2004 national elections, although DMK won the majority of Tamil Nadu's parliamentary seats in both elections, ADMK (under the leadership of MGR's successor, Jayalalitha) retained its strong hold over the very poor and women voters (Frontline 1999; Prasad and CSDS Team 2004).

ADMK's mass-based welfare benefits, although popular with the electorate, have been criticized for their long-term economic and government capacity consequences. Atul Kohli (1990a) writes that under MGR's leadership, the state was poorly ruled "as a personal fiefdom where the economy and administration almost collapsed" (p. 162). Both Kohli (1990a) and Joop de Wit (1996) point to news reports in the mid-1980s that Tamil Nadu fell from its rank as the third most industrialized state in India to thirteenth place under MGR. Scholars argue that MGR's costly welfare benefits catalyzed an economic decline. Once in place, the benefits were almost impossible to curtail. By 1984, the cost of the famous mid-day meal scheme, which provided free lunch in schools, had risen to 10 percent of Tamil Nadu's budget (de Wit 1996). Under MGR, state funding shifted away from long-term planning and investment in industry and infrastructure toward the short-term distribution of welfare. Capital began to leave the state, and new investment slowed. Scholars have also argued that, although MGR neglected industrial development, he handled the fiscal problems that come with populist policies better than had DMK (de Wit 1996; Kohli 1990a). For example, MGR lifted a restriction he himself had placed on the sale of alcohol because the drop in tax revenue was hurting state finances. The repeal of the prohibition was so unpopular among women voters, however, that MGR used the increased tax revenue from the alcohol to finance the mid-day meal scheme from 1982 to 1987 (Subramanian 1999).

Although MGR targeted the lowest strata by providing paternalist benefits, even at the expense of long-term economic soundness, he did not attempt to alter the structures that created marginality in the first place. As Geeta Ramakrishnan, general secretary of TMKTPS, puts it, "ADMK's

[33] Poverty gap is the mean distance below the poverty line, expressed as a percentage of the poverty line. The mean is taken over the entire population, counting the nonpoor as having a zero poverty gap. The measure reflects both the depth of poverty and its incidence. I calculated these figures, using figures of poverty trends in Tamil Nadu in various reports by the Ministry of Finance, Government of India. See http://www.tamilnadustat.com/india.

base is the illiterate masses. They all remember MGR, the actor. ADMK appeals to the group that watches the movies and knows him as a hero. But in reality, the party is more inaccessible than the others."[34] Rather than empowering the lowest strata through local-level government, MGR centralized power in Tamil Nadu, leaving village governing bodies or *panchayats* less developed than in many other states (Kohli 1990a; MIDS 1988). Institutional links that could help common Tamils access ADMK power were largely undermined under MGR. In addition, even though the poverty rate fell more under ADMK than under DMK rule, the Gini coefficient, a measure of inequality, decreased less. During the decade of MGR's ADMK rule, the rural Gini index did not change and the urban Gini decreased by only 2.5 percent, whereas under the decade of DMK rule, the urban Gini index decreased by 7 percent and the rural Gini by 19 percent.[35]

ADMK's lack of redistributive intentions can also be seen in its relations with organized formal workers. By the 1970s, trade unions had gained strength in Tamil Nadu, especially among industrial workers in large firms and among government employees. During the 1970s, DMK had attained some working-class support by offering them an alternative to communist unions – that is, DMK-affiliated unions that promoted class compromise. By the late 1970s, almost all unions in Tamil Nadu supported either DMK or the communist parties and were thus perceived as a threat to ADMK. At first ADMK tried to follow DMK's approach of gaining workers' support by drawing members of existing unions into new ADMK-affiliated unions, which were moderate in strategy. When that failed, ADMK tried to undermine labor's power. In 1978, it banned strikes in an effort to decrease worker militancy, and it permanently stationed the Central Reserve Police Force in industrial areas to assist employers in confrontations with organized formal workers. ADMK also became more involved in mediating labor disputes than DMK or INC had been (Subramanian 1999).

Despite its crackdown on unions and its consequent loss of support among formal workers, ADMK retained its large popular support. MGR served as Tamil Nadu's chief minister and head of ADMK for ten

---

[34] Geetha, Interview, June 10, 2003.

[35] The Gini coefficient is a measure of inequality. It is a number between 0 and 1, where 0 corresponds with perfect equality and 1 corresponds with perfect inequality. The Gini index is the Gini coefficient expressed in percentage form. I calculated these figures using various reports from the Ministry of Finance, Government of India.

consecutive years until his death in 1987 – when two million followers attended his funeral, and literally thousands mutilated and killed themselves in sorrow (Pandian 1991). Except for a brief split in the party after MGR's death, the party remained popular until the mid-1990s. More importantly, MGR's paternalist populist strategies were so effective in securing mass electoral support that both the ADMK and DMK use them today.[36] Even A. K. Padmanabhan, Tamil Nadu's national secretary for CITU, admitted, "ADMK does have a base among the lower working class." He added, "They have the support even though they do not espouse a leftist ideology."[37] This paradox reflects (1) the limited power that leftist unions have held in Tamil Nadu and (2) ADMK's ability to retain power by offering some inducements for lower-class interest groups whose demands do not threaten its role as the guarantor of social order.

It is in this realm that informal workers' organizations willingly fit. In return for the promise of their political support, organized informal workers demanded protection from MGR. Tamil Nadu's competitive electoral context enabled informal workers to make similar demands on subsequent populist leaders as well. As shown in Table 11, under MGR informal workers managed to get targeted protective policies enacted, despite the state's lack of interest in deep structural change. In 1980, MGR began the implementation process of the 1976 Bidi Cess Act and Bidi Welfare Board, making it the first state in India to implement the act. By 1983, Tamil Nadu opened its first health dispensary for bidi workers, located in Chennai, and over the next five years the state implemented twenty-four additional welfare schemes for bidi workers, including children's scholarships. [38] In 1981, MGR enacted the Tamil Nadu Handloom Workers Act to protect informal handloom workers, and in 1982, he expanded its protections to cover all manual workers (including construction workers) through the Tamil Nadu Manual Workers (Regulation of Employment and Conditions of Work) Act. Under this act, the state provided identity

---

[36] In January 1989, DMK returned to power. Although MGR had died and his party was suffering from a brief split, the paternalistic policies that MGR had set in motion set the bar that DMK had to follow to retain power. For the next three years, DMK espoused a paternalistic populism, expanding MGR's welfare schemes. After ADMK returned to power, it too continued the paternalistic policies of MGR (based on multiple interviews with DMK and ADMK party officials).

[37] Interview, July 12, 2004.

[38] Interview, Rajangam, general secretary of Tamil Nadu's Communist Bidi Federation, July 16, 2003.

cards to informal workers, thereby legitimizing them as contributing members of the economy.

The achievements that informal workers made under MGR are significant. As outlined in the previous section, despite Tamil Nadu's progressive social and political movements for social justice, the state government did not pass any legislation designed to protect informal workers until the 1980s. Before that, the few state policies that recognized and protected workers focused exclusively on formal workers. Other policies designed to protect non-elite Tamils identified recipients based on caste. MGR was the first leader to acknowledge informal workers both as a unique subgroup within the meta-identity of "non-Brahmin Dravidians" and as a class of workers distinct from formal workers. The laws that MGR passed not only legitimized informal workers as a separate class with distinct needs but they also enabled informal workers to attain state-supported rights designed for their unique informal labor status. Most significantly, the precedent MGR set during his ten years as chief minister of Tamil Nadu has continued into the present day, regardless of the party in power. How and why did MGR and subsequent populist leaders choose to meet the needs of informal workers? The following section explores how organized informal workers in Tamil Nadu capitalized on MGR's mass-based populism and the state's competitive electoral context to frame themselves as a key interest group for the state's politicians.

3.5 PROJECT FROM BELOW: FRAMING INFORMAL LABOR AS "COMMON" VOTERS[39]

Although MGR's master skills at understanding and using the popular mind to attain support have been claimed to be the rationale for his welfare policies (Barnett 1976b; de Wit 1996; Subramanian 1999; Swamy 1996a), I argue that informal workers' organizations played just as vital a role in attaining state protection under MGR (and thereafter). To gain MGR's attention, these organizations framed their members as (1) a massive vote bank, (2) a core part of MGR's target group of the "common" poor, and (3) a group whose needs did not threaten liberal economic structures. In other words, MGR's populist leadership created an opportunity for informal workers in the state to use him as much as he used them. Moreover, MGR's electoral success pushed competing parties to

---

[39] I borrowed the terms "Project from Below" and "Project from Above" from Collier and Collier (1991).

follow his lead in targeting lower classes for support. The resulting pro-poor competitive electoral context enabled informal workers to employ the strategies they used to attract MGR to attract subsequent Tamil politicians seeking mass-based electoral support. In doing so, Tamil informal workers have created a social contract with the state that recognizes them as a class and supports their social consumption needs.

Informal construction workers in Tamil Nadu began organizing in 1979 – two years after MGR took office as the chief minister. Until that time, no political party had supported or even acknowledged them as a distinct group. The state was then undergoing an economic recession, placing downward pressure on the construction industry. Construction workers were unable to find jobs, and a group of workers in Chennai held demonstrations and presented a memorandum of demands to the state labor minister at the time. In response, the labor minister promised to pass a law that would protect construction workers during economic downturns (Mody 1997). But by the end of the year, nothing had happened. The government's inaction prompted workers to organize into what eventually became TMKTPS – a union formally registered under India's Trade Union Act (1926) and comprising only informally employed construction workers.

According to Geeta, founding member and general secretary of TMKTPS, the union quickly understood that the promise of its members' votes could attract politicians' attention: "It is about the parties wanting power. They always meet our demands just to get voted in."[40] To capitalize on the state's interest in attaining votes, TMKTPS and other informal workers' unions in Tamil Nadu have translated their members' identity as a mass class into a powerful vote bank *available to any politician*. To relay this message, union leaders have highlighted the numbers of informal workers; after all numbers directly appeal to politicians' interests in retaining or attaining electoral support. Even intermediate caste associations – which were not necessarily "poor" – were able to win preferential policies through ADMK as long as they could show that the policies were part of a "mass mobilization drive" (Subramanian 1999: 292).

To credibly offer the promise of a mass number of votes, TMKTPS spent two years, from 1979 to 1981, aggressively expanding its membership. Using the networks of existing masons' guilds, Geeta and her colleagues traveled throughout the state to attract a range of informally employed construction workers into the union. Membership spanned

[40] Interview, July 8, 2003.

from unskilled women "helpers" or *chitals* to skilled, male masons. Today, the union's membership in the state numbers 17,000. Moreover, the union is one of the only (and certainly the largest) organized representatives for informal workers in the construction industry. Given the rapidly growing size of the informal construction workforce, the union holds the power to *claim* a link to a population that is even larger than its direct membership base. The success of the informal workers' strategy of using mass numbers to attract the attention of Tamil politicians has pushed formal workers' unions in the state to be more open to including informal workers. As A. K. Pakmanabhan, CITU national secretary for Tamil Nadu, stated,

During the last twenty years, CITU has increased its attention on the informal sector. The informal sector is entering into the previously formal sector, and the formal sector is being cut in size. Unions know that if we want workers' grievances to be addressed by the government, we must look at the total workforce. We cannot differentiate between informal and formal workers, because politicians only care about getting the most votes.[41]

In addition to highlighting informal workers' numbers, unions highlighted their poverty. Issues of poverty have served as a mass mobilization catalyst in Tamil Nadu since the tenure of MGR. As outlined earlier, poverty was a much higher priority for ADMK than anti-Brahmin caste appeals had been under DMK. With its expanding membership base, TMKTPS held rallies outside state government offices, demanding greater attention to the insecurity faced by the mass group of poor informal workers. On one occasion, union leaders were arrested and spent twelve nights in jail. During these rallies, TMKTPS appealed to ADMK's claims that, unlike DMK, ADMK sympathized with the plight of poor masses. Informal workers, TMKTPS pointed out, were a large subset of ADMK's target population. "Our calls for help were genuine, because there was a real hope at the time that ADMK was different [from other political parties]," recalled Geeta.[42] In return for welfare protection, informal workers offered the promise of their political support and the opportunity for ADMK to claim assistance to its primary target group.

Soon MGR began to respond to the demands of informal construction workers. In 1981, the state government drafted a bill that would protect the working conditions of informal workers and provide them with welfare benefits, such as housing, medical care, day care, and education

---

[41] Interview, July 10, 2003.
[42] Interview, July 8, 2003.

scholarships for workers' children. Whereas the TMKTPS's rhetoric highlighted the needs of all informal workers, the union demanded benefits specific to construction workers, such as fair prices for construction materials and relief for workers who were laid off because of the scarcity of cement. In addition, it demanded a separate law for construction workers that would provide them with a minimum wage, pension, accident compensation, and welfare. Despite these industry-specific demands, in 1982, an election year, ADMK redrafted and enacted the 1981 bill into a law for all manual workers, called the Tamil Nadu Manual Workers (Regulation of Employment and Conditions of Work) Act. Construction was included as one of the several eligible industries under the act. From MGR's perspective, the Manual Workers Act served to appease a broader population of potential voters than a single construction workers act would have. In 1994, construction workers did attain a separate welfare board under the Manual Workers Act.

The third strategy that informal workers' organizations used to attain populist leaders' attention in Tamil Nadu was to frame their demands in a way that did not threaten liberal economic structures. The use of this strategy was particularly apparent among the state's bidi unions, despite their affiliation with CPM. Although the CITU Bidi Union in Chennai had reemerged in 1974 to fight for benefits for informal workers, it was not until 1980, under MGR, that the Tamil Nadu government finally began implementing the welfare provisions that had been promised, but not provided, to informal bidi workers in 1971. According to Bappu, general secretary of Chennai's Bidi Union, "It was easier to convince MGR to implement the Cess Act, since employers are not directly involved. It was better for the government that way."[43] In other words, the bidi unions understood that implementing the Bidi Welfare Act allowed MGR to appease informal workers without upsetting employers.

The year after MGR passed the Manual Workers Act, he won another term in office. During the next three years, TMKTPS and the Bidi Union continued to push for more state attention to their needs, and MGR continued to respond to their demands by enacting protective legislation. In 1983, he fixed a new minimum wage for construction workers, and in 1984, he enacted the Tamil Nadu Construction Workers Act, which aimed to protect the conditions of work in construction. In 1983, Tamil Nadu opened the first health center for bidi workers in the state, and in 1986, the government began to provide pension funds to bidi workers.

---

[43] Interview, June 29, 2003.

Although these efforts appeared at first to be victories for the construction and bidi unions, they were not well implemented (especially the construction laws). Still, Tamil Nadu's construction and bidi unions became known among informal workers' movements in India for their successful strategies in attaining state attention. Even government officials today admit that MGR's efforts on behalf of informal workers were pushed from below. As the head of Tamil Nadu's Construction Workers Welfare Board, Mr. Viruthagiri, said, "Being a government man, I should say these [Welfare] Boards were due to the government vision. But I would be lying if I didn't say they are due to the workers' struggle... Now in terms of implementation, the Boards run well because the unions are involved."[44]

In 1985, the Indian government set up a tripartite working group to examine why existing laws on social security were not being implemented in the construction industry. TMKTPS (along with the construction unions from Maharashtra and West Bengal that are included in this study) was an active participant in this working group. Because existing laws did not cover the growing informal workforce, the working group pushed for the establishment of the Construction Workers Welfare Board to protect informal workers.[45] TMKTPS led the movement at the state and national levels to pressure the state and national governments to implement the welfare board for informal construction workers.

Unfortunately for the construction and bidi workers' movement, MGR died in 1987, and their ability to attain state attention and support entered a brief lull. State politics underwent a period of instability as ADMK split over disagreements on MGR's successor. In the face of a potential political crisis, DMK, led by Karunanidhi, took over the state government in 1989. During his first term in power, Karunanidhi followed his previous strategies (detailed earlier), which focused on the middle strata and paid little attention to informal workers. As a result, the strategies that helped informal workers attract state attention under MGR proved less successful under Karunanidhi. The bidi union invested much of its energy into writing memorandums to Members of the State Legislative Assembly (MLAs) and holding rallies outside state government offices calling for the state to more fully implement existing laws designed to

---

[44] Interview, July 2, 2003.
[45] In 1979, the national government extended the 1948 Employees' State Insurance Act (which provides medical insurance for sickness and accidents, as well as maternity benefits) to construction workers, and in 1980, it extended the Provident Fund to cover construction workers.

protect informal bidi workers. As Rajangam, a long-time bidi activist and now general secretary of Tamil Nadu's CITU Bidi Union Federation, recalled, "In 1988 we had our most major struggles taking place, but the government was in a mess and nothing happened."[46] However, informal workers were able to re-spark state attention to their interests when ADMK returned to power in 1991, with Jayalalitha as the chief minister. Jayalalitha was MGR's protégé (and co-star in Tamil films). She continued MGR's mass-based paternalism, which enabled informal workers to continue applying the same strategies they had used under MGR to attain welfare benefits from the state. The year that ADMK returned to power, the Bidi Union appealed to the national government to pressure the state government to more fully implement the Bidi Welfare Act. Supreme Court Justice Jaganath Misra then gave a direct order to the State Labor Department to ensure more comprehensive implementation of the act. In addition, the Bidi Union appealed to Jayalalitha's claim to care for the "plight of poor women" by highlighting the high percentage of women among bidi workers. In 1993, Jayalalitha expanded the State Labor Department by appointing nine new assistant labor inspectors, one chief inspector, one implementation secretary, and one legal aid secretary just for bidi workers. The new staff members were posted in towns with large concentrations of bidi workers. Recalled Lalli of her efforts as a newly appointed chief labor inspector for bidi, "For three years [1993–96] we implemented the bidi acts so well. The unions used to come to me, and I could help them. Jayalalitha said she stood for poor women, and there I was helping poor women. I was proud of my job."[47] Rajangam, general secretary of Tamil Nadu's Bidi Union Federation of CITU, agreed with Lalli's sentiment: "Under Lalli the unions, the Labor Department, the Provident Fund, and the Welfare Board were all well coordinated. We worked together. And Jayalalitha was happy to be helping poor women"[48] TMKTPS was also successful in attracting politicians' attention. In 1994, ADMK finally granted construction workers their own welfare board to be implemented by the Tamil Nadu government.

In 1996, Karunanidhi's DMK returned to power. To avoid losing the state's interest in their welfare, informal workers' unions worked hard to convince DMK, as they had done with ADMK, that informal workers

---

[46] Interview, July 16, 2003.
[47] Interview, July 9, 2003.
[48] Interview, July 16, 2003.

were organized and could provide a major vote bank. Their efforts appeared to have succeeded. In May 1997, DMK sent three officials from its Ministry of Labor to examine the functioning of welfare boards for informal workers in other states (Harikrishnan, Viruthagiri, and Jeyasngan 1997). Drawing from the findings in Kerala (where informal workers' welfare boards were found to be most advanced), DMK launched an examination of informal workers' needs in Tamil Nadu. The resulting report, published in 1998, reflects the impact that informal worker unions had in altering DMK's attitude toward informal workers. First, unlike DMK's 1975 report that focused only on *non-unionized* informal workers, the 1998 report focused on any work that is legally "unprotected" and included organized informal workers (Tamil Nadu Government 1998: 80). Representatives from informal worker unions, along with employer federations, served as members of the 1998 report committees, collecting and analyzing data, formulating recommendations, and writing the final report. As noted in the report, even employers of informal industries were recognizing organized informal workers:

A redeeming feature which came to the notice of the Committees during their observational visits is the perceptive level of attitudinal change and value-judgment on the part of the employers who by and large have reconciled themselves to the fact that labour is a force to be reckoned with and that a worker has a personality of his own. (Tamil Nadu Government 1998: 80)

Second, the 1998 report linked DMK's leader, Karunanidhi, to DMK's founder, Annadurai. During the 1970s, Karunanidhi had moved away from Annadurai's commitment to the lowest strata groups. Rather it was MGR who had connected himself to Annadurai, making ADMK popular among poor, informal workers. By linking Karunanidhi to Annadurai, the 1998 report brought DMK into the fold of MGR's mass-based populism:

The present Government in the State of Tamil Nadu having firmly pledged in wiping out tears from the eyes of the common man and having committedly resolved to eradicate poverty and misery of the under privileged and the down-trodden has been and is consistently maintaining in all its politics and programmes the avowed principle propounded by our late Chief Minister Perarignar C.N. Annadurai that "smile of the poor is the smile of God." It is in this context that the Honourable Chief Minister of Tamil Nadu, Dr. Kalaignar M. Karunanidhi announced in the State Legislature on March 5, 1997 that separate Committees will be constituted to study the problems and issues of...unorganized labor and suggest ways for resolving their problems. (Tamil Nadu Government 1998: 2)

MGR's populist rhetoric of moral justice, even at the cost of economic efficiency, can be found throughout the report. For example, in recommending more inspectors in the Labor Department, the report notes,

The task is a noble one-doing economic and social justice to more than 90% of the unorganized, under-privileged and most exploited work-force. Hence, cost should not be an inhibiting factor. (Tamil Nadu Government 1998: 88)

Finally, unlike the 1975 report, which focused on extending workers' rights to informal workers, the 1998 report focused on creating new welfare benefits for informal workers as a unique class of workers. As it notes,

The Five-Year Plans have not evolved an integrated comprehensive scheme of social security for unorganized labour. [The] majority of the existing labour laws seek to benefit the organized sector which constitutes merely a little more than eight percent of the total 315 million workforce. *A very bold policy is needed in this respect* [emphasis added]. (Tamil Nadu Government 1998: 79)

Based on the recommendations of the 1998 report, on March 17, 1999, DMK enacted the Tamil Nadu Manual Workers Social Security and Welfare Board. During the election campaigns in 2000, DMK implemented an additional nine welfare boards for other informal sector industries under the Tamil Nadu Manual Workers (Regulation of Employment and Conditions of Work) Act (Tamil Nadu Government 2000–01).[49]

Since 1996, Tamil Nadu's government has shifted back and forth between DMK and ADMK. Informal workers' success in convincing both parties that informal workers could provide an important support base motivated TMKTPS and the Bidi Union to promise a large number of votes to whichever party is in power and to continue equating informal labor with the plebian masses. In March 2002, TMKTPS organized a highly publicized march of all unorganized workers in the state. The march, which lasted for two months, began at the southern tip of the state and ended in the state capital in the north, covering fifteen districts. The primary demands of the workers were welfare related (i.e., identity

---

[49] These are the Tamil Nadu Auto Rickshaw and Taxi Drivers Welfare Board, Tamil Nadu Washer Men Welfare Board, Tamil Nadu Hairdressers Welfare Board, Tamil Nadu Tailoring Workers Welfare Board (implemented July 20, 2000); Tamil Nadu Palm Tree Workers Welfare Board, Tamil Nadu Handicraft Workers Welfare Board (implemented October 18, 2000); Tamil Nadu Handloom and Handloom Silk Weaving Workers Welfare Board, Tamil Nadu Foot Wear and Leather Goods Manufactory and Tannery Workers Welfare Board, and Tamil Nadu Artists Welfare Board (implemented March 14, 2001).

cards for all workers, health care, education scholarships, social security benefits, child care services, and compensation for injuries and sexual abuse). In addition, marchers demanded that "they all be declared below the poverty line" (Special Correspondent 2002e). In other words, organized informal workers were demanding that they be defined – in the state's own terms – as a population warranting the state's support.

The success of this framing can be seen among government officials and in Indian media. In the latter, sentiments of the informal workforce as "poor" and "vulnerable" are prevalent (Nagaraja 1995; Padmanabhan 1995; Special Correspondent 2002a; Sreenivas 1998; Staff Reporter 1999, 2001). This sentiment contrasts with media depictions of formal workers as "overly militant" and "on their way out" (Dhavan 1999; Gangadhar 1995; Subramanian 1995). Similarly, nearly all government officials in Tamil Nadu spoke to me about "informal workers" and "the poor" as one entity. As Tamil Nadu's Labor Commissioner M. Rajaram said, "The two parties [DMK and ADMK] have very little difference in terms of issues. But ADMK has more charismatic leaders. MGR had a vision to create the [informal workers'] welfare boards because he wanted to help the poor."[50] By the early 2000s, informal labor had achieved the power to secure state-provided benefits, even if the benefits were economically inefficient. Exactly two years after DMK established the nine new welfare boards, ADMK returned to power and criticized the boards as a "strain on government finances." The state labor minister under ADMK announced that the nine additional welfare boards would be combined into one board to save government costs (Tamil Nadu Government 2004b). Informal workers' union leaders, who preferred industry-based boards, loudly criticized ADMK's plan.[51] Their criticism pushed opposition parties, such as DMK and CPM, to respond by joining forces to support informal workers' unions and highlighting the mass number of informal workers who needed assistance (Special Correspondent 2002a). DMK featured the reestablishment of the nine welfare boards as a major promise in its 2006 election campaign (DMK 2006: 29). As a further indication of DMK's support for informal workers regardless of cost, other electoral promises included increasing informal workers' pensions (DMK 2006). Informal workers' criticisms and DMK's response were

---

[50] Interview, June 12, 2003.
[51] Although union leaders claimed that having separate boards facilitates their ability to attain industry-specific benefits, some government officials claimed that separate boards simply allow union leaders to attain more politically visibility (multiple interviews, July 2003).

so widely publicized that the ADMK labor minister soon announced that the state government would contribute Rs. 50,000 to help finance a new housing scheme for informal bidi workers, thereby softening the impression that the party did not support informal workers (Special Correspondent 2002b). Under this scheme, the government would construct 10,000 homes over the next five years for informal, women bidi workers. The national government would contribute Rs. 20,000 per home, and the state government would contribute Rs. 5,000 per home; the bidi worker would pay the remaining costs (Tamil Nadu Government 2003a, 2003b, 2004a). In 2005, just prior to the next elections, Jayalalitha increased the amount granted in the education scholarships and added pensions to the Construction Workers Welfare Board (Tamil Nadu Government 2004b, 2005).

Given Tamil Nadu's record for anti-incumbency, it is not surprising that ADMK's last-minute consolations were not enough to win the 2006 elections. More significant than the electoral winner, however, is the *campaign rhetoric*. Despite its already high chances of winning due to anti-incumbency trends, DMK chose to campaign on a pro-informal worker platform, which then forced ADMK to also offer support to informal workers. In other words, informal workers managed to influence the campaign promises of both parties, thereby securing support from whichever party won. This strategy of offering informal workers' votes to any political party that will meet their demands was reflected among individual construction and bidi union members in Tamil Nadu. Thirty-nine of the forty interviewees in Tamil Nadu voted; of these thirty-four voted for either DMK or ADMK (the remaining five voted for either INC or CPI). Not one voter, however, expressed her party choice in ideological terms. Moreover, the unions (even the CPM-affiliated Bidi Union) did not urge their members to vote for a particular party. As one construction worker explained to me, "We don't discuss politics at the union. It causes too many arguments and takes time away from our real fight."[52] Union leaders in the informal sector also repeatedly expressed to me their desire to be viewed as independent of any political party.

This nonpartisan union strategy stands in sharp contrast to that pursued by India's formal workers' unions, most of which are affiliated with a political party (on both the left and right sides of the political spectrum). Although membership in the affiliated political party is not required, formal workers' union members are usually educated in the ideology of that

---

[52] Interview, Shanta, July 3, 2003.

party. The link between formal workers' unions and political parties in India has been so strong that many have argued that it has harmed formal workers' labor movements, causing unions to lose their larger visions in the face of partisan politics (Ramaswamy 1988; Rudolph and Rudolph 1987).[53]

To avoid the perceived trap that formal workers' unions fell into – namely, becoming stifled by party affiliations and partisan ideology – informal worker unions encourage their members to *vote according to their neighborhood*, rather than their party affiliation.[54] Neighborhoods in urban India, as elsewhere, are economically stratified, so that the poor congregate in slums that politicians can easily target. By not dictating members' vote choices, informal workers' unions in Tamil Nadu allow members to interact with politicians as citizens with civic needs. This strategy enables members to combine their work identities with their identity of being "poor." It also creates opportunities for informal workers to ensure a workable home environment. Because informal work is so closely tied with the home, home amenities define working conditions. Almost all the bidi workers whom I interviewed complained about the amount of time they spend either fighting the municipality for water or waiting in line at the neighborhood water pump during the few hours that the water is turned on. The time they spend on getting water for the household is time away from their bidi work, which in a piece-rate wage system, translates into lower incomes. To fight for their civic needs (and ultimately their work needs), informal workers appeal to populist politicians' desire for votes. In turn, votes are amalgamated at the neighborhood level and are sometimes "rewarded" with neighborhood amenities, such as water and paved roads.

Informal workers characterized this system as a superficial exchange of a vote for civic goods. Although the interviewees consistently voted, they were quick to remind me that they "got nothing in return." When pressed on why they then continued to vote despite the lack of return, they expressed their vote choice in terms of an exchange. In return for a vote, interviewees received civic goods. For example, Azara, a bidi worker in Chennai, said, "In this alley, we all vote for CPI, because they give us water. They have an office here, so when we have a problem, we can go to them. So we give them our vote."[55] Others expressed dissatisfaction

---

[53] For an excellent recent critique of this argument, see Teitelbaum (2011).

[54] Union leaders in the informal sector repeatedly expressed their desire to be viewed as independent of any political party.

[55] Interview, July 17, 2003.

when the government did not uphold its end of the promised exchange. For example, Chandra, a construction worker in Chennai, explained, "I voted for DMK, because I thought they would do something good for us. But they haven't done anything. And now if one politician comes to my door asking for a vote, I'm going to throw them right out. These past few years have been so bad."[56] Finally, others said that their actual vote sometimes differed from the vote they announced in public; the latter could change depending on the civic good they could get. As Govinda, a construction worker in Chennai, explained, "We have to say we voted for both parties [DMK and ADMK], because each one has a water tank here, and if we want water from both tanks we have to say we gave votes to both parties. It is better not to talk about it."[57]

Informal workers' lack of ideological commitment to a particular political party was also reflected in their expressions of party loyalty. Support for ADMK was expressed as a loyalty to MGR, despite the fact that he has been dead for more than two decades. Loyalty to the remaining parties (DMK, CPI, and INC) was expressed as a function of the neighborhood. "I vote for party X, because my whole street does," was a common explanation for why they voted for a particular party. On further questioning, however, these loyalties were expressed as an exchange of votes for certain goods. MGR provided food for the poor children, and neighborhood commitments to another party were almost always justified by showing me a nearby water tank, a paved road, or a new dispensary.

This perceived exchange of a vote in return for a civic good was consistent with claims that "they have not received anything in return for their votes." In other words, although votes were seen as a means to attain a few basic (already due) needs, they were not seen as a mechanism that could alter the structures within which people had to live and work. Daily life remained as vulnerable and insecure as always. These comments from informal workers interviewed for this study reflect the central themes of populism, where political parties offer small "gifts" to mass populations in return for votes, but do little to fundamentally improve the socioeconomic status of the lowest strata. Although workers play the game, they had little illusions that a party's provisions were unique or ideologically motivated. In fact, not one interviewee claimed that her party of choice provided more for people than the other parties.

Significantly, although workers did not support any particular political party that could represent their interests at the state level, they

---

[56] Interview, August 11, 2003.
[57] Interview, August 14, 2003.

expressed a strong belief in their ability to attain benefits from the state. This belief stands in sharp contrast to the views expressed by workers interviewed in Maharashtra or West Bengal. Shanta, a 45-year-old construction worker in Chennai, has been engaged in her current work since she was 18. Both Shanta and her husband are illiterate, but their three sons are studying in high school and college. Before migrating to the city of Chennai for her marriage, she worked for a daily wage as a landless laborer on farms. Shanta feels that her work in construction is as difficult as her previous work on farms. She works seven to ten hours a day. She gets one tea break, where the employer provides tea and bread; she does not get a lunch break. The employer does not provide drinking water, toilets, or overtime pay. The subcontractor provides transportation to and from work. Like most construction workers, Shanta has never met or spoken to her employer. Instead, she only interacts with the subcontractor or *maistry*. Despite her harsh working conditions, she does not feel she can make any demands on the *maistry*. Says Shanta, "The *maistries* are struggling just like us. They cannot give us anything. We make all our demands to the government. They will give us something."[58]

In addition to attaining state attention and benefits for informal workers, leaders have secured an important position for informal workers' unions. As Mr. Balaraman, secretary of the new Domestic Servants Welfare Board in Tamil Nadu, explained, "The trade unions are the main interface between the workers and the government today."[59] The state, therefore, uses informal workers' unions as a vehicle through which it can interact with the massive and dispersed population of informal workers. For example, as part of the identity information required for welfare board membership cards, informal workers must write the name of their trade union. Today, nearly all members of the Construction Workers Welfare Board are members of a union.

In many ways these findings reflect Przeworski and Wallerstein's (1982) conception of the state as the administrator of class compromise. As long as this state is democratic, it must also ensure that "the class coalition that forms the compromise can win popular support in elections, which implies that interests of those excluded from the particular coalition must also be taken into account" (Przeworski and Wallerstein 1982: 236).

---

[58] Interview, August 8, 2003.
[59] Interview, December 17, 2008.

3.6 PROJECT FROM ABOVE: CAPITALIZING ON INFORMAL LABOR SUPPORT

Since the late 1970s, informal workers in Tamil Nadu have appealed to populist politicians' interest in retaining power. As outlined in the previous section, informal workers' organizations have done so by framing their members as part of the "common, poor masses," offering them to any party as a potential vote bank in return for state recognition and protection, and making demands that do not force the state to challenge liberal economic structures. The success of this three-pronged strategy can be found not only in the many protective laws the Tamil Nadu government has passed for informal workers but also in the way leaders across parties assert their commitment to poor workers and repeatedly acknowledge the massive numbers of informal workers needing protection. Through such expressions, Tamil politicians acknowledge the political and economic benefits of capitalizing on informal workers' support.

Political Benefits of Informal Workers: Securing Popular Support

Although the passage of laws for informal workers has been followed by haphazard implementation, the legislation has served a primary purpose for Tamil leaders since MGR – namely, attracting mass political support from informal workers. Because Tamil parties do not have the costly monitoring mechanisms needed to ensure that informal workers actually vote according to their promises, politicians rely on union leaders' public pledges and then tailor benefits that are salient only to informal workers. These strategies help increase the chances that informal workers' vote promises will be realized.

Today, government officials in Tamil Nadu are quick to point to the electoral appeal they believe informal workers' welfare boards have had. In 1994, for example, ADMK's Jayalalitha created the Construction Workers Welfare Board shortly before beginning her election campaign. As Viruthagiri, the head of the Construction Welfare Board in 2003, said simply and candidly, "In 1994, Jayalalitha [ADMK] created the Construction Board... It was very politically motivated. She needed the votes."[60] The popularity of the Construction Workers Welfare Board spurred DMK to respond to informal workers' requests in its competition with ADMK. As T. K. S. Elangovan, organization secretary of DMK, explained, "DMK has support from urban backward castes [middle caste

---

[60] Interview, July 9, 2003.

groups] and government employees. The rest of our support depends on our performance. So we have to perform."[61] As noted earlier, Karunanidhi formed nine new welfare boards to accommodate sixty-four additional informal sectors in 2000. This was in response to demands from informal workers' unions for the same benefits received by construction workers. Moreover, as Viruthagiri explained, DMK was following ADMK's electoral strategy: "This was an election year. I even had a meeting with senior officers, where they were very open about the importance these boards have in securing votes."[62] To spread the word on the upcoming welfare boards and secure votes from interested groups, DMK invested in an intense publicity campaign – buying advertisements in local newspapers and making announcements while driving through villages and towns.[63]

To ensure popular credit for the boards, Karunanidhi personally unveiled each of the nine boards in a massive and much publicized rally on the main boulevard in Chennai (Special Correspondent 2000). During the announcement, Karunanidhi also distributed cash benefits to several families who suffered from occupation-related diseases or injuries. Finally, he used the occasion to award certain trade unions and factories with a "Good Industrial Relations Award," because the Confederation of Indian Industry (CII), India's primary federation for industries, had rated the state of Tamil Nadu first in terms of peaceful industrial relations.

Karunanidhi appointed the state minister of labor to chair the nine welfare boards, thereby signaling the political motivation behind them. One month after unveiling the welfare boards, Karunanidthi personally handed the identity cards to the workers at the Secretariat's office. Also present were State Labor and Transport Minister K. Ponmudi, Labor and Employment Secretary R. Rathinasamy, and Labor Commissioner P. A. Ramiah. Again, the moment was very well publicized. At the time, the general secretary of Tamil Nadu's branch of CITU, T. K. Rangarajan, referred to DMK's progress in establishing the boards as a "pre-election gimmick" (Special Correspondent 2001). In 2006, when DMK returned to power, party leaders continued to be swayed by the promise of mass support from informal workers. DMK not only reversed ADMK's unpopular decision to combine the nine welfare boards into one but also created three new welfare boards for three new categories of informal

---

[61] Interview, December 19, 2008.
[62] Interview, July 2003.
[63] Interview, Jhiru M. Viruthagiri, September 9, 2003.

workers and added four new informal employment categories to be eligible for protection under the 1982 Manual Workers Act. In 2006 and 2007, DMK strengthened the Construction Workers Welfare Board – increasing the monthly pension and maternity assistance amounts, eliminating all registration fees for workers, increasing the number of staff, forming district-level monitoring committees, and offering training services to registered members (Tamil Nadu Government 2006b, 2007a, 2007c, 2007d). In 2008, DMK's Department of Labor announced that it would build a free construction university for the state's informal construction workers. The only requirement for entry would be that workers must be members of the Construction Welfare Board.

Once again, government bureaucrats and party leaders candidly affirmed that DMK's focus on informal workers was motivated by the promise of electoral support. As the secretary of the Construction Workers Welfare Board, Alagasan, explained, "The government is interested in this [the Construction Welfare Board], because it is a vote bank. All political parties are interested in the unorganized [informal] sector. You have to see the numbers. 93% of the workforce! And within that construction is second to agriculture in terms of employment." He added proudly, "It is about the numbers, and we have twenty lakh [2 million] construction workers already in our Board."[64]

As part of their effort to tap the mass of informal worker votes, Tamil leaders have crafted symbolic personas that appeal to poor workers. MGR billed himself as a fellow "mass worker" who understood that improvements in the lives of the poor could only come from improvements in employment. MGR always played a poor, heroic worker in his films, and he repeatedly spoke about his personal history to the public (Pandian 1991; Subramanian 1999). Although MGR was born into a professional Malayali (non-Tamil) family, the death of his father when MGR was an infant impoverished his family. The notion that MGR intimately understood the plight of the poor worker continues to be pervasive. Members of DMK and ADMK continuously reminded me that "because MGR knew what it felt like to be in a pinch, he worked for the poor worker."[65] Informal workers also reiterated that they believed MGR's personal experiences motivated him to make the changes needed to improve their lives. "I voted for ADMK because I thought they would do something good for us. MGR knew we were suffering," stated Kaadar, a Chennai-based

[64] Interview, December 18, 2008.
[65] Various interviews including Rajaram, Tamil Nadu commissioner of labor, and V. Raaja, deputy commissioner of labor, June 2003.

construction worker who recalled the hope she had placed in the ADMK government in the late 1970s.

Today, ADMK continues to live off of the success of MGR's public image among informal workers. The present-day ADMK leader, Jayalalitha, does not fashion herself as "one of the poor workers," but rather as a "trusted confidante of MGR, the poor worker." Although Karunanidhi does not enjoy the same public image as MGR, DMK has recently begun to formulate a similar, worker-based history for Karunanidhi. As Mr. Shanmugam, general secretary of DMK's trade union federation, Labor Progressive Federation (LPF), explained to me, "Karunnanidthi accepted all our recommendations for informal workers, because he himself is a laborer. He was a village artist. He comes from an unorganized [informal] workers' family."[66]

Particularly noteworthy in DMK's efforts toward informal workers is its emphasis on defending its track record with informal workers against ADMK's record. Since 2000, DMK's election manifestos for state and national-level elections have detailed its achievements in advancing informal workers' welfare and its promises to further improve informal workers' welfare if elected (DMK 2001, 2004, 2006). As DMK's labor minister, Annabarasan, proudly explained, "Our [party's] priority is supporting informal workers. And, unlike ADMK, we do it. We talked about establishing fourteen welfare boards already in our campaign. It is in our manual. And within two years we have fulfilled our promise."[67] In recent years, DMK began requiring weekly progress reports from the informal workers' welfare boards. As a testament to the political nature of the boards' success, monitoring reports are presented in terms of progress before and after DMK came to power (Tamil Nadu Government 2008a).

Informal workers' strategy of appealing to Tamil leaders' interest in securing mass electoral support from the plebian masses has enabled informal workers to secure the state's targeted attention. Tamil Nadu's pro-poor, competitive electoral context has enabled this attention to be secured regardless of the party in power – as seen in both parties' election campaign promises, the laws both parties pass to protect informal workers, the way each party assesses its own achievements in comparison to opposition parties, and the symbolic personas that each party's leaders portray. The perceived political benefits of appealing to informal workers have become so entrenched in Tamil's populist politics that

---

[66] Interview, December 18, 2008.
[67] Interview, December 17, 2008.

leaders of both parties address informal workers' interests whether or not previous years' efforts earned them a victory. In return for the mass political support Tamil Nadu's populist leaders have sought since MGR, informal workers have attained a unique level of state recognition and protection in Tamil Nadu.

Economic Benefits of Informal Workers: Reconciling Populism with Liberalization

Their acknowledgment and protection of informal workers have enabled populist leaders in Tamil Nadu to pursue liberal economic reforms by assuring support from the very groups most disaffected by the reforms. As shown in Chile and Brazil, populism *can* coexist with neoliberalism (Pereira et al. 1993; Roberts 1995). Although the fiscal austerity of neoliberal policies may preclude populist leaders from delivering on their traditional promises of higher wages or subsidized consumer goods, it does not prevent populist leaders from offering targeted material benefits to specific groups in return for political support. These targeted benefits are often less costly and more visible than traditional clientelist promises. Such efforts signal a distinction that populist leaders make between the material rewards for political support at the micro level and a neoliberal pursuit at the macro level. This distinction is important to our understanding of the impact of neoliberal politics on labor.

Since the Indian government launched the 1991 liberalization reforms, DMK's and ADMK's populist leaders have supported the reforms at the state level. Informal workers have served as an essential peg in the state's economic reform project, and informal workers' tacit acceptance of the reforms has been critical to the state government's ability to implement them. At the time that this study began, ADMK held the seat of state government. The party was attempting to straddle the fine line between maintaining its populist policies and initiating new liberalization reforms. Within her first year of becoming chief minister for the second time, Jayalalitha instituted several welfare schemes to decrease female infanticide, improve welfare policies for the elderly, and expand MGR's mid-day meal program. These policies were enacted alongside a renewed commitment to liberalization and increased cooperation with the right-wing party, BJP, which was in power in the national government. As *The Hindu* reported in April 2003, "Ms. Jayalalithaa has ensured that the reforms affect only the politically indifferent middle class, not the voting underclass" (Venkatesan 2003).

Informal workers' unions fought hard to resist the government's liberalization efforts. The Bidi Union organized several widely publicized marches against the government's decrease in cigarette taxes and the anti-smoking bans initiated by the World Health Organization (WHO); these policies increased competition in the bidi industry and pressured bidi employers to further reduce labor costs. Construction workers marched against the increased use of imported, prefabricated construction materials that were eliminating the need for the lowest skilled construction laborers. These marches against state policies were conducted alongside efforts to work with the state to attain welfare benefits: the two were not viewed as mutually exclusive. The attempts to attain welfare benefits, however, proved to be more successful than the attempts to alter the liberalization policies of the state. Although the state has enacted and implemented welfare benefits for informal workers (as detailed earlier), it has not yet repealed any of its laws designed to increase competition or liberalize the economy.

Like ADMK, DMK used informal workers to pursue the parallel tracks of populism and liberalization. To assert its interest in the common man, DMK claims that it is a labor party. Karunanidhi's son is named "Stalin" as a tribute to Joseph Stalin. As DMK Organization Secretary Elangovan said, "There is no real difference between CPM and DMK. Karunanidthi is a Marxist, and we like Marxist philosophy."[68] Mr. Shanmugam, general secretary of LPF, reiterated the sentiment: "There is no communism anymore. We [DMK] practice the principles of Marxism and Leninism more than CPM does. We believe in the principles."[69] At the same time, however, because DMK supports liberalization policies, it has shied away from holding employers accountable for labor by formalizing the workforce or making the structural changes necessary to protect all labor. For example, to provide incentives for multinational corporations to locate in Tamil Nadu, DMK has provided them with free real estate and justified the lack of unions. By Elangovan's own admission, "DMK has always been sympathetic to labor, but we have not done much for formal workers."[70]

Instead, DMK uses informal workers to bridge the gap between its claims to protect labor's interests and its commitment to liberalization. Specifically, providing welfare benefits to informal workers enables DMK to take direct credit for protecting a vulnerable, plebian mass while

---

[68] Interview, December 19, 2008.
[69] Ibid.
[70] Ibid.

simultaneously pursuing a liberalization agenda that absolves employers of costly labor protections. As Elangovan explained, "The formal sector already has laws in place. But the informal sector is full of individuals who are alone with no organization, and DMK thought they should be supported, and their grievances should be heard... It is the duty of the government to provide them with a forum."[71] The "forum" Elangovan referred to was the state welfare boards. In other words, the DMK asserts the moral duty of a paternalist state, rather than pursuing a programmatic agenda toward workers. Alagasen, secretary of Tamil Nadu's Construction Welfare Board, was quick to note the difference between welfare benefits for informal workers and traditional class conflict: "The Board has no big controversy. It is just helping the poorest workers."[72] Labor Minister Anabarasan proudly claimed, "We have many trade unions. But we have no industrial disputes in our state. It is a very peaceful environment."[73] Mr. Balaraman, secretary of the new Domestic Service Welfare Board, summed up DMK's dual stance on populist labor protection and liberalization: "DMK government is a labor government. Our Chief Minister is particularly interested in labor welfare. You can see his election manifesto. But this doesn't mean we are anti-employer. We just have to protect the weak."[74]

To defend their attention toward informal workers, DMK officials openly point to the political and economic benefits of informal workers' support. For example, Elangovan defended DMK's attention to informal workers in terms of their numbers: "The only difference [between DMK and CPM] is that CPM speaks openly of economic class differences, and DMK speaks of socially backward classes and Vedic class differences. But since 90% of the socially backward classes are in the informal sector, we [DMK] end up also speaking about economic differences."[75] As detailed earlier, the number of informal workers translates into potential electoral votes. Other DMK officials focus on informal workers who operate in industries that are booming in the new liberalized economy. For example, Alagasen, the secretary of Tamil Nadu's Construction Welfare Board, noted, "With the increased IT and real estate businesses these days, construction has also boomed. After agriculture, it provides the most jobs. So the government must be interested in its workers."[76] In contrast to

---

[71] Ibid.
[72] Interview, December 18, 2008.
[73] Interview, December 17, 2008.
[74] Ibid.
[75] Interview, December 19, 2008.
[76] Interview, December 18, 2008.

construction workers, the DMK government exhibits a lower level of interest in bidi workers, whose industry is considered to be declining under liberalization. As Shanmugam, general secretary of LPF, said, "Bidi workers have gotten many benefits, but now the industry is declining and so will their benefits. With the ban on smoking, bidi work will disappear in a couple of years."[77] Indeed, except for the state's contribution to bidi housing, the State Department of Labor when DMK was in power has exhibited less interest in welfare services to bidi workers than did the ADMK government.

The presence of pro-poor, populist leadership in Tamil Nadu has provided an opportunity for informal workers to capture politicians' attention by framing their needs into an attractive vote bank that represents politicians' commitment to the plebian, poor mass. Tamil Nadu's competitive electoral context has enabled informal workers to put themselves on the agenda of any political party seeking power. On a secondary level, informal workers frame their members' demands in terms that do not conflict with the state's liberalization agenda. In turn, members express their power as neighborhood-based voters with basic civic needs. While individual members appeal to politicians to meet their basic civic needs, union leaders turn to politicians to meet their members' collective welfare needs. As a result of these strategies, organized informal workers in Tamil Nadu feel entitled to state-provided welfare benefits and empowered to vote for politician-provided civic goods. To lend further support to this argument, let us now examine what happens when a pro-poor, competitive party context *and* a state-driven liberalization agenda are absent.

[77] Ibid.

4

Communism's Resistance to Change

In sharp contrast to the informal workers' movements in Tamil Nadu analyzed in Chapter 3, those in West Bengal have not succeeded in attaining material benefits from the state. Only one-third of the sixty informal workers interviewed in West Bengal from 2002 to 2004 received any type of material benefit (either work or welfare related) as a result of joining a union (as opposed to thirty of the forty interviewees in Tamil Nadu and more than half of the forty interviewees in Maharashtra).[1] In addition, the type of benefit received in West Bengal differed from those received in Tamil Nadu and Maharashtra. Of the twenty-one interviewees who received a benefit in West Bengal, nearly all received work-based benefits, as opposed to welfare benefits. These benefits were largely confined to members of the politically affiliated construction union. Moreover, the benefits (whether work or welfare related) received by workers in West Bengal were provided by unions, not by the state. Politicians in West Bengal have rarely been directly involved in improving the livelihoods of the state's informal workers. That benefits received in West Bengal were not consistent across organization type or industry and were largely confined to work-based benefits provided by a union indicates that the "new" informal workers' movement outlined in Chapter 2 was less successful. By 2004, informal workers in West Bengal had failed to create a movement that could withstand the pressures of

[1] Because West Bengal is the only state in this study to have independent and politically affiliated construction unions, more interviews were conducted there than in the other two states. Therefore, in percentage terms, the lack of material benefits received in West Bengal is even more striking.

flexible production structures and simultaneously assure some justice to poor workers.

This finding is surprising given West Bengal's history of revolutionary, class-based politics that, as detailed later, began in the early nineteenth century. From 1977 to 2011, West Bengal was ruled by the Communist Party of India-Marxist (CPM). CPM won consecutive elections based on a promise of guaranteeing benefits for workers. Yet, informal workers have rarely been a CPM priority. Drawing from the state framework outlined in the Introduction, in this chapter I examine the evidence for the "low-success" case of West Bengal, arguing that CPM's unchallenged leadership, its entrenched organizational structure and social base, and its lack of interest in liberalization reforms (until recently) made it difficult for unions in West Bengal to frame informal workers' demands in terms that appealed to CPM's interest in retaining power.

In addition to serving as a low-success case, West Bengal provides insights into how shifts in the state's electoral and economic context can alter the effectiveness of informal workers' movements. In 2004, nearly twenty-five years after the Tamil Nadu government began directing benefits to informal workers, the West Bengal government began to showcase its efforts to improve informal workers' welfare. Although informal workers receive little material support from the state government, they are beginning to enjoy the legal right to support and are playing a larger role in the government's rhetoric and agenda, thereby bringing West Bengal closer to the "medium-success" case of Maharashtra. This increase in the state's attention to informal workers can be explained by the rise of an opposition party in West Bengal and the concurrent shifts in CPM's electoral strategy and rhetoric on economic liberalization. These findings provide important clues to the limited impact that class-based social movements can have on informal workers in the absence of conducive political and economic frameworks from above. As well, the failure of informal workers to align with a left party in West Bengal, especially in contrast to their success in aligning with a left party in Kerala, raises questions about the context in which left parties can alter the structural bases of inequalities.

4.1 WEST BENGAL: FEW TO SOME STATE BENEFITS FOR INFORMAL LABOR

Before 2004, the West Bengal government had instituted few protective measures for informal workers, and government officials did not express interest in recognizing informal workers as a distinct group with unique needs. Since 2004, the government's rhetoric toward informal workers has shifted, and officials proudly showcase the protective welfare measures the state government has begun to put into place. Implementation of these measures, however, remains limited.

West Bengal has a high official minimum wage for bidi workers relative to the other two states (see Table 9). This high wage reflects the successes of the state's bidi workers' movement during the 1960s when unions held employers accountable to a formalized bidi workforce. Since the bidi workforce has become increasingly informal, however, the bidi workers' movement in West Bengal has been less successful. Female workers interviewed in the state reported earning as low as Rs. 30 daily, despite the official minimum wage of Rs. 79. Subramanyam Thakur, secretary of AITUC, the union federation affiliated with the Communist Party of India (CPI), and general secretary of the National Bidi and Cigar Federation, said, "In West Bengal, we admit that we have accepted the below minimum wage rate, because otherwise the employer runs to [neighboring state] Orissa, and that causes unemployment in West Bengal. Enforcement is weak and the [bidi] movement is very weak. But what else can we do?"[2]

The West Bengal government has also shown limited interest in providing welfare benefits to the state's bidi workers. The Bidi Welfare Committee and Fund are under the jurisdiction of the national government, but state governments are responsible for monitoring the fund and implementing the welfare benefits. West Bengal's labor minister in 2003, Mohammed Amin, was strikingly uninvolved in the Bidi Welfare Fund even though, unlike Tamil Nadu and Maharashtra, West Bengal hosts one of the Bidi Welfare Fund's nine state-level Advisory Committees, which Amin chairs.[3] State-level Advisory Committees are a key avenue through which state governments can monitor and pressure the national government to address bidi workers' issues. Unlike Tamil Nadu government officials, Amin displayed little interest in the Fund, and he did not take personal responsibility for it. Rather, he spoke of it as a project that belonged to the national government. This is despite his acknowledgment that West Bengal's "informal workforce is larger than its formal sector

[2] Interview, June 3, 2003.
[3] Each of the nine State-level Committees represents a regional cluster of states. West Bengal's Regional Bidi Welfare Office located in Kolkata is responsible for overseeing the bidi welfare boards in the states of Assam, Arunachal Pradesh, Maghalaya, Nagaland, Manipur, Tripura, Mizoram, and West Bengal. In addition to the Bidi Board, the Cinema Workers Welfare Board (1981) is also located in West Bengal.

workforce, and the informal sector is only increasing," and "so far not much has been done for them [informal workers] by the West Bengal government."[4]

Aarti Dasgupta, a Member of the Legislative Assembly (MLA), head of the Bidi Workers' CITU Union Federation in West Bengal, and a senior member of the State Advisory Committee for bidi welfare, shared Amin's apathy toward the Bidi Fund: "The welfare card is basically good, and the trade unions try to help workers with the applications. But the problem is in the implementation. There are so many middlemen that by the time the benefit reaches the worker, so much has been cut."[5] Like Amin, Dasgupta did not express any responsibility for the proper implementation of the Bidi Fund. Rather, she considered it a sub-optimal project of the national government.

In contrast to state-level government officials, national-level officials in West Bengal have assumed responsibility for the Bidi Welfare Fund. In 2003, N. K. Prasad, who was a regional welfare commissioner employed by the national Ministry of Labor, served as the vice-chairman of the State Advisory Committee in West Bengal. Although this set-up should have theoretically allowed the national-level welfare officials to establish close relations with the state government, Prasad did not pursue such a relationship. He reminded me several times that he was part of the national government, not the state government: "The states cannot do much. It is the regional commissioners that are responsible for implementation." Like Amin, he reiterated that West Bengal's government did not focus much on informal workers. "Different state governments have more or less focus on informal workers, and West Bengal has shown less interest. But the central government now has a much greater focus on these workers," said Prasad. Not surprisingly, Prasad held a different view from Amin and Dasgupta on how well the Bidi Fund is being implemented in West Bengal: "West Bengal makes up by far the largest share of beneficiaries of the Welfare Fund." However, Prasad had no reports or written material to support his claim, which according to the annual reports of the Ministry of Labor, was false (GOI 2002a). Regardless of the facts, Prasad felt the need to exaggerate the success of the Bidi Fund, in contrast to the views of the state-level government officials.

In construction, the West Bengal government, like all state governments, holds direct responsibility for protecting workers. However, the

---

[4] Interview, November 19, 2003.
[5] Interview, November 17, 2003.

state's official minimum wage in construction (at Rs. 95 daily) is lower than that in the other two states (see Table 9). This reflects a recent effort by the state government to attract more developers.[6] Workers report receiving between Rs. 40 and Rs. 80 daily. As examined in greater detail later, the amount of effective wages correlates with the type of union to which workers were affiliated. In terms of welfare benefits, the government did not operate the Construction Workers Welfare Board until 2006 – more than two decades after the parallel one was implemented in Tamil Nadu. In 2003, union leaders, union members, and then State Labor Minister Amin acknowledged that the Construction Welfare Board would be set up in West Bengal. However, Amin also pointed to the government's lack of commitment to such a board: "Under the central law, employers will have to pay 1 to 2 percent [of their profits] into the board fund. This will include state public works, and at the moment they [public employers] are unwilling to do so. And if the public sector government employers don't pay, how can we expect the privates to pay?"[7] Although Amin was open about the deficiencies of his government, he expressed little interest in pushing for change.

The one law that the West Bengal government did pass for informal workers in January 2001 is the State Assisted Scheme of Provident Fund for Unorganized Workers. This fund helps informal workers and employees in small-scale industries prepare for retirement. Workers and the state government must contribute Rs. 20 per month to the fund. The money is deposited in a bank and earns interest at the rate of the regular pension fund (which is approximately 9 percent); the interest is paid by the state government. At retirement (age 55), workers receive the entire amount (West Bengal Government 2001). This law was spearheaded by Shubash Chakrabarty, an active member of CPM and West Bengal's minister of transport and sports in 2003. Although he was proud that the law finally passed, he admitted in 2003 that not much had been done by way of implementation: "It was under our constant pressure that the state government finally passed the [Provident Fund] policy. I had my greatest satisfaction on hearing the government's announcement after raising our slogans for more than ten years. It has not been implemented properly, but at least the policy is there."[8] State Labor Minister Amin also confirmed that the Provident Fund was a good policy, but had not been well

---

[6] Interview, Mohammed Amin, November 19, 2003.
[7] Interview, November 19, 2003.
[8] Interview, Shubash Chakrabarty, December 17, 2003.

implemented. In fact, the annual report of the State Labor Department did not even report on the fund's implementation until 2007.

The state government's lack of interest in protecting informal workers was reflected in the few state-provided benefits received among the workers I interviewed from 2002 to 2004. Of the twenty bidi workers interviewed in West Bengal, only six were members of the Bidi Welfare Board, and not one had received a welfare benefit from it. One member said she had received a wage increase (a worker benefit) since joining the union. Of the forty construction workers interviewed, only one had received a welfare benefit from the state (a pension); none had received a work-based benefit from the state. Benefits received by union members in West Bengal were provided by the unions, not by state. The independent construction union provided more welfare-oriented benefits, whereas the CPM-affiliated unions (in construction and bidi) used their political power and control over the police to provide more work-based benefits. In both cases, politicians and political parties of the state were not directly involved.

A Shift in Attention

Since 2004, West Bengal's government officials have increased their attention to informal workers. In 2007, the state government introduced the West Bengal Bidi Workers Welfare Scheme to supplement the national government's Bidi Welfare Fund. The state government now provides Rs.10,000 to each female beneficiary building a house (in addition to the national government's subsidy of Rs. 40,000), as well as Rs. 10,000 for beautification and construction of infrastructure to each bidi worker constructing a home in a registered housing cooperative. In addition, West Bengal has instituted a unique benefit in which the state government provides Rs. 2,500 to the state electricity board for the electrification of each bidi house. This effort was facilitated by the fact that the same person headed both the state-level Department of Labor and the Department of Electricity. Bidi workers in West Bengal can obtain funds from the State's Provident Fund for Unorganized Workers after retirement.

As mentioned earlier, the state government formulated the rules for the Construction Workers Welfare Board in 2004, set up the board in 2005, and began operating it in 2006. Unlike the Bidi Fund, the state government does not provide direct funding to the Construction Board. Rather, it provides administrative support, and the Construction Welfare Board is funded through worker fees (Rs. 20 per month and an initial registration fee of Rs. 20) and welfare taxes collected from builders.

In return for becoming members of the board, workers are promised accident and death insurance, a pension, health care support, education scholarships for children, maternity benefits, and a housing loan. In 2007, construction workers became ineligible for the State Pension Fund for Unorganized Workers.

In addition to providing welfare benefits for bidi and construction workers, the state government is attempting to support other informal workers. In 2008, the government expanded the State Provident Fund for Unorganized Workers to include forty-three occupational categories of informal workers. In 2009, the state government began setting up the West Bengal Unorganized Workers Welfare Board for all informal workers.

The implementation of these new efforts has been uneven. The state government has now committed its local representatives to assist national government officials and trade unions in confirming bidi workers' informal work status, registering bidi workers, and issuing identity cards through "registration camps." As a result, the number of applications for a housing subsidy under the Bidi Fund jumped from 168 in 2006 to 14,267 in 2007. In addition, the state government is computerizing identity card registration to facilitate their management. By the end of 2007, however, only 617 beneficiaries had received the first installment of payment to begin construction of their homes (West Bengal Government 2007). By March 2009, that number had increased to 800 out of 16,000 approved bidi workers, and 270 beneficiaries had received their second installment of funds (West Bengal Government 2009c). Similarly, by March 2009, the state had released funds for the electrification of more than 16,000 bidi homes, but only 3,700 houses had been connected to the grid (West Bengal Government 2009b). To date, no bidi workers have received assistance under the scheme that supports infrastructure development in bidi housing cooperatives (West Bengal Government 2007).

For construction workers, the state government launched a massive publicity campaign to increase awareness of the Construction Workers Welfare Board – organizing information camps and registration drives that included city- and village-level politicians, trade union leaders, and bank officials in each state district. It placed advertisements in all local newspapers and distributed brochures; government officials were given improved internet connections and cars to facilitate the publicity efforts. As a result, 71,510 construction workers were registered with the Construction Board by March 2009. By 2009, however, only 205 workers had received a benefit from the board (West Bengal Government 2009a). As

Labor Commissioner Chakrabarty admitted, "The Construction Board has not yet been very popular, but that is because we need to do more education."[9]

Despite these uneven results in implementation, state government officials now express a commitment to informal workers and pride in the state government's recent efforts to support these workers. Since 2007, the State Labor Department's annual report, *Labour in West Bengal*, has included a section detailing the state's efforts in social security and welfare provision for informal workers. Included in this section are annual progress reports on the Provident Fund, the Bidi Fund, and the Construction Board. The current minister of state in the Labor Department, Anadi Kumar Sahu, shares the department head position with the labor minister and is responsible for informal workers (along with employee state insurance); the labor minister remains responsible for traditional industrial relations. As Sahu admitted, "West Bengal did get started a bit late on the informal sector, but we were not the last to start."[10] In contrast to my interviews in 2003, where most government officials were uninterested in the Provident Fund for unorganized workers, in 2009 government officials repeatedly pointed out its uniqueness and its progress. As Labor Commissioner Chakrabarty proudly expressed, "There is no hesitation in admitting we were late starters. But there is a good reason – we already had the Provident Fund scheme that included construction workers until recently. You can't find such a Provident Fund scheme anywhere else in India."[11] Even CPM members, who earlier shunned welfare measures for informal workers as an attempt to undermine formal workers' movements, now acknowledge their necessity. "As the Communist party of India-Marxist, we have to be more concerned about the informal sector. It is 93% of the labor force after all," exclaimed Paras Basu, treasurer of CITU's All India Bidi Workers Federation and CPM member.[12]

Currently, all projects for informal workers are implemented by the Labor Directorate, which is significant given that this office, headed by the labor commissioner, has traditionally been responsible for managing industrial relations and enforcing labor laws for formal workers. That West Bengal's labor commissioner is now responsible for extending welfare to informal workers illustrates a major shift in the government's attitude toward labor. As Labor Commissioner Chakrabarty, explained,

[9] Interview, April 22, 2009.
[10] Ibid.
[11] Ibid.
[12] Interview, April 19, 2009.

"Industrial relations have already improved in West Bengal. Workers and management have become more pragmatic in our state. So enforcing industrial relations is not the only function of the Labor Directorate anymore. It used to be. But now we also do welfare for informal workers."[13] To facilitate its handling of this added responsibility, the government has increased the Labor Directorate's resources and staff to include contract workers, known as "self-employed labor organizers."

In the following sections, I explore the reasons behind both West Bengal's earlier failure to procure state-conferred benefits for informal workers and its recent attention to informal workers. As a primary explanation for its earlier failures, I explore West Bengal's entrenched, hegemonic governing style; as a secondary explanation, I explore its anti-liberalization agenda. These factors stifled informal workers' ability to attain their leaders' attention. To explain the state government's recent attention toward informal workers, I explore CPM's status as a member of the national government's ruling coalition from 2004 to 2008 and the rise of a popular opposition party in West Bengal. These forces pushed CPM toward a pro-liberalization agenda and forced it to address competing party challenges for the first time in three decades. The long-term effects of these recent shifts in government attention to informal workers' movements remain to be seen.

Before expanding on these arguments, let us first examine Bengal's radical class-based agenda for social justice, which showed early promise for formal and informal workers, but ultimately failed to deliver material gains for informal workers.

4.2 COMMUNISM: A RADICAL CLASS AGENDA FOR SOCIAL JUSTICE

In Tamil Nadu, caste-based social movements did not at first yield benefits to informal workers, but the resulting political and economic framework from above created a context in which informal workers' movements could eventually succeed. In West Bengal, social movements that expressly addressed class-based inequalities (alongside Bengali ethnic nationalism) offered initial hope to informal workers, but the political and economic framework from above undermined the ability of informal workers' movements to succeed.

Scholars of South Asia have written extensively on how West Bengal's class-based movements arose from its unique class and caste structure (Chakrabarty 2000; Franda 1973; Kohli 1987, 1990a, 1990b; Park 1949;

---

[13] Interview, April 22, 2009.

Sen Gupta 1989). As in Tamil Nadu, there were few Brahmins in Bengal, and other high castes were virtually nonexistent; together Brahmins and other high castes formed only 6 percent of the state's population before independence (Mallick 1998).[14] Unlike in Tamil Nadu, the majority of the population did not organize against Bengal's high-caste members. Some have argued that the material heterogeneity among intermediate castes, or *jotedars*, across villages undermined their ability to organize. Because some *jotedars* controlled rural production and labor and had access to education, Brahmins did not have a monopoly over land ownership and rural intelligentsia.[15] Others have argued that the ethnic heterogeneity of urban elites prevented their forming a coalition and undermined urban workers' ability to direct their resentment toward a single group of privileged Bengali Brahmins.[16]

Rather than forming upper-caste parties, urban Bengali elites mobilized lower and intermediate classes to resist rural landowners and non-Bengali, urban industrialists (neither of whom shared interests with the urban Bengali elites).[17] Part of the inspiration for these radical turns came in the early nineteenth century when Bengali elites, who migrated to cities to gain access to education and to work in the British civil service,

---

[14] Most of Bengal's remaining population comprised of lowest-caste members and Muslims. For more on West Bengal's caste and class structure, see Chatterjee (1982) and Kohli (1990b).

[15] Although Bengali Brahmins owned land prior to British colonialism, they simply collected revenues for the *nawabs* (Muslim rulers). Despite the heterogeneity among *jotedars*, it is important to note that lower-caste movements did arise in Bengal. Among the most famous is the Tebhaga Movement of 1946, a militant campaign where sharecroppers demanded they give landlords only one-third (as opposed to half) of their harvested crop (see Majumdar 1993).

[16] Bengali Brahmins, known as the *bhadralok* or "gentlemen," operated in the spheres of the civil service, arts, and scholarship, whereas non-Bengali, high-caste migrants served as major traders and industrialists (Mallick 1993; Timberg 1978). Much has been written about the Bengali ethnic nationalism that prevented Bengali elites from joining forces with upper caste leaders outside Bengal, as in INC. Hindu Bengali elites resented INC for giving concessions to Muslims and for favoring a North Indian party leadership. Early Bengali leaders, such as Shubhash Chandra Bose, called for a militant approach to independence, which conflicted with then INC leader, Mahatma Gandhi's call for nonviolence. These differences led to Bose's removal from INC and greatly wounded Bengali elite pride. For more information on why the Bengali elites did not join hands with INC, see Kohli (1990b).

[17] Before independence, Muslim political parties had also appealed to lower-class interests by offering an alternative to the hierarchical Hindu caste system and tenancy reform to rural workers (of both low and intermediate castes). As elsewhere in India, the British government allied with Muslim parties. The British, the Muslims, and lower-caste rural Hindu workers shared an antagonism toward the landed, upper-caste, Hindu Bengali elite.

arts, and academia, became influenced by the ideals of modernism. In a statement against landed privilege, some elites stopped financing their lifestyles with income from their land and launched social movements to reform the exploitative aspects of Hinduism, increase public education, and overthrow British imperialism. In the early twentieth century, some Bengali elites went to study in England, where they became attracted to the principles of Marxism; others joined Bengali nationalists who went to Mexico and Moscow to meet members of the Comintern. After converting to communism, they returned to Bengal in the 1930s and led radical movements that provided the rural masses and a growing industrial proletariat with a socially just, Bengali alternative to British, Muslim, and INC rule (Franda 1973). The partition of Bengal after independence forced Muslim party leaders (who also attempted to meet the needs of low-caste Hindus) to leave India, and most large landholdings ended up outside the borders of India.[18] Having few ties to either land or industry, being newly influenced by intellectual trends from abroad, and facing little opposition in the state, the Bengali elite became instrumental in leading a radical movement that combined an ethnic Bengali heroism with concern for class-based justice.

Significant for informal workers, these movements fought to hold landlords and industrialists accountable for all workers' welfare. Structural changes, including most of the labor protections that formal workers in India enjoy today, were meant to eradicate unprotected, informal work. In 1933, for example workers formed the Bengal Bidi Union to demand protections for all bidi workers. The union, which was the first bidi union in India and the second union in India to be formally registered (the first was the Kolkata Tram Workers Union), led numerous strikes involving workers across the country. In 1966 (an election year), the union convinced the ruling-party INC to pass the Bidi and Cigar Act and the Welfare Cess Act to protect working conditions for the newly formalized bidi workers. During this same period, CPM split from the original Communist Party of India (CPI) to advocate a more militant approach that could better address the needs of Bengal's majority rural population.[19] To this end, CPM launched forced land redistribution movements among landless peasants, and some CPM leaders participated in a tribal peasant

---

[18] At independence the state of Bengal was divided into the Hindu majority state of West Bengal (in present-day India) and the Muslim majority state of East Pakistan (present-day Bangladesh).

[19] CPI was founded by M. N. Roy, a Bengali, in Tashkent in 1921. Although it established its first presence in Bengal during the 1930s in the countryside, its loyalty to the Soviet Union eventually drew its focus toward urban issues (Mallick 1993).

uprising in the tea plantations of northern Bengal, which turned into the famous Naxalite movement.[20]

Although INC ruled West Bengal from 1947 to 1967, the state's radical groups gained support among Bengal's formal and informal workers during this period. Shortly after independence, the Bidi Union severed its affiliation with INC to join CPI.[21] In 1967, the United Front (UF), a coalition of fourteen leftist groups of varying extremism, surprised scholarly expectations by defeating INC in the state elections (Weiner 1959). As in Tamil Nadu, INC's mishandling of the 1964 drought, which led to severe food shortages, rising prices, and high unemployment among the lowest strata, provided a perfect window of opportunity for opposition parties to enter politics (Franda 1969).[22] UF helped unprotected industrial workers demand benefits from employers by ordering police to stay out of all labor conflicts. More than 75 percent of the workdays lost under UF rule were due to strikes, and the annual number of *gheraos* (a form of protest in which workers prevent managers from leaving the workplace) increased from less than 100 before 1967 to 811 in 1967 and 517 in 1969 (Ray 2000).[23] In 1972, West Bengal became the first state to institute a minimum wage for bidi workers (Rs. 70 per 1,000 bidis). Although UF catalyzed capital flight, a decline in industrial production, and intermittent periods of President's Rule (when the national government assumes authority to rule a state to regain order), its commitment to fighting the structures that created class inequality secured the support of both formal and informal workers (Franda 1973).

In 1977, CPM, a leading party in UF, won the West Bengal state elections.[24] For the next three decades, CPM's success on the electoral

---

[20] Soon after the 1967 rebellion, Naxalite sympathizers were expelled from CPM. The Naxalites formed a new break-away party, called the Communist Party of India-Marxist-Leninist (CPI-ML). Since then, competition for rural support has grown between CPM and the Naxalites. The Naxalites, however, chose an extraparliamentary path for action and therefore never established formal rule like CPM did.

[21] The union was originally affiliated with INC, because most of its members were Muslim and INC had allied with Muslim parties. Interview with Debashsish Roy, Secretary of CITU Bidi Union, Kolkata, November 18, 2003.

[22] INC's demise in West Bengal can also be attributed to the increasing corruption and factions that had infected the party. As well, its traditional strategy of ruling through a network of local elites proved less effective in the context of West Bengal's more flexible caste structure.

[23] Numbers attained from Government of West Bengal, *Labor in West Bengal*, cited in Kohli (1990a).

[24] INC ruled the state from 1973 to 1977. Indira Gandhi, then prime minister and head of INC, had launched a State of Emergency at the time and supported INC's power in West Bengal's state government.

front was a matter of record: it won every state government election from 1977–2011, making it the longest running, democratically elected communist party in the world. CPM remains rooted in the class-based social movement that formed the party, and it has maintained its power based on a platform of social justice and commitment to labor.

This backdrop would suggest a favorable environment for the protection of workers and the eradication of informal work. Yet, informal workers remained extant under CPM rule. Moreover, their attempts to organize as a separate class with unique interests fared poorly under West Bengal's CPM rule. Rather than serving as a historical peg in CPM's agenda of class equality, informal workers only recently surfaced in CPM's rhetoric, just as the party's electoral success and economic agenda started to show their first signs of vulnerability. Let us now examine the political and economic framework of the party from above that undermined the effectiveness of informal workers' movements in the state.

4.3 PROJECT FROM ABOVE: ENTRENCHING POWER

Informal workers' failure to attain either formal protection or welfare benefits in West Bengal can be largely attributed to CPM's hegemonic rule that relied for decades on an entrenched organizational and social base. Its anti-liberalization stance further hampered informal workers' leverage in the state. CPM's organizational form became entrenched through its strict adherence to the principle of "democratic centralism," in which the party position, once adopted by party leaders, became binding on all party members. CPM's democratic centralism resulted in its tight-knit, highly disciplined structure (Franda 1969; Kohli 1990b), which had both positive and negative effects. Atul Kohli (1987) extols the structure for giving the party the political autonomy from the dominant classes that it needed to channel government resources toward the lower classes. In contrast, Amrita Basu (1992: 47) critiques it for stifling "creative grassroots participation," especially among women. Raka Ray (2000) argues that it shaped the types of issues addressed by women's groups in the state. I find that CPM's entrenched organizational structure, alongside its anti-liberalization rhetoric, not only failed to eradicate informal labor (as originally intended) but also inhibited the party from altering its approach to fit the changing needs of the state's workers. It stands in contrast to Tamil Nadu's populist, flexible governing style.

CPM's unchallenged organizational structure translated into an entrenched social base that excluded informal workers. Although CPM tried to alter the structures that created class-based exploitation, it took a reformist approach toward the class struggle. After being repressed by the national government when it pursued a purely revolutionary approach in the late 1960s and watching the defeat of leftist parties during the 1970s in Kerala, CPM secured its electoral success in West Bengal by moderating its socialist principles, thereby reassuring the property classes (Basu 1992; Kohli 1987). In rural areas, CPM offered palatable development incentives to employers and poverty-alleviation programs to the lower strata, which together secured substantial rural support. In urban areas, CPM offered employers a formally protected workforce controlled by the government, but did little to secure urban support through poverty-alleviation efforts. As a result of this approach, CPM did not identify urban informal workers as a target group that could guarantee electoral support or advance industrialization under liberalization. Instead it long viewed informal workers as a reserve army that would eventually be formally employed. Movements that legitimized informal labor through state-sanctioned welfare were especially unwelcome.

Reformist Rural Development

CPM's reliance on rural support after it gained electoral power in 1977 created a reformist rural development agenda that facilitated agricultural growth and alleviated rural poverty. However, this agenda undermined rural labor organizing efforts both among agricultural workers and among nonagricultural workers in the informal and formal sectors. As a result, CPM neither eradicated informal labor nor sought to legitimize informal workers as an organized class or voter group.

As part of its reformist strategy, CPM relied on the electoral support of rich peasants; it thus pursued nonrevolutionary development policies by offering capitalist farmers irrigation, seeds, fair prices for agricultural produce, and reduced taxes. As Atul Kohli (1987: 99) writes in his analysis of CPM's ideology, "The party line stressed that 'land redistribution,' while a useful 'propaganda slogan,' should not be made into a 'slogan of action.'" Only large, absentee landowners were deemed by CPM as "enemies." Kohli (1987: 100) adds, "Exploitation, in this view, is not a function of 'surplus appropriation' but of parasitic life-styles." This approach resulted in significant economic gains in the agrarian sector. Between 1980 and 1990, West Bengal had the highest agricultural growth in the country, with an annual increase in food production of 7.1 percent, as opposed to the national average increase of 3.2 percent.

Over that decade, the number of tube wells increased, and paddy and rice production doubled. By the end of CPM's rule in 2011, West Bengal's agricultural productivity ranked fourth in the country.

In contrast to its earlier radicalism that sought to attain employer protection for all workers, CPM's reformist approach discouraged rural workers from organizing against their employers, especially because employers formed a key support base for the party. During the 1990s, although West Bengal was the fourth most productive state in terms of agriculture, the state's male laborers had the lowest relative agricultural real wages of any Indian state (Mallick 1998). CPM did little to enforce the payment of minimum wages or equal pay for men and women.[25] In addition, CPM did not forbid rural employers from hiring workers informally. In the bidi industry, for example, UF's earlier attempts to hold employers responsible for labor had pushed capital to rely almost entirely on informal, rural workers.

In addition to dissuading workers from making demands on employers, CPM undermined informal workers' ability to organize against the state. CPM's secure power at all levels of rural government gave politicians little incentive to meet informal workers' welfare demands in return for their votes. Because avenues for action were restricted, after losing their formal status in the 1960s, bidi workers did not reorganize until 1989.[26]

To compensate for its decreased radicalism, CPM increased its attention to rural poverty alleviation. In contrast to Tamil Nadu's populist parties, CPM launched rural programs, such as tenancy reform, registration of sharecroppers, facilitation of credit for small landholders, and strengthening of village government bodies (or *panchayats*), that tried to alter the structures that caused rural poverty. Under CPM's rule, the number of people living below the poverty line in rural West Bengal decreased from 56 percent in 1977 to 27 percent in 1997. Although West Bengal has less than 4 percent of the total agricultural land in India, it holds nearly 20 percent of land distributed through land reforms. In addition,

---

[25] Interview with Aarti Dasgupta, November 17, 2003. CITU's West Bengal bidi union was the only CITU union that was headed by a woman (Aarti Dasgupta), and it was the only one that expressed an interest in ensuring equal wages for men and women. Indian laws stipulate that equal wages be paid to men and women for equal work in the same place. Bidi employers skirt these laws by hiring men in the head office to perform certain tasks (such as labeling bidis), where they earn higher incomes, and hiring women to manufacture bidis in their homes (where they earn lower incomes). For an insightful analysis of CPM's failure to initiate progressive reforms concerning gender, see Basu (1992).

[26] Interview, Debashsish Roy, November 18, 2003.

60 percent of West Bengal's land is owned by small and marginal farmers, as opposed to the 29 percent national average (Chaudhuri 2002).[27]

There is little question that CPM's rural programs are responsible for its electoral support among lower-middle- and middle-income rural groups (Kohli 1987; Mallick 1993; Rudra 1981).[28] Its conservative land reforms reduced some dependency on landlords but ensured tenants' dependence on political means (and thus the political party in power) to retain proprietary claims.[29] Today, CPM officials openly admit that their support base is rural. Said State Labor Minister Amin, "We have given [rural Bengalis] power, land reform, a decentralized *panchayat*. Our base is definitely peasants, since we did so much for them."[30] Party propaganda, newspaper interviews, and election speeches by party officials repeatedly voice this line. Until its defeat in the national parliamentary elections in 2009, CPM had won eight consecutive parliamentary elections at the national level and seven Legislative Assembly elections at the state level. No state in India has ever experienced such party stability. Moreover, election statistics show that despite its reformism and recent electoral defeats, CPM continues to enjoy a strong share of votes from the rural poor (Bhattacharya 2004; Yadav 2004).

Because CPM's ideology of rural reformism brought it so much electoral success for so long, the party had little incentive to revisit its rural strategies. Rural informal workers, alongside rural formal workers and employers, have clearly benefited from CPM's poverty-alleviation policies. CPM did not, therefore, find it necessary to explore how it might better accommodate the unique needs of informal workers as a distinct voter group.

Reformist Urban Omission

As in rural areas, CPM's strategy in urban areas was reformist and often suppressed workers' struggles against employers to attract investment.

---

[27] For more detailed analyses on the impact of CPM policies on West Bengal's rural economy, see Kohli (1987) and Sen Gupta (1989). For a critique of these claims, see Mallick (1998).

[28] It is worth noting that CPM's tenancy reform programs were similar to informal workers' welfare boards in that they registered sharecroppers so they could enjoy security, increased incomes, and a legal status. CPM did not extend this program to include nonagricultural, informal workers in rural areas.

[29] For an interesting look at CPM's agrarian politics in Kerala and West Bengal, see Herring (1989).

[30] Interview, November 19, 2003.

Yet, while suppressing formal workers' movements, CPM did not offer investors an alternative workforce that was informal and flexible. Rather, it offered investors a formally protected labor force that the government could control. Although this strategy attracted some capital, it did not meet its promise of mass employment. Nor did it ensure formal protections for all workers; most workers in West Bengal (as elsewhere) continued to operate informally. Moreover, in contrast to its attention to the needs of poor rural voters, CPM's electoral strategy did not prioritize poor, urban voters (in either the informal and formal economies). As a result, its urban agenda led to neither industrial growth nor urban poverty alleviation. It also undermined the party's ability to identify informal workers as a potential vote bank that could guarantee electoral support among the urban poor or facilitate industrial growth under liberalization.

Although on paper and in their rhetoric, CPM resisted the 1991 economic reforms, its actions were more complicated. On one hand, it embraced the push for privatization that accompanied Indian liberalization. In April 1993, CPM launched new incentive schemes (such as tax concessions and streamlined application procedures for corporate credit) to attract domestic and foreign private investment to West Bengal. In September 1994, CPM unveiled its new industrial policy that emphasized large foreign investments and joint ventures (Pederson 2001; West Bengal Government 1994). As then Chief Minister Bhattacharya said, "For the first time, we provided a clear [positive] policy on the private sector" (Majumdar 1998). Shortly after the 1994 industrial policy was announced, the state government revived the West Bengal Industrial Development Corporation (WBIDC) and appointed Somnath Chatterjee, a high-ranking CPM Member of Parliament (MP), as its chairman to signal its importance.[31]

On the other hand, and in contrast to Maharashtra and Tamil Nadu, CPM did not embrace the call for flexible, informal work that normally accompanies liberalization. Rather, CPM leaders criticized informal work as inferior to secure, formal work. Just after the 1991 reforms were announced, CPM supported labor unions that resisted new liberalization policies, and party members today continue to criticize the rise in workers' vulnerability resulting from liberalization efforts. In its 2009 election manifesto for the national Parliament, CPM lambasted neoliberal policies for being "anti-people," increasing unemployment, and decreasing

---

[31] Somnath Chatterjee was kicked out of CPM in 2008 for supporting the INC position on India's nuclear deal with the United States.

wages (CPM 2009: 1). CPM promised "to protect the interest of the working class, by preventing the introduction of anti-labor laws" (CPM 2009: 10). Specifically, it promised to "discourage contractualisation and casualisation of work" (CPM 2009: 22).

To reconcile its resistance to flexible production with its embrace of privatization and market competition, CPM tried to shift its public image away from being labor-friendly toward being an investor-friendly labor controller. To attract investment, it did not offer investors the right to informal work, but rather the promise that West Bengal's government could control its (protected) labor force. In an interview with *The Hindu*, then Chief Minister Buddhadeb Bhattacharjee said, "We have got to convey the message that we are an industry-friendly government and that we encourage private capital." Bhattacharjee warned workers that CITU "will have to agree; otherwise the impact would be disastrous." He went on to assure that CITU is indeed "slowly realizing" that CPM's message is correct (Bhattacharya 2000).

In 1999, the West Bengal government announced a much-publicized project called "Destination Bengal," which aimed to increase foreign industrial investment in the state (Dasgupta 1999). The project, which was implemented by the WBIDC, sponsored meetings with more than 100 corporations, chambers of commerce, and the state industries minister. Destination Bengal launched a series of first-ever efforts by the state government to "sell" West Bengal's advantages at the annual meetings of the Confederation of Indian Industry (CII). The government claimed that its primary advantage (alongside a stable government and the absence of communal tensions) was its control over labor.

As a signal to potential investors CPM de-registered thousands of unions in the state – a move that received wide publicity across the nation (Bandyopadhyay 1995; Banerjee 1999; "Bengal Uses Statistics" 1997; Dutta 1995; "Militancy Melted Down" 2000; Mukerjee 1997; Standard 1997). Although formal workers retained their legal right to claim benefits from their employers, this move symbolized the power that CPM held over its formal workforce. After 1991, the number of strikes declined and lockouts initiated by management increased; from 1990 to 1996, there were eight times as many lockouts as there were strikes in West Bengal. By 1996, West Bengal had the highest number of workdays lost due to lockouts of any state in India (Banerjee et al. 2001). The state did not intervene to reduce the rising trend of lockouts.

In many ways, CPM's post-1991 urban strategy promised a European-style class compromise and was in line with the reformist policy it had adopted toward urban workers since it attained electoral power in 1977.

Unions not affiliated with CPM had always struggled to exist against competition from CPM-affiliated unions, which enjoyed resources and power because of their close relationship with the ruling party. At the same time, CPM often suppressed CPM-affiliated union attempts to create class conflict. For example, CPM's first industrial policy encouraged small enterprises and public sector growth to reduce the power of big business (both foreign and Indian), increase employment, and strengthen workers' influence on the factory floor (West Bengal Government 1978). Yet West Bengal's first CPM chief minister, Jyoti Basu, welcomed businesses into West Bengal by forbidding workers' strikes. From 1977–1995, the number of strikes in the state fell from 200 to 10 (Pederson 2001).

To justify its attempts to curb labor unrest, CPM officials framed their policy choices as an attempt to help workers. As State Labor Minister Amin explained, "In West Bengal, we [the government] just try to open the workers' eyes. Workers shouldn't do anything that can harm the industry because that will only hurt themselves. A strike is really a last resort, and violence is not advised. We always had this message, but now it is even more."[32] Not surprisingly, employers reiterate this frame. As an official from Larsen and Toubro, a Danish construction company and the largest contractor for the Vivekananda Bridge project in Kolkata, explained,

> We used to avoid jobs in Kolkata because there was too much political interference and labor demands. The local workers were not suited to our needs, and they would not allow us to bring our own labor. But now it is a much more stable environment, and they [government and unions] do not make any demands on us. So we are increasing our work here. In fact, we do not like having any unions on our site. It is a sensitive issue, but we prefer to resolve the problems ourselves.[33]

Despite the inflow of some investment, CPM's claims that labor reformism would increase massive investment and employment did not materialize. West Bengal's national share of licenses for industrial investment declined from 7 percent in 1977 to 1 percent in 1991, and its national share of factory production decreased from 10 percent in 1977 to

---

[32] Interview, Mohammed Amin, November 19, 2003. This same sentiment can be seen in speeches by an earlier labor minister, Krishna Pada Ghosh (1981). See excerpts in Mallick (1993, 194).

[33] Larson and Toubro is the largest contractor for one of the four construction projects being administered by the Hooghly River Bridge Commission (HRBC), a statutory organization under the State Ministry of Transport. The HRBC manages the construction of flyovers and bridges in Kolkata, but contractors handle labor issues. CITU's construction union has fought to organize workers under HRBC projects with varying degrees of success. Interview with Larson and Toubro, November 2003.

5 percent in 1997. CPM's offer of a controlled formal workforce appears to have been less attractive than other states' offer of an informal, flexible workforce. Moreover, employment in West Bengal was stagnant between 1977 and the mid-1990s (with the exception of the public sector and the informal sector), and real wages decreased under CPM rule (Pederson 2001). From 1993–1999, job growth declined and is currently below that of the national average. These figures are surprising, given the above average 6.7 percent growth in state domestic product (SDP) during that same period. In short, the state government's reforms spurred growth that was not labor-intensive (West Bengal Government 2004).[34]

Unlike its rural reformism, CPM's urban reformism was not counterbalanced with successful poverty-alleviation efforts (among either formal or informal workers). Newspaper articles on West Bengal rarely mentioned urban, small-scale industries as a focal point of CPM activities.[35] Urban issues, to the extent they were covered in the media, focused almost exclusively on industrialization efforts. When asked about "the poor," CPM officials whom I interviewed only referred to the rural poor.

CPM has long been aware of its tentative support from urban voters, especially in the slums. From 1977 to 1985, for example, it blocked elections to the Kolkata Municipal Corporation (KMC) due to the "fear of losing the city to Congress [INC]" (Kohli 1990a: 151). This fear was realistic, arising from the party's decision to focus on the countryside and the subsequent increase in urban poverty and the continuing decline of civic amenities, such as transportation and sanitation (Sen Gupta 1997). Rather than allowing elections during this period, CPM redrew the borders of the KMC to include areas with a high concentration of Bangladesh refugees, who had resented INC ever since partition.[36] During the late 1980s, CPM extended some efforts toward slum dwellers – legalizing slums; offering public sewerage, water, and electricity in slums; and setting up Basti (slum) Federations and Citizen Committees to help slum dwellers resolve disputes. Only then did CPM allow an election to take

---

[34] State Labor Minister Amin concurred during a personal interview that West Bengal has increased incentives to attract foreign business in high-skilled industries, such as information technology and petro-chemicals. These projects do not aim to increase unskilled or low-skilled employment opportunities.

[35] This observation is based on a review of all articles held in the Center for Education and Documentation, Mumbai, India, from 1997 to 2007. The sample of articles was nonrandom, and the point is thus illustrative, rather than generalizable.

[36] During the 1970s, CPM attracted support from Bagladeshi refugees by helping them attain permanent homes, voter registration cards, food ration cards, and telephones.

place, which it won by a thin margin that required it to create a coalition with other leftist parties.

CPM has also suffered from its weak urban support at the state government level. In 1977, its share of votes from the Kolkata district in the State Legislative Assembly was less than 40 percent, and CPM had to enter a coalition with other leftist parties to win the district. In 1982, its support from the Kolkata district dwindled further, and by 1987, CPM suffered its worst defeat by losing its majority to INC in the Kolkata district. In her analysis of the 1987 Legislative Assembly elections in West Bengal, Prasanta Sen Gupta (1989: 888) argues that CPM's loss of urban support was "due to the continuing unemployment, industrial stagnation, flight of capital, and closed factories, especially around Kolkata." In 1996, when CPM lost more Legislative Assembly seats to INC, even the leftist magazine, *Frontline*, had to acknowledge the impact of the urban vote. Drawing from election data from the New Delhi-based Center for the Study of Developing Societies, *Frontline* reporter, Sajal Basu, wrote, "The anti-Left Front swing worked in Kolkata and two other urban districts," and then added, "But CPM has a continuing grip over rural Bengal" (Basu 1996).

Basu's article reflected CPM's approach to urban voters. Despite its losses in urban districts, CPM had little incentive to revisit its strategy of reformist urban omission, because it had never relied on urban voters for its electoral success. In fact, the increasingly low proportion of urban votes for CPM in West Bengal made party officials satisfied to rely even more on their rural majority support. As State Labor Minister Amin plainly stated, "We [CPM] have stiff opposition in the city. We are the minority in Kolkata because we have no solution for the urban problems. So urban voters go against the establishment. That is understandable."[37] Yet he did not express any plans to attract urban voters. "We make up for our urban deficit with our rural vote," he assured me.

To divert blame for urban poverty and industrial strife away from the party, CPM presents the national government as the enemy of urban areas. Unlike the rural enemy (large absentee landlords), the national government as the urban enemy is too big for CPM to tackle. Until India launched the 1991 economic reforms, all industrial investments required licenses issued by the national government – a power the national government lacked over rural production and taxes (Weiner 1959). Therefore, influencing the national government became a key part of

[37] Interview, November 19, 2003.

ensuring industrial growth at the state level. Given the tense history between CPM and INC (which was in power in the national government until 1989), this strategy was difficult for West Bengal to implement. Instead, CPM blamed its industrial failures on INC and the national government (Pederson 2001). By the early 2000s, these tactics still permeated CPM's offices, despite the lifting of national government control over state-level industry. When explaining the lack of attention paid to urban informal workers in West Bengal, for example, State Labor Minister Amin said, "The state government is in a major financial crunch, so for now there is no scheme for the informal sector. It is a serious crisis we are going through, and the Center [national government] is not providing any help to us."[38] CPM government officials and union leaders in 2003–04 repeatedly voiced this sentiment during my interviews.

CPM's urban policies and its commitment to a controlled, protected workforce did not eradicate informal work. Therefore, informal workers launched new movements to protect their welfare. Yet CPM continued to focus on building relations with (and strengthening control over) formal-workers' unions and ignored informal workers' distinct class movements. Let us now turn to how informal workers from below experienced these challenges from above.

4.4 PROJECT FROM BELOW: FAILING TO FIT INTO STATE INTERESTS

Just as Tamil Nadu's competitive populism and pro-liberalization agenda provided informal workers with an ideal opportunity to fight for state protection, CPM's entrenched organizational structure and social base, combined with its anti-liberalization rhetoric in West Bengal, restricted informal workers' ability to fight for state protection. First, CPM's strict adherence to labor reformism constrained unions' abilities to make demands and initiate struggle. Second, CPM's long unchallenged rule cemented an electoral strategy that focused on rural voters and undermined informal workers' ability to frame themselves as an important vote bank. Finally, CPM's criticism of liberalization policies and resistance to flexible production undermined unions' ability to frame informal workers as a vital peg in a new economy.

West Bengal's informal workers' unions are either CPM-affiliated CITU unions or politically independent. CITU unions are the largest,

[38] Ibid.

wealthiest, and most prevalent unions in West Bengal. Unlike in other states, there is a CITU union for informal workers in construction; established in 1978, West Bengal's CITU Construction Union began including informal workers in 1986. Today 80 percent of its members in West Bengal are informal workers.[39] Therefore, my interviews in West Bengal cover three unions, rather than two: a CITU bidi union, a CITU construction union, and an independent construction union. As I describe in this section, despite their commitment to including informal workers and their unique ties to the state, CITU unions face substantial challenges in West Bengal.

CITU Unions in West Bengal: Targeting Neither the Employer Nor the State

Under CPM rule, CITU unions (as CPM affiliates) received substantial political and financial support. CPM provided CITU with leverage in tripartite bargaining and conciliation procedures, as well as resources to open new offices and hold annual meetings and rallies. On the rare occasions where they did launch a strike, CITU unions did not face the threat of police intimidation. To capitalize on these advantages, smaller unions allied with CITU, which further bolstered CITU's strength (Fernandes 1997).

In return for government support, CITU cooperated with CPM's reformist labor policy. As a result, CITU informal worker unions in West Bengal's construction and bidi industries exhibited conservative tactics. For example, as general secretary of the CITU Construction Workers Federation of India, Debanjan Chakrabarti, explained, "We use the labor court and only threaten strikes if the government or the employer doesn't negotiate. Or we do half-day strikes."[40] The CITU Bidi Union leaders expressed a similar conservatism. According to Debashish Roy, head of Kolkata's CITU's Bidi Union, "We don't hold strikes anymore because there are no factories left in Kolkata. We have tried to hold area-wide strikes among home-based bidi workers, but they are very hard to organize." Since 1977, CITU has held one bidi strike (in October 2003) in the rural district of Murshidabad.[41] As Dasgupta, senior member of CPM and head of the CITU Bidi Union, bluntly stated, "If you ask me, I think

---

[39] Interview, Debanjan Chakrabarti, November 18, 2003.
[40] Interview, November 18, 2003.
[41] Interview, Debashish Roy, November 18, 2003.

being affiliated to the ruling party is a handicap. It is hard for us to fight in a very revolutionary manner. We have to be low key."[42]

Some union leaders justified CITU's moderation by reiterating that CPM's power in West Bengal has ensured that the government does negotiate and unions do not need to resort to strikes. Other union leaders bemoaned CPM's moderation, but noted it was their only option in the face of recent liberalization policies that have increased unemployment: "We can't just jump to strikes. Especially now when it is a real bread and butter question," complained Debanjan Chakrabarti.[43] CITU's conservatism, however, is not a new result of liberalization; since the late 1970s, CPM has not intervened in either the construction or bidi industries when employers refused to pay minimum wages. In a study conducted by bidi unions in the neighboring state of Madhya Pradesh, West Bengal's bidi workers were said to have surprisingly low wages for a communist state: "The West Bengal Government is doing little to benefit the bidi rollers... and even West Bengal unions are of the view that the minimum wages fixed by the West Bengal Government are impractical," wrote a journalist reporting on the study (Shastri 1996).[44]

Unlike in Tamil Nadu and Maharashtra, CITU unions in West Bengal have not held rallies against the state, because for so long the state under CPM was CITU's major protector. In the CITU Construction Union, if workers take their concerns to the government at all, they employ the traditional channels of industrial dispute resolution, rather than confronting elected politicians (as in Tamil Nadu). As Chakrabarti said, "We always present our main demands to the labor commissioner. We can't first go to the labor minister."[45] The labor commissioner is the administrative civil servant, whereas the labor minister is the elected politician from the ruling party. Because it relies so heavily on CPM, it was difficult for CITU to confront state officials while CPM was in power. As Ajay Dasguputa, a senior member of CPI and long-time labor activist, said, "CPM has created a rift between workers and the government. CITU stopped its struggle. All this militant talk in West Bengal is bogus. CITU doesn't fight!"[46]

---

[42] Interview, November 17, 2003.
[43] Interview, November 18, 2003.
[44] Bidi union leaders repeatedly told me that the real bidi organizing in West Bengal is taking place in rural areas. Due to time and resource constraints, I was not able to examine the extent of this organizing in the rural districts of Bengal. However, several conversations indicated that organizing efforts even in rural areas were not particularly successful or innovative.
[45] Interview, November 18, 2003.
[46] Interview, November 24, 2003.

Moreover, CPM's long unchallenged strategy of reformist rural development and urban neglect undermined informal workers' ability to capitalize on the power of their votes to make demands on the state. As Debashish Roy, the head of Kolkata's CITU Bidi Union, explained, "The bidi vote counts for very little in urban areas." In fact, the urban bidi unions in West Bengal were especially inactive. Instead, CITU's bidi union leaders, as well as some bidi members, defended the state government and directed their criticisms toward the national government. As Rathan Nath, a male CITU bidi member, said, "It is the national government who should be improving our lives. They are the ones with the money. The state government has no money, so how can they fix things?"[47]

CITU's present conservatism stands in contrast to its earlier struggles. Sayfun Nisha, a bidi roller in Kolkata, has been a member of the CITU bidi union for thirty years. A 55-year-old widow, Sayfun, is Muslim and comes from a family of bidi rollers. All six of her children have left the bidi trade and are working as home-based, informal workers in the box-making business. Only her eldest daughter went to school. "We used to go to the boss's shop and even his house to demand more wages and equal wages for men and women. We used to fill trucks with bidi workers and go to the governor's house to fight. Now no one wants to go anywhere. None of the girls want to fight and struggle anymore."[48]

Rather than leading a radical class struggle of workers against employers (as was done in the past in West Bengal) or of citizens against elected politicians (as in Tamil Nadu), CITU construction unions in West Bengal use their political muscle to threaten low-level contractors. This strategy secures some protection for union members on a case-by-case basis. Most of the CITU construction members I interviewed said the primary benefit they receive from the union is that union leaders pressure their immediate contractors to pay their wages on time. Although some complained that they do not always receive the minimum wage, nearly all members agreed that the union helps them secure work. CITU does this by using its connections to CPM, which in turn controls the police. CITU offers workers protection against police harassment, as well as the ability to strong-arm contractors into hiring CITU members and paying them their wages.

Take, for example, Jyotsna Bhoya, who has been a member of the CITU construction union for four years. Jyotsna is 28 years old, illiterate, and a member of the lowest or "scheduled" caste of sweepers.[49] Her parents

---

[47] Interview, December 9, 2003.
[48] Interview, November 19, 2003.
[49] Scheduled castes are also known as "Dalits" in India.

migrated to West Bengal from the neighboring state of Bihar. Jyotsna was married at age 15 to a sweeper and now has four daughters. The family lives in a rented home, where they have access to water and electricity. However, her home is in the rural outskirts of Kolkata, and she commutes two hours on the train each way to come find work in the city. Like many women, she said the union identity card helped protect her against police harassment during her long commute to and from work beginning before sunrise and ending after sunset. Like her parents, Jyotsna works as a sweeper for the KMC's Public Works Department (PWD), which builds roads and public toilets.[50] After working for seven years on an informal basis, Jyotsna demanded a permanent job; the contractor fired her. As she explained, "I joined the union to get my job back. Now the contractor has to listen because the union is so strong and holds hands with the big men [i.e., the CPM government]." According to Jyotsna, in addition to helping her secure more stable work (although it is still not legally permanent), the union has also helped force the contractor to increase her wage. Indeed, her wage of Rs. 80 per day is higher than the standard Rs. 40–50 per day received by women affiliated with the independent construction union in West Bengal.[51]

CITU officials point to their ability to secure some protection against exploitation in West Bengal to justify their lack of agitation toward employers and the state. As Chakrabarti said, "The Left Front is in power in West Bengal. So we are able to pressure contractors for money. In other states, contractors do not listen to us, so we always have to agitate." Ranjit Guha, general secretary of West Bengal's AITUC, concurred: "The organization aligned to the government in power will always enjoy some privileges, and CITU definitely uses its political wing [CPM] to get these privileges."[52] He cited examples where employers in the power sector, who relied on CPM for certain licenses, agreed to CITU demands because of their need to ensure good relations with CPM. "AITUC can only fight for the rights of the workers, but this doesn't guarantee anything. CITU can guarantee something," said Guha.[53]

---

[50] Because the municipal government contracts construction work to private companies, the contract laborers employed by the construction company for construction and maintenance (i.e., sweeping) join the construction workers union.

[51] Interview, December 16, 2003.

[52] AITUC is the CPI-affiliated union federation. Although CPI is a major partner of CPM in the state's ruling Left Coalition, AITUC must compete with CITU for membership. Interview, November 24, 2003.

[53] Ibid.

CITU's guarantee, however, is completely dependent on CPM. Without the CPM's backing as the governing party, CITU unions have little bargaining power over employers. CITU unions are also subject to CPM's electoral strategy concerning employers. To prevent capital flight and secure electoral support from employers, for example, CPM drew back on protecting workers from employer exploitation. Today, CITU bidi members do not receive minimum wages, pensions, or welfare benefits in West Bengal. Without CPM's support, CITU bidi unions have been unable to exert power over bidi employers.

Moreover, CITU construction unions' strong-arm strategies with contractors do not assist the working class a whole; rather, they favor union members over non-union members. Shoba Baktu is one of the few women leaders I met in West Bengal's CITU construction union. She is a 45-year-old, illiterate, scheduled caste member. Married at the age of 7 to a fish seller, she has been working in construction for sixteen years. When asked what her primary responsibility was as a union committee member, she answered, "I have to keep out new workers, and protect our [CITU] workers in the bazaar."[54] CITU uses its connections with CPM to attain space for construction workers to stand on the railway platform. The union organizers work with the railway police to ensure that only CITU members can stand there and so gain access to potential employment. In addition, CITU members are protected against harassment from both police and local mafia/strongmen. Many of the women I spoke with said they joined the union specifically for that protection against police harassment (on the railway platform or a city street corner), as they sought employment. "The union has no purpose. But if we didn't have the union, we wouldn't get the work. The union calls all the contractors for us, and we just stand here, waiting for them. The police know not to bother us. We can't go to different markets because the others won't let us in," said Putin Haldar, a member of Kolkata's CITU construction union.[55]

In Kolkata, members view the CITU unions as a broker between the workers and the contractor on one hand, and the workers and the local police on the other hand – not one respondent considered unions to be a link between workers and employers or politicians.[56]

---

[54] Interview, December 10, 2003. The 'bazaar' refers to the space in which construction workers stand while they wait for contractors to pick them up.

[55] Interview, November 21, 2003.

[56] Although all CITU members said they voted for CPM, it was difficult to discern actual party loyalties in the presence of CITU union leaders.

Although CITU unions in West Bengal did not exercise much resistance in practice, they exhibited a strong commitment to traditional worker struggles and a lack of enthusiasm toward the alternative informal workers' movement outlined in Chapter 2. CITU union members not only critiqued CPM's reformism but also pledged faith in its expressed commitment to protecting formal workers and eradicating informal work. In line with CPM, they viewed welfare boards as only a partial measure to regularize workers and thus an unwelcome compromise. This position stood in contrast to that taken by CITU unions in other states, where members recalled with pride their earlier radical struggles against capitalists while acknowledging that such struggles had limited success and could not continue today.

Among Kolkata's bidi unions, CITU remained determined to formalize bidi workers once again, and their primary demand was to attain identity cards for workers from employers. This formal recognition of work by the employer would make the employer responsible for providing each worker with a pension, minimum wage, and other work-based benefits. As Dasgupta, head of the bidi union, explained, "Right now the Bidi Workers Welfare Fund provides some welfare from the government, but nothing from the employer. These workers are counted by the government, but not the employer. CITU wants the employer to recognize its workers!"[57] Unlike CITU leaders in other states, Dasgupta remained committed to the terms of traditional class conflict and collective bargaining via union leaders. As one bidi union member explained, "We usually stand outside the factory office and the leaders go inside and talk."[58]

As a result of this strategy, implementing the Bidi Welfare Board is not a top priority for bidi union leaders in West Bengal. Among the twenty women bidi members I interviewed, only six were members of the welfare board. They attained the identity card two years ago, yet none have yet received any welfare benefit from the board. Two male members I spoke with (outside my female interview sample) had received some welfare benefits from the board, but neither spoke positively about it. "The medicine is cheap quality, the education scholarships are only for star students, and everything else requires so much paperwork, we lose our wages trying to get them," cried Rathan Nath, a male bidi roller in Shyam Bazaar.[59] Moreover, unlike in other states, West Bengal's bidi union leaders did not assume responsibility for attaining the cards

---

[57] Interview, November 2003.
[58] Interview, Nathu Bibi, December 10, 2003.
[59] Interview, December 9, 2003.

for their members. Rather they viewed this as the responsibility of the national government.

The CITU construction union displayed a similar posture. Half the members I interviewed said their primary demands were for a secure wages and permanent employment. Several members also spoke of the need for occupational safety provisions by the employer. Chakrabarti, head of CITU's Construction Workers Federation, claimed that attaining the welfare board is one of the union's primary goals. However, he also immediately blamed the national government for its absence: "So far the Welfare Board has not been passed in Bengal because it is very costly. The center didn't give the state any money to implement it." Although many construction union leaders knew about the welfare boards, only two of the union members I spoke with had heard of them. Workers who demanded welfare benefits, such as medical expenses, a home, and an identity card, considered either the union or the employer as the responsible agent for such provisions. The state was absent in the discussions.

Also in line with CPM's electoral strategy, CITU unions in West Bengal resisted liberalization policies. The CITU bidi union in West Bengal, for example, has been fighting to ensure the local manufacturing and selling of bidis. Because the minimum wage in Kolkata is higher than that in rural districts (within West Bengal), bidis are often manufactured in rural areas, shipped to Kolkata (where they get a Kolkata-based brand label), and then sold in Kolkata at a higher price. Unions in other states rarely addressed such policies. Although CPM began opening West Bengal's economy to foreign investments, its claims to resist liberalization policies made it impossible for CITU unions to frame informal workers as an important peg in the national government's new economic policies.

Non-CITU Unions: Limited Effectiveness

In contrast to the CITU unions, I found that unions affiliated with non-CPM parties were more open to alternative informal workers' movements; however, their effectiveness was hampered by CITU's entrenched organizational and social base.

Like CITU unions, unions affiliated with other leftist parties have expressed their disapproval of CPM's reformism. However, unlike CITU unions, they have attempted to resist it. Ranjit Guha, general secretary of AITUC in West Bengal, carefully explained, "In general we consider the West Bengal government to be a friend of the worker. And in principle it doesn't work against workers. But when the government does something against the proclaimed interest of the workers, we oppose it. For example, the honorable Chief Minister interprets militant struggle as bad, but we see it as enthusiastic struggle. He says it is unhelpful. We disagree." Guha went on to explain that his union also opposes the "inaction of West Bengal's Labor Minister... It [West Bengal's government] should be more pro-worker and implement the labor laws better."[60] Although AITUC has resisted CPM's reformism more than has CITU, it has not made major strides in developing new forms of struggles among informal workers.

Independent unions also present an alternative organizing model among informal workers in West Bengal. The Nirman Mazdoor Panchayat Sangam (NMPS), founded by Aran and Mina Pande in 1985, is the only independent construction workers union in the state.[61] It first formed as a spin-off of the Eastern Railways Union. During the early 1980s, when railway employees were being laid off, some were rehired on a contract basis, which made them ineligible for the railways union. Others were forced to find new jobs, and many turned to construction. Aran Pande, also a railway employee and long-time union member, quit his job and dedicated his life to organizing construction contract workers. Using their contacts in the Eastern Railways, Aran and his wife, Mina, spent three years mobilizing membership, attaining an office, and registering the union with the state.

Unlike the CITU construction union, NMPS has actively fought for the establishment of a welfare board. In 2001, the Pandes met with the leaders of TMKTPS, the Tamil Nadu construction union, to attain guidance on the struggle. Since then, NMPS has organized weekly "reading circles" throughout West Bengal to educate construction workers on the benefits of a welfare board.[62] In contrast to the CITU construction workers, more than half of the twenty NMPS members whom I interviewed knew about the welfare board and expressed to me its potential benefits. Many said they joined the union to attain access to this board, and one-third said they joined the union to obtain an identity card, which would "allow someone to find them in case of an accident." In addition, unlike in CITU, 70 percent of NMPS members interviewed said the biggest benefit

---

[60] Interview, November 24, 2003.

[61] Technically, the union is affiliated with the Hind Mazdoor Sabha (HMS) Federation, which is affiliated with a political party called Janata Dal. However, because Janata Dal is weak in West Bengal, NMPS operates as an independent union.

[62] A "reading circle" is the term NMPS uses for a group of workers, organized by neighborhood, that gets together to discuss strategies and educate themselves.

they had received from the union was education on their rights. Finally, NMPS leaders appeared to be more involved in the personal lives of the members, often providing them with medicine, marriage loans, legal assistance, and youth training against alcohol, drugs, and sexually transmitted diseases. For some members, this assistance provided them with a welcome alternative to relying on favors from local CPM representatives and strongmen.

Like the unions in Tamil Nadu, NMPS has pressured elected state officials. It has written letters and met with MPs, MLAs, the state labor minister, and the state governor. It has even appealed to the prime minister of India. Between September and November 2003, the union held a monthly rally outside state government offices.

Despite its efforts, however, NMPS has not achieved much success. More than members of any other union included in this study, NMPS members expressed their frustration with the governing party and its restrictions. "In a democratic structure the MPs and MLAs are considered the representatives of the people. So we tried to use the MPs and MLAs to pressure our state government into action. But our government is run by the mafia. They don't do anything. And if we dare demand something of them, they think we are launching a conspiracy to throw them out," explained Aran Pande.[63] Because NMPS lacks the political connections to the police that CITU has, most NMPS members are not able to stand in the marketplace to seek work. Rather, they must form personal relationships with contractors and so become wholly reliant on them. They also earn approximately 40 percent less than CITU construction workers, because NMPS is not able to place the same pressure on the contractors as can CITU.

NMPS leaders felt that they could never compete with the resources and power that CITU enjoys because of its affiliation with CPM. Currently, the NMPS membership is approximately 4,500, but its major challenge is competing with CITU unions for members. "Since everything has been politicized here, people think that the ruling party will give more protection to the workers," Pande explained. In addition, NMPS cannot pressure the government alongside CITU, because "they always have to go along with their party. They don't oppose the government like we do."[64]

Although the Pandes expressed pride in the union's growth over the past twenty years, they also expressed frustration with the inability of

---

[63] Interview, November 20, 2003.
[64] Interview, November 25, 2003.

NMPS to secure identification cards for their members. "If we could get the ID card granted under the welfare board, we could prove that these people are workers and that they are owed some things," explained Mina Pande.[65]

Finally, NMPS relies heavily on its networks with other non-CPM affiliated organizations, which enable it to expand in new areas. For example, it works with a local doctor in one area who is close to a ward counselor from an independent party. In another area, it has joined hands with a local branch of the Backward and Depressed Classes League (DCL), an independent organization founded by the scheduled caste leader, Dr. Ambedkar, and registered in 1952.

4.5 SHIFTING POLITICS: A SHIFT FOR INFORMAL LABOR

In recent years, CPM has begun to revise its social base and its resistance to liberalization and flexible production. In large part, these shifts can be attributed to the challenges posed by CPM's long-held reliance on reformism, rural development, and urban omission on the state-level electoral front. In addition, CPM's status as a coalition partner with INC in the national government from 2004 to 2008 encouraged it to join INC in supporting informal workers. These shifts in West Bengal's political and economic frameworks have, in turn, shifted the conditions for effectiveness among the state's informal workers' movements. As a result, informal workers have begun to emerge on the state's policy agenda for the first time. Although the substantive implications of these changes are yet to be seen, they have the potential to shift West Bengal to a medium-success case for informal workers' movements, if informal workers take advantage of the opportunity.

On the political side, CPM has been forced to alter its social base because its electoral success has been threatened for the first time since it came to power. The primary opposition party that has emerged in the state is the All India Trinamool Congress (TMC), a local offshoot of INC, founded in 1997. Like CPM, TMC offers voters a Bengali alternative to INC. However, unlike CPM, TMC targets urban voters. In recent years, it has also tapped rural voters who are frustrated with CPM's reformist attempts to attract private investors. Its appeal to rural voters was most vividly illustrated in the 2008 Nandigram case, in which TMC made

---

[65] Interview, November 27, 2003.

strategic use of CPM's suppression of rural protests against the party's land grab for private capital.[66]

The defection of urban voters from CPM to TMC has been primarily responsible for CPM's municipal- and state-level electoral losses. By the late 1990s, some formal workers' unions began to express resistance to CPM's reformist policies (Banerjee 2002). In 2000, when CPM condemned all militant union activity, the general secretary of CITU criticized CPM for "deviating from the communist ideology" and "suffering from a bourgeois influence" (Banerjee 2000). Because CPM's urban reformism did not alleviate urban poverty, poor urban workers (most of whom are informally employed) also began to express their dissatisfaction with CPM. As Indian political analyst, Prasanta Sen Gupta (1997: 912), argues, CPM's loss of support from the urban poor "may be attributed to complacency and arrogance . . . [T]he Left Front underestimated their opposition."

In particular, CPM underestimated TMC's ability to attain electoral advantage by targeting poor urban voters. In 2001, CPM lost the Kolkata municipal elections to TMC. This was the first time since 1977 that CPM did not control the state's capital. To win these elections, TMC had targeted the dissatisfied slum youth and migrants in squatter settlements whom CPM had ignored. Municipal election data showed that CPM's loss was due to its decreasing influence among "the urban poor, lower middle class sections and the so-called 'unorganised' [i.e., informal] stratum of the working class" (Dwaipayan and Nigam 1996: 28). As slum dweller activist, Mira Roy, explained, "After watching them in power for 30 years, *bastis* [slums] are withdrawing their support from CPM. They are not providing enough services. The hospitals are terrible. They have not upgraded any of the services, despite the population boom, and there are no jobs for the youth."[67]

---

[66] In 2006, the West Bengal government under CPM used the 1894 Land Acquisition Act to expropriate land for the automobile company, Tata Motors, to produce the "Nano," a small, cheap car designed for the mass market. More than 13,000 people held claims on the acquired land, of whom more than 2,000 refused to accept the government's compensation for the land.

[67] Interview, Mira Roy, November 2003. In 2003, TMC mimicked CPM in evicting squatters even though it had relied on squatter votes to enter power at the city level. According to Kolkata's mayor in 2003, Subrata Mukherjee (TMC), "Migrants are good for our vote, but they are trouble for our Corporation. They use our services, but they do not pay taxes and they send all their earnings home to other states" (interview, Mukherjee, December 17, 2003). Although the CPM government at the state level had the power to

TMC's strategy of capitalizing on CPM's failure to meet urban needs also cost CPM popularity at the state and national government levels. Since India launched its liberalization reforms, CPM's share of seats in the state legislature has dropped – from 64 percent in 1991 to 53 percent in 1996 to 49 percent in 2001. In 1991 and 1996, CPM lost seats to INC; in 2001, both CPM and INC lost seats to TMC, which took an impressive 20 percent of seats in its first contested election (GOI 1991, 1996a, 2001b). In an interview after the elections, West Bengal's Chief Minister Buddhadeb Bhattacharjee admitted that, during the 2001 State Assembly elections, CPM enjoyed less support in urban and semi-urban areas, "mainly because of problems such as unemployment and rising prices" (Menon and Chaudhuri 2001: 12).

In the 1999 elections to the national parliament, CPM and TMC each received 44 percent of the votes from West Bengal's lower classes, indicating a weakening of CPM's unchallenged hold on lower-class voters; much of TMC's support came from urban lower-class members (CSDS 1999). In 2009, CPM lost its majority in West Bengal's national parliamentary elections for the first time since it came to power in 1977. In 2011, CPM faced its most crushing defeat, losing control of the state government to TMC. Although detailed analyses of these elections remain to be done, preliminary reports suggest that TMC gained support from both urban voters and CPM's long-standing loyalists from rural areas.

After the 2001 municipal and state elections, CPM reexamined its strategy toward urban residents. First, it appeased urban middle and upper classes by launching several "beautifying the city" campaigns, which involved evicting refugees from their squatter settlements without provisions for their resettlement. Many attribute CPM's 2001 loss in the KMC elections to this shift in stance toward refugees in Tollynalla canal, one of CPM's major vote banks in the 1977 election.[68] As Mira Roy, a long-time worker for UNAND (an NGO that fights for the rights of urban squatters in Kolkata) said, "The Left entered power on the backs of refugees and workers, and now they are evicting poor refugees in squatter settlements and cracking down on strikes! They have lost all their radicalism."[69]

---

control the evictions around the canals due to its control over irrigation, it supported the evictions.

[68] This topic was raised by several activists, urban intellectuals, and city government officials in Kolkata.

[69] Interview, November 2003.

As part of its efforts to reexamine its strategy toward urban residents, CPM began to address some of the welfare demands of informal workers. As detailed earlier, in 2001, CPM passed the Pension Fund for Unorganized Workers, the state's first welfare policy for informal workers. The catalyst behind this fund was an eclectic and energetic man, Shubash Chakrabarty – a long-time CPM member and the minister of transport and sports in 2003. Of all the CPM officials I spoke with in 2003 and 2004, Chakrabarty was the only one who had been willing to resist CPM's apathy toward the urban poor. He confidently admitted to me the deficiencies in his own party: "Even though I am a part of them [CPM], I have spoken out for and against them. They have not addressed the issues of the poor. Especially the urban poor."[70] Despite resistance from his own party, Chakrabarty managed to initiate several programs for the urban poor in West Bengal, including a campaign that enrolled 60,000 poor mothers and 120,000 children into India's National Health Insurance Scheme for cancer, leukemia, and heart and kidney disease. Since 1980, Chakrabarty has led an annual rally in Kolkata where informal workers in the transport industry (including truck and bus drivers, rickshaw pullers, and railroad hawkers) call for government benefits such as pensions, subsidies for food and edible oil, and medical aid. Chakrabarty's efforts to challenge CPM were not at first well received by the traditionally disciplined CPM. Even as it launched the 2001 Pension Fund for informal workers, CPM State Secretary Anil Biwas advised Chakrabarty to "quit [the party] if he felt the government has done nothing for the poor" (Staff Reporter 2001).

Like MGR in Tamil Nadu, Chakrabarty defined his target population as the broad category of "the poor," rather than the more specific group of informal workers. During our conversation, Chakrabarty repeated several times, "I work for the poor, not the informal sector."[71] Moreover, Chakrabarty never referred to his efforts in terms of "workers' struggles," but rather as "humane efforts for the poor." By framing informal workers' demands in these terms, Chakrabarty not only increased informal workers' attractiveness as a large vote bank for CPM but also fit their support into CPM's reformist development ideology.

CPM's move to finally alter its stance toward informal workers in 2001 may be partly explained by the large electoral support informal workers promised, just as the media highlighted CPM's threatened electoral

---

[70] Interview, September 2003.
[71] Ibid.

prospects (Frontline 2001; Menon and Chaudhuri 2001). Unlike in Tamil Nadu, where MGR's populist legislation to protect informal workers was received with positive press, the media strongly criticized CPM's shift toward populism. CPM's long-standing resistance to urban informal work was deeply entrenched in the party's ideology, and newspapers lampooned CPM for showing interest in informal workers merely to attain votes (Namboodiri 1998; Statesman 2001). As one editorial warned, CPM's "support for unorganized [i.e. informal] labor is a cruel joke. And no one is fooled by the gesture" (Statesman 1999). However, the shift was effective: in 2005, CPM regained control over the KMC, and in 2006 it increased its share of seats in the state legislature to 60 percent.

This media critique, however, only captured part of CPM's interest in informal workers. In addition to trying to attain votes in 2001, CPM was also beginning to adjust its stance toward liberalization and flexible production. For the first time since it gained power under Jyoti Basu, there was a new party chief minister in West Bengal, Budhadeb Bhattacharjee. Bhattacharjee entered office in 2001 with a commitment to revise CPM's economic ideology by expanding its market orientation and its acceptance of privatization. As *The Economist* reported in 2008, CPM "believes the state's future lies in industry, not just farming" ("Nano Wars" 2008: 63). In 2004, CPM attained power in the national government by joining the ruling INC-led coalition. Although CPM continued to resist many INC policies and ultimately left the coalition over a dispute around the India-U.S. nuclear deal, it joined INC in signing a Common Minimum Program.[72] As the Program acknowledged, the 2004 election was viewed as a popular call for "parties wedded to the welfare of farmers, agricultural laborers, weavers, workers, and weaker sections of society" (GOI 2004: 1) Of the six principles of governance outlined in the Program, the third targeted welfare for informal workers, promising "to enhance the welfare and well-being of farmers, farm labor and workers, particularly those in the unorganized [or informal] sector, and assure a secure future for their families in every respect" (GOI 2004: 1). As part of this commitment, CPM began to alter its long-held stance against liberalization's call for flexible labor and instead agreed to promote and protect informal workers as a central part of the newly reforming Indian economy. As the minister of state in West Bengal's Labor Department explained to me,

[72] This document, which has become increasingly popular as coalition governments have become the norm in India, lays out a ruling coalition's minimum objectives of governance.

"In our state, CPM began interest in the informal sector in a major way in 2004. Manmohan Singh was Prime Minister and CPM supported the Common Minimum Program."[73]

At times, the party's positions on liberalization and informal work contradicted one another. For example, in its 2009 Election Manifesto, CPM pledged to constrain informal work by promising to "discourage contractualisation and casualisation of work." In a subsequent statement, however, it promised to "improve the legislation on Unorganized Sector Workers... and set up special welfare boards for [informal] fish workers, providing them with identity cards and social security schemes" (CPM 2009: 22–23). As detailed earlier, since 2004 CPM has initiated several welfare schemes for informal workers, including expanding the 2001 Pension Fund, enacting the Construction Workers Welfare Board, expanding the Bidi Workers Welfare Fund, and creating welfare boards for additional informal worker groups.

4.6 CONCLUSIONS

This chapter provides support for my regime-type explanation regarding the effectiveness of informal workers' movements: informal workers in West Bengal have failed to attain material benefits because of the absence of a conducive economic and political framework from above. In West Bengal, CPM's long entrenched organizational and social base, coupled with its lack of interest in liberalizing, has made it difficult for unions to frame informal workers' demands in terms that would appeal to the ruling party's interest in staying in power. For decades, CPM retained power by enforcing a reformist ideology and focusing on rural interests, which constrained urban workers' struggles. CPM's entrenched political power also limited informal workers' ability to make new demands on the state by appealing to its interest in attaining their votes. Finally, CPM's criticism of liberalization policies undermined informal workers' ability to convince the state government to privilege informal workers as a vital part of the new economy.

To the extent that informal workers in West Bengal have attained some benefits for union members, those benefits have been provided by unions in the construction industry, rather than by the state across industries. Independent construction unions have used their own resources to provide members with welfare benefits; CPM-affiliated construction

---

[73] Interview, April 22, 2009.

unions have used their relationships to the party in power to force employers to provide jobs and on-time wage payments to their members. The latter experience is unique among the three states in this study. In both cases, the state government has rarely shown much interest in acknowledging informal workers' distinct class location and their specific interests. Such an acknowledgment has been viewed as legitimating unregulated work, which in turn has been considered antithetical to CPM's expressed commitment to formal workers' rights.

Yet, in an attempt to attract capital, West Bengal's CPM government has recently begun to relieve employers of their responsibility for worker welfare. As illustrated in the state's bidi industry, once CPM fails to enforce worker rights, unions (even those affiliated with CPM) are unable to ensure benefits to their workers. This situation raises important questions as to whether informal workers' unions in West Bengal will be able to create a movement that can, on one hand, ensure some social justice to the state's workers as structures of production become increasingly flexible and, on the other hand, accommodate CPM's entrenched organizational and social base and rhetorical resistance to liberalization.

CPM's increased support for informal workers has coincided with the electoral challenges it faced at the state government level from TMC and its status as a partner with the pro-liberalization INC coalition at the national government level. As a result of these forces, CPM has begun to appeal to new vote blocs and to support some flexible production. In turn, these shifts in CPM's political and economic frameworks provide informal workers an opportunity to frame themselves as (1) a large vote bank and (2) an important resource in facilitating government efforts toward flexible production. These shifts have already yielded several new laws designed to provide government-supported welfare benefits to informal workers. If West Bengal's informal workers are able to capitalize on these opportunities, they may be able to secure more improvements in their daily lives – bringing West Bengal closer to Kerala, where informal workers enjoy substantial success under an electoral context in which CPM competes for votes with INC by offering pro-poor policies.

We have now found support for the two extreme cases in our state framework. The experience in Kerala further supports the argument that West Bengal's lack of success with informal workers is primarily due to the absence of electoral competition and resulting social movement mediation. However, questions remain as to what informal workers operating in states without pro-poor competitive elections can do to attain some success. In such cases, can a state's commitment to liberalization offer informal workers any opportunity to gain power? If so, state conditions in which pro-poor competitive elections are absent but a state-driven liberalization agenda is present should yield more successful informal workers' movements than those in West Bengal, but less successful than those in Tamil Nadu. Let us now turn to this final case to examine this claim.

5

The Minimal Gains of Accommodation

The state of Maharashtra provides our final case of how state factors affect the amount and type of benefits that informal workers attain. In this study, Maharashtra exemplifies a "middle success" case for the new informal workers' movement outlined in Chapter 2. Like in West Bengal (examined in Chapter 4), informal workers in Maharashtra have had limited success in eliciting benefits from the state. The state's informal workers are forced the Maharashtrian government to show some interest in providing minimal levels of welfare. Twenty-three of the forty informal workers interviewed for this study received a material benefit in Maharashtra (as opposed to thirty of the forty in Tamil Nadu and only twenty-one of the sixty in West Bengal). In contrast to West Bengal, of the benefits informal workers attained in Maharashtra, nearly all were welfare benefits and relatively few were work-based benefits, indicating a greater focus on the new informal workers' movement. Unlike Tamil Nadu (examined in Chapter 3), however, most of the welfare benefits were provided by the unions, rather than the state, indicating less success in institutionalizing the new movement into the state's political agenda.

Drawing from the state framework outlined in the Introduction, I argue in this chapter that informal workers' limited success in attaining state-provided welfare benefits in Maharashtra can be attributed to the state's commitment to liberalization and its electoral context, which has been largely uncompetitive and never pro-poor. Maharashtra's political leadership encountered some competition in the 1990s, but all the competing parties have appealed to intermediate and elite caste members and been impervious to mass demands for social justice and equity.

Informal workers, therefore, have not had ample opportunities to use their mass, plebian, or "poor" vote bank to attract politicians. Maharashtra's economic policies, however, have provided informal workers with a small window of political opportunity to attain welfare benefits. Since the early 1990s, Maharashtra's government has pursued liberalization policies (including deregulation and privatization) alongside an active, pro-business industrial policy that includes building export-promotion zones and reforming labor laws. These policies have undermined workers' ability to pressure employers and have stifled some of the strongest workers' struggles in India. At the same time, they have enabled the state's informal workers to attain some welfare benefits for their members by claiming to be a partner in the state's economic agenda. To do so, informal workers have convinced government officials that (1) informal workers are an essential peg in the government's drive toward industrialization and economic growth and (2) the government must provide for workers' basic needs to prevent their refusal to work informally.

5.1 MAHARASHTRA: SOME STATE BENEFITS FOR INFORMAL LABOR

The Maharashtrian government has instituted far fewer protective measures for informal workers than has Tamil Nadu's government. In relation to West Bengal, in 2002–04, Maharashtrian state officials indicated more interest in providing support to informal workers but by 2009 they showed less interest.

Maharashtra's official minimum wage in construction (Rs. 113.65) was higher than that of West Bengal and Tamil Nadu; however, reported wages were lower than those found in Tamil Nadu and among some CITU-affiliated construction workers in West Bengal. Women workers interviewed in Maharashtra consistently reported earning Rs. 50/day for unskilled manual work; for the same work, men earned Rs. 100/day. Workers who lived on construction sites also received shelter.

Implementation of the Construction Workers Welfare Board has been slow. Unlike in West Bengal, however, Maharashtra's Labor Department officials expressed keen support for the board and openly criticized their own government for the delays in ratifying it. Hemant Deshmukh, Maharashtra's minister of labor in 2003, is a long-time labor activist who has organized farmers in northern Maharashtra. Deshmukh candidly remarked to me, "Maharashtra is still not enacting the construction board. There is government delay and there is really no excuse. The board has been opposed by industries, so ministers are delaying it."[1] In 2007, the Maharashtrian government finally began the process of enacting the board by formulating its own state-level rules. Because much of Maharashtra's construction work is done by migrant workers who live on construction sites for an unspecified amount of time, the state's proposed Construction Welfare Board includes common welfare benefits (such as education scholarships and health care), as well as site-specific benefits such as water facilities, toilets, day care centers for workers' children, canteens, and housing. By 2009, the Construction Board had been constituted, but it did not yet include representatives from capital and labor and had therefore not begun to provide benefits. Again, Labor Department officials spoke candidly about the government's delays. Arvind Kumar, labor commissioner and chairman of the Construction Board in 2009, expressed a keen interest in informal workers: "We must admit that it [completing the Construction Board] is going very slowly. My colleagues are advising me to take it slow. They are nervous about bringing the tax money into government hands and having accusations about corruption. It is a very sensitive issue. It is important to make it tripartite to keep the corruption charges low."[2]

Of the twenty construction workers interviewed in Maharashtra, none had received a direct welfare benefit from the state. However, 70 percent reported that they received a benefit from their construction workers' organization. As detailed later, many of these benefits were provided in partnership with municipal governments.

In the case of bidi, Minister of Labor Deshmukh in 2003 worked closely with unions to pressure the government to improve work conditions. In 1998, bidi unions engaged in a much-publicized, month-long statewide strike until the state government agreed to form a committee to review minimum wages (Staff Reporter 1998). The official minimum wage for bidi was increased to Rs. 40 in 2001. In 2003, Deshmukh chaired the wage committee, which again increased the minimum wage and bonuses for all bidi workers in the state: it increased the minimum wage to Rs. 50 and the "dearness" allowance to Rs. 10–20, resulting in Rs. 60–70 per 1,000 bidis.[3] Not surprisingly, employers, especially

---

[1] Interview, January 20, 2004.
[2] Interview, April 28, 2009.
[3] The dearness allowance was implemented in 1991 to ensure that minimum wages accounted for inflation by linking them to the Consumer Price Index (CPI).

in urban areas, have employed innovative strategies to avoid complying with these laws. Bidi workers interviewed in Maharashtra reported earning Rs. 30/day, which was the same wage as in West Bengal and nearly half of what was found in Tamil Nadu.[4]

The most striking gains for bidi workers in Maharashtra have resulted from the state's implementation of the Bidi Welfare Fund. In 2002, Maharashtra's government committed to build 10,000 houses under the auspices of the Bidi Welfare Fund, with ownership of each house in the name of a woman bidi worker. The national and state government each agreed to provide Rs. 10,000 per worker toward the construction costs of the house; the worker had to pay the remaining amount. A local developer (Pandhe Group of Industries) has been responsible for the construction of the homes and has received the proceeds of all commercial space sold from the land. This project received massive media attention, because it was the first of its kind to be implemented in Asia. In March 2004, India's President, Abdul Kalam, participated in a ground-breaking ceremony for the first 300 homes (Monteiro 2003; Singh 2002). By 2008, 7,695 houses had been constructed in Sholapur district, and 328 houses had been completed in the districts of Gondia, Bhandara, Ahmednagar, Sindhudurg, and Nanded. In addition to houses, by 2008, the Bidi Welfare Fund had delivered education scholarships to more than 50,000 students, health benefits to nearly 850 workers, and marriage and funeral assistance to more than 100 bidi families (Maharashtra Government 2008).

Of the twenty bidi workers interviewed in Maharashtra, all had welfare identity cards from the Bidi Welfare Fund, and more than one-third had received education scholarships for their children. One member had received a grant from the fund to support her health care expenses resulting from kidney failure. Finally, 75 percent reported that the union had increased their knowledge about their rights and helped them connect with government benefit schemes.

Maharashtra is also noted for the programs it has enacted for informal workers outside the bidi and construction industries. In 1969, Maharashtra enacted the Maharashtra Mathadi, Hamal and Other Manual Workers (Regulations of Employment and Welfare) Act, the first welfare board for informal workers in the country.[5] Under this act, workers engaged

---

[4] Some workers reported that they earn Rs. 88/1,000 bidis. However, they have to purchase inputs with their wages: 1 kilogram of leaves (Rs. 35), 200 grams of tobacco (Rs. 14), and one bundle of string (Rs. 7).

[5] Mathadi refers to porters working on the docks.

in loading and unloading, fishermen, salt-pan workers, and other casual labor employed on the docks could attain an identity card by registering with the Mathadi Workers Welfare Board. In 1970, the Mathadi Welfare Act was extended to include workers in grocery stores who are responsible for loading, unloading, stacking, carrying, weighing, and measuring food.

As in the construction and bidi industries, the Mathadi Board was funded by a tax placed on employers, government contributions, and workers' membership fees. In return, the board provided medical service, pensions, and traditional work-based benefits, such as bonuses, paid vacation, and workers' compensation. Like the earlier Bidi Board and unlike contemporary welfare boards, the Mathadi Board also served as an avenue through which workers could attain employment and payment. In short, the Mathadi Board aimed to provide informal workers with the benefits received by formal workers. By 2006, the Mathadi Board had more than 15,000 members. However, according to its annual audit report in 2006, the Maharashtra government had not appointed a full-time chair or secretary to the Mathadi Board since 2002. The report concluded, "We are of the opinion that there is a lot of gap between expectations of the Act and the Scheme" (Bhave 2006: 19).[6]

From 2002 to 2004, the state government was attempting to enact new protections for informal workers. Steps were taken to provide licenses for street vendors and welfare boards for domestic workers, hand and power loom workers, and sweepers.[7] As expected, the middle and upper classes criticized these proposals (Times News Network 2002). As the *Times of India*, a leading English-language newspaper in the state, sarcastically reported, "Chief Minister Sushilkumar Shinde pronounced this decision [to enact a domestic workers welfare board] taken by his cabinet with the gravitas usually reserved for serious matters of the state" (Times News Network 2003). In addition, in 2003, Khot, the state secretary of labor who was responsible for drafting labor legislation, was actively involved in creating an umbrella welfare board for all informal workers. This board would provide pensions and invite employers' voluntary contributions in return for a loyal workforce.

---

[6] At the time of my fieldwork, the Mathadi Board was no longer active, because the Mathadi Union had weakened in the face of increased informalization. The rise and subsequent demise of the mathadi movement parallel those of the early bidi movement (outlined in Chapter 2); an alternative mathadi movement for informal workers has not yet emerged.

[7] A Bill for the Domestic Workers' Board was introduced in Maharashtra's Legislative Assembly on July 25, 2008.

The Maharashtrian government's interest in protecting informal workers should not be overstated. Although in early 2003 both Khot and Deshmukh told me that the state government should finalize this umbrella welfare board within a few months, by the end of 2003, the proposal had been tabled. In 2005, Maharashtra had stopped its state supplement for bidi workers' homes, after the national government doubled its grant contribution. Officials acknowledged a need to reverse the current inertia toward informal workers' protections. When speaking about the tabled informal workers welfare board, for example, Khot admitted, "The Labor Minister got too involved, and he is useless. He doesn't care at all about the poor."[8] Although Maharashtra, on occasion, has ensured welfare provisions for informal workers, the sustainability of these efforts remains to be seen.

Let us now turn to the reasons why informal workers have obtained minimal welfare gains in Maharashtra, but not more. As a primary explanation, I explore Maharashtra's electoral context, which has undermined informal workers' ability to appeal to political leaders' interest in a mass vote. As a secondary explanation, I explore the state government's commitment to liberalization, which has given informal workers a political opportunity to fit themselves into the state's economic agenda and so obtain minimal gains.

5.2 DOMINANT CASTE POWER

Students of South Asian politics may find it unsurprising that informal workers have had little success in forging an effective movement in Maharashtra. Unlike West Bengal, Maharashtra's social structures and political history have not been conducive to successful class struggle among poor workers. Although caste has served as a central organizing principle in Maharashtrian politics, as it did in Tamil Nadu, Maharashtrian politicians have continuously appealed to the interests of intermediate and elite castes, rather than lower castes. Intermediate caste members have gained power through the Indian National Congress Party (INC), which has dominated Maharashtrian party politics more than in any other state. The political success that INC secured by appeasing intermediate castes in Maharashtra encouraged the opposition parties that emerged in the 1990s to do the same. The state has, therefore, not produced leaders that appeal to poor, mass interests to attain power. Members of the

---

[8] Interview, March 25, 2003.

intermediate castes have become nearly unchallenged leaders, successfully stifling radical movements from below. This political context has undermined the success of the state's informal workers' movements.

Maharashtrian state politics has been dominated by the intermediate castes of Marathas and Kunbis. Most members of these castes were rural peasants, many were landowners, and nearly none were employed in the urban informal workforce. As in Tamil Nadu and West Bengal, the highest caste of Brahmins (who comprised only 4 percent of the region's population) held cultural hegemony and ownership over the means of production in pre-colonial Maharashtra (Palshikar and Deshpande 1999). As the Indian nationalist movement grew in the early 1900s, however, Brahmins began to lose political power to the Marathas and Kunbis. Together, Marathas and Kunbis comprised 31 percent of the population; their members owned agricultural land, enjoyed ritual status in the society, and controlled village-level political institutions. Maratha-Kunbis could, therefore, use the power of their numbers and their local status to position themselves as essential players in the independence movement. In 1930, Marathas and Kunbis joined the INC that was then dominant in western Maharashtra and the leading force in India's independence movement.

In the decade after independence, Maratha-Kunbis attempted to take over INC's leadership positions. Frustrated by INC's urban, non-Maharati, Brahmin leadership between 1947–60, a group of Marathas and Kunbis split from the party to form the Peasants Workers Party (PWP). PWP led a separatist movement, called Samyukta Maharashtra, for the creation of a state for Maharati-speaking people. Eventually, INC (under the leadership of a non-Maharati chief minister, Y. B. Chavan) joined PWP's battle for a separate state, because it could not sustain its power in western India without the numerical support of the Marathas and Kunbis. On May 1, 1960, the national government (also under INC) conceded, and the state of Maharashtra was created along linguistic lines. Maratha-Kunbis led the new state under INC, which remained unchallenged until 1995. Even when party competition emerged in the 1990s, Maratha-Kunbi interests continued to dominate the state's politics.

Although earlier accounts framed Maratha-Kunbis' influence in Maharashtra in terms of a radical, secular manifestation of caste and class consciousness (Mandelbaum 1970), contemporary accounts agree that it was largely driven by elites for elites (Lele 1990). Primarily peasants involved in agriculture, Maratha-Kunbis are diverse in terms of wealth, power, and status. It was the elite members of the Maratha caste, however, who became politically active and joined INC and PWP. These elites capitalized on the large numbers of their caste by uniting the diverse set of Marathas and Kunbis under a single, anti-Brahmin, peasant identity (Lele 1990). Elite Marathas offered masses an alternative to the existing Brahmin INC leadership. Unlike in Tamil Nadu, where the anti-Brahmin movement was similarly led by elites, Maharashtra's Maratha-Kunbi elites never tried to meet mass interests to secure power. In their rhetoric, Maratha leaders of INC claimed to represent the middle masses of the "bahujan samaj" – non-Brahmins and non-Dalits (members of the lowest caste). To this end, they initiated some land reforms that ended absentee landlordism, primarily among Brahmins.[9] They also launched the Employment Guarantee Scheme (EGS) in 1965, which was sanctioned by the state in 1978. The EGS simultaneously met the needs of rural peasants by providing some employment guarantees and those of rural landlords by externalizing a portion of their labor costs with state subsidies and preventing mass insurrection among peasants.[10] The benefits of the EGS to peasants and landlords reflect Maharashtra's use of welfare boards to benefit informal workers and employers.

To a larger extent, however, Maratha leaders of INC met the needs of agricultural elites, most of whom were Marathas or Kunbis and were related to INC leaders through blood or marriage. Because India relied on a planned economy until the early 1990s, for decades INC leaders could provide large and medium-sized landowners with access to state resources, subsidized fertilizer and electricity, cheap credit, and irrigation. In return, local elites ensured their clients' electoral support for INC by exercising their economic control over mass labor and their social control at the village level. In addition, many INC ministers were also members (often leaders) of the state's infamous cooperatives (primarily in sugar), which helped them directly control rural factory workers (Lele 1990).

INC's attention to agricultural elite interests, often at the expense of other state interests, continues to the present day in Maharashtra. In 2000, a report on the state's finances criticized then Chief Minister Vilasrao Deshmukh for driving the state into its worst financial crisis (Special Correspondent 2002c). Deshmukh increased spending for a minority of

---

[9] For an excellent analysis of Maharashtra's EGS, see Herring and Edwards (1983).
[10] For an insightful comparative examination of Maharashtra's and Kerala's land reforms, see Herring and Hart (1977).

rich farmers by providing electricity subsidies to sugarcane growers who owned pump sets, rescheduling debt for the cooperative banks (many of which made loans to INC ministers), and increasing support for the cotton federation. The 2004–05 state budget ran a Rs. 10 billion deficit (Maharashtra Government 2007). When the budget was released, it was heavily criticized for subsidizing farmers' cotton and sugar production, power needs, and irrigation. Today, Maharashtra's cooperatives have become nearly synonymous with corrupt, inefficient, government-backed production (Bunsha 2002; Special Correspondent 2002d).

In addition to accommodating the interests of agricultural elites, INC's Maratha-Kunbi leadership also appealed to the urban Brahmin minority in the state. This is ironic, because Maratha-Kunbis first sought power to oppose Brahmin dominance. Some scholars argue that Maratha-Kunbis accommodated Brahmins in order to channel capital from industry to Maratha caste members in agriculture (Vora 1996). Others argue that the Maratha leadership merely failed to block efforts by then-prime minister and national INC leader, Indira Gandhi, who wanted to undermine the Maharta-Kunbi's hold over the local INC party by increasing national support for capitalist, industrialist expansion (Palshikar and Deshpande 1999).

Regardless of the motivation, Maratha-Kunbis' ability to control rural institutions and accommodate urban elites entrenched their power within INC and undermined opposition until the mid-1990s. As a result they have had little political incentive to enact policies that meet the welfare needs of poor workers. Although its per capita state domestic product is nearly 50 percent higher than the national average, the share of the state's population below the poverty line matches the national average (Maharashtra Government and UNDP 2002). Maharashtra's economic development policies have been heavily concentrated in a few coastal cities, such as Mumbai and Pune, which have drawn massive rural–urban migration in search of employment. In 2002, more than 42 percent of the population was urban, as opposed to 28 percent at the national level. The state's employment opportunities have declined since 1980. This has resulted in the world's largest concentration of poor, urban slum dwellers. Finally, the state budgets have been highly biased against welfare spending, so much so that in 2000, even the World Bank (which had long been pursuing an agenda of reduced government spending) criticized the state of Maharashtra for inadequate spending on education and health care (Sharma 2000).

Failed Opposition from the Left and Right

Despite the urgent need to improve the poor's welfare in Maharashtra, opposition parties have not successfully filled the vacuum left by INC. Those that emerged from the left were stifled by INC's entrenched power, and those on the right have appealed to the interests of an elite minority.

Perhaps the most famous attempt to create a party to meet the needs of poor workers was launched by Dalits. At the end of the 1800s, as the boom in cotton production spurred railroad construction, Dalits (who worked informally as agricultural laborers, poor cultivators, or village artisans) joined the mass migrations to cities in search of work. Even in the cities, however, Dalits continued to lack access to means of production and relied on their own labor power as a means of subsistence. Most secured work as low-level laborers in textile mills, sweepers for the municipal government, and drivers in the public transport system; some joined the British military.[11] As a result of these experiences, some Dalits began organizing around a dual identity of caste and class.[12] Jyotibhai Phule, for example, created Satyashodhak Samaj, one of the first radical, non-Brahmin movements in Maharashtra designed to improve the treatment of Dalits and women.[13] From the 1920s onward, B. R. Ambedkar rose to lead the Dalit movement, achieving a nearly god-like status among supporters.[14] As the first Dalit to graduate high school, Ambedkar went on to attain graduate degrees from Columbia University and London University and become a barrister of law; Ambedkar was actively involved in the nationalist movement and was one of the principal drafters of the Indian constitution.

In 1930, Ambedkar helped found the Independent Labor Party (ILP) to address both caste- and class-based exploitation by uniting peasants, urban workers, and left parties. Although ILP fared well in the 1937 Mumbai elections, it fell apart shortly thereafter because Ambedkar

---

[11] In 1890, Dalits were kicked out of the military, because the British adopted the martial caste theory (where only members of the upper caste of Kashatriya could join the military). Still, the Dalits' brief experience with military training is thought to have made a significant impact on Dalit consciousness and education. The military Dalits became active in the Dalit movement (see Gokhale 1990).

[12] As with the Maratha movement, the Dalit movement relied on elite Dalits claiming to represent mass Dalits (see Gokhale 1990).

[13] During the same period, Brahmin-led Hindu reform movements were also growing. Although they did not alter social practice, they created a context within which Dalits could demand reforms to Hindu caste discrimination.

[14] Unlike Phule, Ambedkar rejected the possibility of Hindu reform and instead advocated conversion to Buddhism.

rejected joining a coalition with what he felt were elite-run communist parties. Without the coalition, ILP could not match INC's power. The following year Ambedkar formed the Republican Party of India (RPI), which again aimed to alleviate the joint caste- and class-based inequalities faced by Dalits. However, RPI was also unable to undermine INC's strong hold and was split into several factions; it never managed to make inroads into the urban sector and today is a minor player in the state-level party politics (Gokhale 1990).

The second radical attempt to oppose INC's intermediate and elite caste focus was launched by the Communist Party of India (CPI), which organized workers within the rapidly growing textile industry in Mumbai.[15] Unlike Kolkata's British-owned jute industry, Mumbai's textile industry was pioneered by Indian entrepreneurs. By 1926, Mumbai had more than eighty textile mills, which employed 125,000 workers – or 25 percent of the city's working population at the time. During the second half of the 1920s, the textile industry experienced a serious economic crisis caused by overproduction, Japanese competition, limited help from the colonial state, and unwise industrial capitalization. To resist the resulting fall in wages, N. M. Joshi and R. K. Bakhle, both moderate middle-class men, organized textile workers into the Girni Kamgar Union (Mumbai Textile Labor Union) in 1928. Girni Kamgar, a militant union affiliated with CPI, dominated Mumbai's labor movement and became one of the country's largest unions. As the governor of Mumbai, Sir Frederick Skyes declared in 1932, "Mumbai City [has come] to be regarded as a seething base of nationalist agitation and anti-colonial politics, as well as the epicenter of working class political action" (quoted in Chandavarkar 1994: 7). Between 1929 and 1940, the textile industry had eight general strikes, as well as hundreds of smaller strikes.

After independence, however, the communist-led workers' movement did not pose a threat to INC power. Because textile work in Maharashtra was often casual and insecure, migrant workers retained their village links

---

[15] In addition to the urban workers' movements I cover in this section, Maharashtra also witnessed rural movements, which were not sustained. In 1978, Sharad Joshi mobilized rural masses in the poorest regions of the state to form the well-known farmers' movement, Shetkari Sanghatana. The movement lost ground after six years of success. Amrita Basu's study of Shramik Sangathana, a large tribal women's grassroots organization for landless laborers in rural Maharashtra, illustrates how Shramik Sangathana's refusal to enter electoral politics facilitated its desire to pursue militant goals through the early 1980s, but it also led to weak organization and unsustained growth by 1987 (see Basu 1992).

through kinship networks and ties to their land. In addition, they created local caste associations in receiving cities, which in turn reproduced the regional and caste distinctions that dominated rural life (Chandavarkar 1994).[16] These primordial ties undermined efforts to organize along traditional class movement lines. The communist leadership remained largely upper-caste Brahmin, while INC captured the support of intermediate caste Marathas and Dalits (Basu 1992).

In addition, INC in Maharashtra drew support from the national-level office to undermine the state's communist workers' movement. For example, INC split the communist labor movement by creating a rival textile union. INC also supported the rise of local caste-based organizations to undermine cross-caste, class-based organizations. Finally, it worked with big business to support the rise of Shiv Sena. Shiv Sena began as a social movement in 1966 targeting unemployed, urban youth who claimed the government and employers were favoring minorities (especially Muslims and Dalits) and migrants (especially Bangladeshis and South Indians). In return for Shiv Sena's help in rallying support for INC and against CPI, INC supported Shiv Sena's campaign attacking South Indian migrants who were accused of taking Maratha's low-level white-collar jobs (Lele 1990; Ray 2000).[17] By 1970, Shiv Sena had become known as an influential arm of the INC party, so that in 1973, when then Prime Minister Indira Gandhi declared a state of emergency to wipe out all opposition and left-wing parties were forced to go underground, Shiv Sena was allowed to continue operating above ground. Maharashtra's textile movement ultimately died with the end of the 1982 Mumbai textile strike, which involved 240,000 workers, lasted eighteen months, and became renowned for being one of the largest and longest strikes in Indian history.

By the early 1990s, the Maratha-Kunbi leadership of INC had suffered several setbacks, such as internal factions and mounting corruption charges. Moreover, INC had frustrated two of its key vote banks: landowners were suffering from low rates of agricultural production, and Muslims accused it of mishandling the growing communal violence erupting throughout the state. To address its declining popularity, the party elected Sharad Pawar as chief minister. Pawar was one of the only ministers in Maharashtra to have mass appeal and to implement the few

---

[16] Most textile workers were Dalits and other low-caste members who had migrated from the rural districts of Konkan and Deccan.

[17] South Indians, such as Krishna Menon, were leading communist union leaders at the time.

pro-poor programs that pepper the state's history.[18] He is often credited by party members for establishing the Mathadi Board in 1969.[19] Unlike Tamil Nadu's leaders, however, Pawar did not succeed in sustaining INC power through his mass-based appeal. Instead, his endeavors became symbols of government corruption.[20]

INC's declining popularity opened an opportunity for Shiv Sena, which became a state-level political party in 1984, to emerge as the primary opposition party. During the early 1990s, Shiv Sena drew some support from middle- and lower-class Maratha-Kunbis who were not benefiting from INC's elite focus. Shiv Sena's non-Maratha leadership also appealed to those who suffered from the Maratha dominance of INC, and its Hindu conservatism attracted Hindu Dalits who resisted the Dalit movement's call to convert to Buddhism (Palshikar 1996a).

By the mid-1990s, however, Shiv Sena focused on appeasing intermediate- and high-caste urban Hindus by joining a coalition with the well-organized, right-wing, national Hindu Bharatiya Janata Party (BJP) (Palshikar 1996b).[21] This coalition defeated INC in the 1995 state elections and the 1996 national parliamentary elections – marking INC's first defeat in Maharashtra. As part of its Hindu revivalist stance, the

---

[18] Pawar initiated the Zhunka-Bhakar Yojana Scheme, which promised to construct 25,000 low-cost houses for the urban and rural poor every year. He also reserved more seats in government jobs and education for non-Maratha members of Other Backward Castes (OBCs) and increased the OBC leadership in INC. He created development boards for the two poorest districts of the state, Vidarbha and Marathwarda. Finally, in a symbolic gesture to the state's Dalits, he renamed Marathwada University after Ambedkar. In 1999, Pawar left INC to form the National Congress Party (NCP).

[19] Interview, Mr. Binsali, NCP Spokesman, April 29, 2009.

[20] Pawar's connections with the mafia and his fights with other INC leaders, such as Sudhakar Naik, hurt the party's organization. Since Pawar, INC's leadership has suffered from multiple corruption charges. Accused of excessive spending and cronyism, Chief Minister Deshmukh was removed from office in the middle of his term by the national INC in January 2003. Deputy Chief Minister Chaggan Bhujpal of NCP was also removed from office in 2004 because of a scandal involving him and the state police force. Bhujpal is an influential member of the OBC community, and he comes from a poor, rural district of Maharashtra. He had earlier been a member of the Shiv Sena, but later joined NCP. Finally, Chief Minister Sushilkumar Shinde received heavy criticism for his massive sixty-nine-member cabinet and for using state funds to fund personal favors. In 2000, the state's debt to income ratio rose from 11.6 percent in 1995 to 18.93 percent due to bad loans given by state cooperative banks to MLAs and MPs and to bad infrastructure financing. Moreover, 49 percent of the loans were being used to pay salaries and interest, rather than productive investments. The government has also been criticized for not handling the state drought well (see Bunsha 2002).

[21] BJP was in power in the national government from 1998 to 2004.

Shiv Sena–BJP coalition challenged Maratha-Kunbi achievements within INC by placing Brahmins in leadership positions. The coalition abolished the State Minorities Commission, which aimed to protect education and employment quotas for minorities; ended the Srikrishna Commission, which was investigating the communal riots of 1993; and dropped the abuse cases Dalits had brought against elite Mahars (Palshikar 1996a). Shiv Sena–BJP leaders also undermined INC power among rural elites by initiating inquiries into the practices of government-owned rural banks and of sugar cooperatives that were traditionally led by INC ministers. Fearing prosecution, many bank and cooperative leaders left INC to join Shiv Sena. Using this elite-focused strategy, Shiv Sena won several municipal elections (including in Mumbai), as well as seats in the state legislature and national parliament.

Not surprisingly, the Shiv Sena–BJP coalition's focus on elite interests alienated Muslims, Dalits, and poor urban workers and pushed them to return their electoral support to INC. As a result, the coalition has not won a state election in Maharashtra since 1995, and INC has remained the entrenched power base in the state.[22]

Unlike Tamil Nadu, Maharashtra's INC party has not had a mass-based leader whose interest in securing votes would have enabled informal workers to make demands on the state. Rather it has held onto power by appealing to intermediate and elite caste interests, even in the face of growing opposition in recent elections. Even the local media has criticized INC for campaigning on promises "not to the poor who make up the bulk of the city's population, but to the middle classes" (Swami 2002). Unlike West Bengal, Maharashtra's dominant political parties have not emerged out of class-based movements, and poor workers' movements have been violently suppressed.

In this context, it is surprising that informal workers have managed to attain any state benefits at all in Maharashtra. Bidi workers are receiving education scholarships, health care, and homes in Maharashtra, and construction workers are receiving child care services, some training, and some health protection. Let us now examine the possible explanations for the limited successes of informal workers' movements in Maharashtra.

[22] As well, INC's victories can be attributed to the rise of another regional opposition party, the NCP, which Sharad Pawar started in 1999 when he split from INC. NCP is often credited for absorbing the rural Maharashtra vote from INC and Shiv Sena (Palshikar et al. 2004). Because NCP joined a coalition with INC, INC was able to replace its own loss of rural support with NCP's rural vote share.

5.3 PROJECT FROM ABOVE: ENSURING ECONOMIC GROWTH
THROUGH INFORMAL LABOR

Despite politicians' lack of interest in pro-poor, mass appeals, organized informal workers have attained some welfare benefits in Maharashtra by capitalizing on the state's support of liberalization and privatization. This economic agenda has relied on the ready labor supply of poor, urban, informal workers, which in turn has given informal workers a small political opportunity to insert themselves into the government's agenda. Without the concurrent opportunity to insert themselves into the state's electoral strategy, however, the success of informal workers' movements in Maharashtra remains limited.

Although rural elites from the Maharata-Kunbi castes have dominated Maharashtra's government, agricultural production has fared poorly in the state. From 1960–70, the land area under production of cereals and pulses remained stagnant, and the yield per hectare declined. From 1960–75, agriculture's share of state income declined by 10.5 percent, whereas growth in the industrial and service sectors grew at 5 percent. From 1976–86, agricultural production dropped by another 10 percent, although the industrial and service sectors grew by a nominal amount (Maharashtra Government 2002–03). In 2002, irrigated land comprised only 17 percent of the state's gross cropped area.[23] Nearly all the land under irrigation today belongs to wealthy landowners who can engage in cash crop production (primarily in sugarcane, onion, and some cotton). However, production has been inefficient; elite producers are organized into tax-exempt cooperatives that receive substantial support from the state government. Aside from cooperatives, Maharashtra's subsistence crop production remains dismally low. By 2002, the state's food grain production per capita was 45 percent lower than the national average (Maharashtra Government 2002–03).

As indicated by these statistics, INC has long relied on industrialization to fuel Maharashtra's economy. By the late nineteenth century, Mumbai had become India's major port, a leading commercial and financial center, the largest cotton market in Asia, and a nodal point for the cotton piece goods trade. Until the 1940s, Mumbai was India's largest and most prominent industrial hub and employed more than one-quarter of the nation's labor force. In 2002, Maharashtra's share of the nation's population was 9 percent, whereas its share of the nation's factories (in

---

[23] The share of irrigated cropped area is a key indicator of agricultural development, and 17 percent is considered very low for a rich state like Maharashtra. Growth in the irrigated areas has even been as low as 15 percent.

number) was 11.7 percent, and its per capita gross industrial output was 114 percent higher than the national average (Maharashtra Government 2002–03). As a result of the state's support of industrialization, by 2002, Maharashtra's per capita income was 38 percent higher than the national average, and the state contributed 13 percent of the national GDP (Maharashtra Government 2002–03).

Since the early 1990s, the state's commitment to industrialization has expanded to include liberalization reforms to accelerate the flow of investment in infrastructure, and facilitate private-sector growth. Such policy reforms include deregulation, disinvestment, and opening capital markets. As well, the Maharashtrian government supports private businesses by offering fiscal incentives to promote industry and relaxed labor laws to increase firms' global competitiveness (Maharashtra Government 2001). Of the three states examined in this study, Maharashtrian political parties are the most committed to private-sector industrialization. To win the 1995 state assembly elections, Shiv Sena capitalized on public resentment of INC's support for privatized industrialization and foreign direct investment by promising a reversal in the state's economic agenda. Once elected, however, Shiv Sena increased incentives for domestic and foreign private-sector investment in infrastructure development, and it built five export-oriented industrial parks and nine industrial estates (Maharashtra Government 1995). Moreover, development under Shiv Sena remained highly concentrated in the state's urban centers.

On returning to power in 1999, INC continued to liberalize alongside a pro-business industrial policy. When outlining its future vision for the state, then Chief Minister Deshmukh of INC declared, "We [Maharashtra] do not want to compare ourselves to other Indian states as we are always better [than them]. What we have decided is to adopt the Chinese and South Korean model for rapid development" (Special Correspondent 2000). This sentiment was repeated in nearly all my interviews with Maharashtra state officials, regardless of caste, class, or party. Then Deputy Chief Minister of Maharashtra Chaggan Bhujpal said that his government "is very concerned about the downtrodden-lower caste minorities, but we want Maharashtra to be like Shanghai."[24] Trying to be like Shanghai meant a focus on rapid economic growth, rather than attention to wealth distribution or poverty alleviation.

Significantly, the state's industrial production has long relied on an informal, urban labor force. Raj Chandavarkar (1994) meticulously details the use of informal labor in the state's booming textile industry

---

[24] Interview, November 6, 2003.

of the early twentieth century. In the late 1980s and early 1990s, INC Chief Minister Sharad Pawar increased incentives to shift the state's industries from an exclusive reliance on large factories in sugar and textile toward technology, collaboration with transnational corporations, and small industries which by definition are not regulated and depend on informal workers (Maharashtra Government 1993). From 1988–95, 8,000 small factories were built in the state; agriculture was rarely mentioned as a development agenda during these years (Palshikar and Deshpande 1999; Vora 1996).

As a testament to the government's continued reliance on unregulated labor, state officials blame organized labor for any problems arising from Maharashtra's rapid liberalization and industrialization. State Deputy Chief Minister Bhujpal explained, "We aren't there [where Shanghai is] yet. Our main problem is that we have democracy, which creates a labor problem. We can't deal with these problems quickly like China. We are liberalizing, but since we are a democracy, we have to do it so slowly."[25] Although Maharashtrian government officials embrace the idea of a liberalized economy, they bemoan the reality of India's liberal democracy. 2003 Joint Labor Commissioner Gajebhiye admitted, "The government blames labor for all the problems of the reforms... but I don't agree." Instead, Gajebhiye emphasized the need for more labor-intensive growth as opposed to the current capital-intensive program. Voicing the government's pro-business leaning, he said, "We need to be more like China; we need a strong government that doesn't appease labor. We should have no unions and no strikes, just production. Only then can we decrease the costs of production like China." He continued, "Employers can't afford workers anymore, and we want to decrease the losses of the industries." Casual labor is considered "crucial for the survival of Maharashtra's economy."[26] Indeed during the 2004 state elections, a leading English-language newspaper noted the irony in INC's victory, given that voters claimed "employment" was their primary concern and INC was rated the worst party in the country in terms of increasing formal employment opportunities (Deshpande and Birmal 2004).

The perception that costly labor laws are a primary obstacle to higher economic productivity has catalyzed considerable debate around labor reforms designed to increase informal employment. The two most controversial reforms are the 2001 amendments to the Industrial Disputes

[25] Ibid.
[26] Interview, March 2002.

Act and the proposed amendments to the Contract Labor Act (Special Correspondent 2001a). The Industrial Disputes Act protects workers' right to strike and job security in factories employing more than 100 workers. In 2001, the Maharashtrian government restricted these protections to cover only workers in factories employing more than 300 workers, thereby increasing the number of unprotected workers (Maharashtra Government 2001). The Contract Labor Act is a national-level law that bans the use of contract labor, except in a few restricted situations. The government of Maharashtra is now in the process of crafting a state amendment that overrides this act in almost all cases. Maharashtra's 2001 Industrial Policy called for a reduction in the number of inspections of labor laws. In addition to promoting informal employment for formal companies, the Maharashtrian government encouraged unregulated self-employment. "They completely glorified it. They even gave the Department of Employment and Self-employment its own Secretary, separate from Labor," explained 2009 Labor Commissioner Arvind Kumar.[27]

In addition to reforms that would increase informal employment, the Maharashtrian government has tried to decrease formal employment. The press criticized the government in 2002 when P. R. Siddhanti, labor advisor to Mumbai's Chamber of Commerce, announced that nearly all of Maharashtra's share of the National Renewal Fund, which was originally designed to retrain formal workers who were laid off due to liberalization, was instead being used to encourage formal workers to take early retirement (Date 2002). In the same year, INC also froze the salary raises for 8,300 government employees (Bunsha 2002).

Nearly all Maharashtrian government officials interviewed for this study said these reform efforts have undermined urban workers' bargaining power. However, they also repeatedly expressed a lack of interest in reversing the situation. The 2003 joint commissioner of labor, Gajere, noted, "Since the reforms, strikes have decreased, workers' attitudes are changing, and lockouts have increased. Even militant unions are bargaining with employers.... [T]he trade union movement here will become like the U.S.: not completely dead, but almost."[28] The 2003 state labor commissioner, Gajebhiye, framed the decline in worker's movements as beneficial to workers' interests: "Necessarily unions come together against

---

[27] Interview, April 29, 2009.
[28] This sentiment was echoed by the state minister of labor, state secretary of labor, and the state labor commissioner. Interviews, February 6, 2003; March 25, 2003; December 12, 2003, January 20, 2004.

anything pro-industry...However, the future of trade unions is very bleak. Now much fewer disputes come to my office. Workers are realizing that we need to look out for industry. It is in their [workers'] interest, or they will lose their jobs."[29] The 2003 state secretary of labor, Khot, went so far as to express relief about the crisis in formal workers' collective action: "The government is terrified of formal-sector leaders. I am fed up with them and their strikes. But their militancy is declining. Now they just have the power of nuisance."[30]

Although government officials resented formal workers' collective action, they expressed an interest in working with informal workers. Deshmukh, the 2003 state minister of labor, felt that the government could be more useful to informal workers, because formal workers were already protected by the law and educated on their rights. Deshmukh, who had been a labor activist for forty years – leading a formal-workers' union and, more recently, working with informal workers in rural Maharashtra – said, "Workers are enlightened here [in the city]. We have good leaders and good workers. But in the informal sector, workers are much poorer and more ignorant. They need the Government's help."[31] Gajere reiterated this sentiment: "We now have laws in place to take care of exploitation among formal workers. They are very knowledgeable and they don't need us [the government] anymore. But for informal workers, where there are no laws, the government must come in with protection."[32] Khot was explicitly dedicated to informal workers: "We have so many schemes for the formal sector, but 92 percent of workers are in the informal sector! They are the ones we must focus on now."[33] When interviewed, Khot had already drafted a social security proposal for all informal workers and was working on establishing a welfare board for domestic workers. The 2009 labor commissioner, Arvind Kumar, reflected on the outcome of that earlier commitment: "Labor has been crushed in Maharashtra. Our government is completely subservient to industry. The Labor Commissioner now really only exists for the welfare boards."[34]

With the exception of Labor Minister Deshmukh, state government officials' interest in informal workers was expressed in terms of potential

---

[29] Interview, March 4, 2003.
[30] Interview, March 25, 2003.
[31] Interview, January 20, 2004.
[32] Interview, February 6, 2003.
[33] Interview, March 25, 2003.
[34] Interview, April 29, 2009.

benefits to employers, the state, and their joint interest in private-sector growth. Khot's proposed welfare board for domestic workers did not require employer contributions. "But," he argued, "after some time, employers will want to contribute because they will see the board is for them too."[35] Khot reasoned that a primary advantage of the domestic workers' board is staff loyalty to employers, whereas his proposed insurance scheme for all informal workers would benefit the government financially: "The government will thank me for my ideas once they see how much money it brings in for them that they can use on infrastructure development. Once we do it, everyone will follow."[36] As in other states, government officials equated informal workers with "the poor." Although Khot expressed a keen commitment to assisting the poor, he emphasized that the poor are working informally, and "informal workers are needed for industrialization;" hence it is in the state's interests "to keep them [informal workers] loyal."[37]

Gajebhiye pointed to stability as a primary benefit of minimal state attention to informal workers: "We do need to do something about informal workers, because the current situation will result in violence. They are over-exploited and need at least minimum relief." He was quick to add, "Industry will agree to this as long as government doesn't guarantee anything beyond the minimum."[38] Shiv Sena Secretary Anil Desai viewed assistance to informal workers as a necessary step toward privatization: "Privatization is the need of the hour . . . and the informal sector is getting a lot of attention as a result. We support this." In Mumbai, where Shiv Sena has controlled the municipal government since 1990, party leaders have implemented micro-credit projects for urban self-employed workers and tried to attain licenses for street vendors.[39] Desai insisted that assistance for informal workers must not undermine "the basic fabric of society. The poor should get their due, but they shouldn't interfere with the view and decent living in Mumbai."[40] Here, Desai is referring to the battle over public space that is taking place between "unsightly" street vendors and slum dwellers versus middle-class residents in Mumbai. Like Gajebhiye, Desai's commitment to informal workers is secondary to his primary commitment to middle-class urban residents.

[35] Interview, March 25, 2003.
[36] Ibid.
[37] Ibid.
[38] Interview, February 6, 2003.
[39] These programs have been implemented through the Shiv Udyog Sena.
[40] Interview, January 14, 2004.

Let us now examine how informal workers convinced Maharashtra's government officials to target informal workers as a partial solution to the state's concerns with formal labor.

5.4 PROJECT FROM BELOW: FINDING A POLITICAL VOICE IN THE ECONOMIC AGENDA

The electoral context in Maharashtra has not enabled informal workers to convince politicians to meet their needs in return for votes. Moreover, the state's commitment to rapid, private-sector industrialization and global competitiveness has squelched traditional union organizing. Rather than using the power of their mass vote or explicitly resisting the state's economic policies, Maharashtra's informal workers have used the power of their informal labor to frame themselves as an essential partner in the state's development agenda. Informal workers in Maharashtra reiterate their ability to impede the state's attempt to remain competitive by offering their flexible labor in return for basic welfare benefits; they have also threatened the state (not employers) with violence, resistance, and death if no welfare is given. As in Tamil Nadu and West Bengal, Maharashtra's informal workers have emphasized their distance from formal workers, projecting interests that are compatible with capital. This strategy has been particularly welcomed in Maharashtra.

Formal Workers Resist Liberalization and Private-Sector Industrialization

Informal workers' strategies stand in sharp contrast to those of formal workers, who vehemently resist Maharashtra's pro-market development agenda. As noted earlier, Mumbai's early industrialization process did not create the common identity among exploited workers that is normally associated with early capitalism.[41] Rather, as Chandavarkar (1994) details in his history of Mumbai's early working-class politics, it was the colonial state's use of force during industrial strikes that catalyzed political solidarity among Mumbai's workers and gave them a single enemy to rally against. In much the same vein, Maharashtra's recent efforts to liberalize the economy and bolster private-sector growth have provided

---

[41] On one hand, mill owners' reliance on labor-intensive technology unified workers by congregating them on a shop floor and in neighborhoods, and by increasing their power to disrupt production by withholding labor. On the other hand, because labor was largely informal, workers retained their links to diverse kinship networks and home villages, which divided their class-based identities.

formal workers with a new common enemy – the state that triggered a decline in formal employment.

Since the early 1980s, Maharashtra's unions have been noted for being weak and fragmented (Ramaswamy 1988). On April 25, 2001, however, unions affiliated with the spectrum of political parties from CPM to Shiv Sena came together in an unprecedented display of unity in a statewide strike protesting "globalization," "liberalization," and anti-labor industrial policies. This strike received massive media and public attention. Some journalists accused unions of merely assisting political parties ten months before the state assembly elections. As the *Times of India* reported, "Wooing the disenchanted working class is slated to become every party's brand new mantra" (Mishra 2001). Most, however, saw the strike as a serious barometer of workers' unified resentment against the state and national governments (Balakrishnan 2001; Chakrovorty 2001; Koppikar 2001; Times News Network 2001). At the heart of workers' unified resentment is the state's commitment to labor flexibility as an essential ingredient to ensuring firm competitiveness in a liberalized economy. According to Gajere, liberalization has shifted formal workers' primary demand "from higher wages to job security," which by definition is absent in informal work.[42]

Informal Workers Make Strategic Organizational Choices

As with formal workers, the state government's pursuit of competitive industrialization and officials' unbending support for capital have squelched informal workers attempts to demand class compromise in Maharashtra. In contrast to formal workers' unions, however, informal workers' organizations in Maharashtra have tried to enable their members to capitalize on the state's economic agenda, rather than resist it.[43] Union leaders in the construction and bidi sectors expressed this strategic choice as the only option they had given the state government's proven autonomy from poor workers' demands.

Informal Construction Workers. As an illustration of Maharashtra's unwelcome landscape for unions, the primary construction workers'

---

[42] Interview, February 6, 2003.
[43] One exception is that, at the national level, bidi unions are fighting the national government's reduction of taxes on mini-cigarettes. These policies have decreased the price of mini-cigarettes, which has increased competition in the bidi industry. The National Federation of Bidi Unions is fighting to reverse this policy.

organization in Maharashtra, NIRMAN, has organized as a nongovernmental organization (NGO). It is the only informal construction workers' organization in the country that is not a registered trade union. The decision to be an NGO, rather than a trade union, was a strategic one, spurred by the onslaught of economic reforms in the state.

In the early 1960s, Maharashtra's construction workers organized into unions. As noted in Chapter 2, in 1962 Sundar Navelkar, one of the first female lawyers in India and a member of the Communist Party of India-Marxist-Leninists (CPI-ML), started India's first construction union for contract workers in Mumbai. The United Labor Union was an independent union with loose ties to the Maoist Red Flag Party. As an organizer in the Naval Dockyard Workers Union, Navelkar recognized the need to organize workers building the wharfs, who were almost all literate, male migrants from Kerala. After waging numerous strikes against employers and public hunger strikes, the union attained minimum wages, a bonus, and unpaid holiday leave for its members under the Contract Labor Act. Some employers agreed to provide free housing and water for on-site workers. Although she is proud of these successes, Navelkar lamented that the "gains protected by law were rarely enforced" and achievements were "never institutionalized into law." By 1990, she left the union, "because the state was not enforcing the laws and all [her] time was spent in court trying to force employers to comply with the law."[44]

As Navelkar's union fizzled, G. S. Madhukant, a young student at the College of Social Work (CSW) in Mumbai, formed a new registered trade union for informal construction workers in Mumbai, called Nirman Mazdoor Panchayat Sangatam (NMPS). NMPS used nonviolent means, such as court cases, to secure the formal benefits for informal workers that Navelkar's union had sought. In addition, it increased its attention to welfare needs by starting a registered NGO, called NIRMAN, that was affiliated with CSW. The NGO provided NMPS members with health care services and day care centers for their children. Despite NMPS's nonconfrontational approach, according to Madhukant, "the state became more suspicious of all trade unions after 1991...It created major problems for us."[45] State funding for NIRMAN's projects was cut, employers building public-sector projects threatened to fire workers

---

44 Interview, August 4, 2003.
45 Interview, May 15, 2003.

who joined NMPS, and the head of NIRMAN, who was a labor sympathizer, was replaced by a social worker with no union background.[46]

The Maharashtrian government's interest in industrialization, coupled with its adherence to meeting elite interests, forced construction workers to retract their demands for formal benefits from employers. At the end of 1991, NIRMAN separated from NMPS, because NIRMAN's funders explicitly stated that they did not want to be associated with a trade union.[47] The construction workers' movement has been critiqued by labor sympathizers for acquiescing to donor demands. As State Minister of Labor Deshmukh said, construction workers are weak, "they do not put enough pressure on the government. Most of the workers are migrants, so they shift from site to site, and the industry minister is not bothered to do anything."[48]

These critiques, however, miss the strategy behind NIRMAN's decision to meet donor demands to separate from unions. Rather than pressuring the government as a union, which in the past has been impervious to workers' demands, NIRMAN has tried to capitalize on its seemingly nonthreatening NGO status, thereby enabling it to become the only organization in the country to mobilize construction workers who live on work sites. NIRMAN works with municipal governments to provide housing, clean water, sanitation facilities, and health care to on-site workers. As State Labor Secretary Khot explained, "NGOs cannot intimidate. They know if they use strong tactics, I will kick them out of my office and never let them return. And they are too small, so they can't afford to be militant. The government should use them more, and they are." This image has helped NIRMAN form relationships with municipal governments and builders.

Most new construction in Maharashtra is regulated by municipal governments, who own the land, distribute construction licenses, and manage the water and firefighting facilities. "Without their [municipal] permission you can't construct anything. They have all the power, not us [State Labor Department]," explained M.A. Sheik, Maharashtra's deputy labor commissioner in charge of issues concerning construction workers. Therefore, NIRMAN pressures municipal governments to extract funds

---

[46] Because NIRMAN is affiliated with CSW, a public college, the state government has control over NIRMAN's personnel.

[47] Interviews with NIRMAN founder, G. S. Madhukant (May 15, 2003), and current NIRMAN Head, Vayjanta (April 24, 2003).

[48] Interview, January 20, 2003.

for welfare programs from builders, who rely on the municipal governments to attain approval for their construction projects. As Dr. Telang,
joint executive health officer in the Mumbai Municipal Corporation,
explained, "Builders never complain about paying [for malaria treatment
for their workers], since they need the licenses from us [the Municipal
Corporation]. And we must demand the malaria treatment to protect
the surrounding community from infections."[49] NIRMAN also uses its
nonthreatening NGO status to convince municipal government officials
to rely on it to implement municipal corporation programs. For example,
NIRMAN works closely with Dr. Deshpande, head of the Urban Health
Post in the New Mumbai Municipal Corporation, to help him meet his
targets under a citywide malaria prevention program. "I enjoy working
with NGOs, like NIRMAN, because they can take us to the people, and
the workers trust us immediately."[50]

NIRMAN also uses its NGO status to form direct relationships with
builders, which have enabled it to provide day care centers for on-site
workers. The day care centers provide a vehicle through which NIRMAN
staff can form relationships with on-site workers, especially women. Once
they gain the workers' trust, NIRMAN staff members organize them to
demand more benefits from the builder or the municipal government.
As Vayjanta, head of NIRMAN, explained, "We found that workers
don't want to fight. They are so afraid of losing their jobs." Even though
workers are reluctant to strike, NIRMAN frames its services to employers
as ensuring labor peace: "We explain to builders that these services will
help prevent disruptions in production. Employers support us, because
they see women are less distracted by their kids, and fewer workers stay
home because they have malaria." As a result of this message, NIRMAN
has been able to work with five of Mumbai's major private builders to
provide day care services, basic sanitation, and basic malaria control and
treatment for workers living on construction sites.

NIRMAN's strategy has several drawbacks. Its unique target population of on-site construction workers has undermined its ability to use the
power of votes to affect state policy toward informal workers. On-site
workers are migrants who move with a builder from site to site. Most
often, they are not registered voters in Maharashtra. Lacking a permanent
address or access to any civic amenities, these construction workers pose

[49] Interview, July 3, 2003.
[50] Ibid.

little threat to politicians. Moreover, because workers follow builders and do not have a stable residence, NIRMAN is unable to maintain sustainable relationships with them and is thus unable to mobilize them to campaign for or against particular politicians. In addition, NIRMAN does not institutionalize employer responsibility into law. NIRMAN must pressure each employer on each project to improve working and living conditions.

Nevertheless, NIRMAN is the largest organization for construction workers in the state, is actively involved in the construction workers' movement at the national level, and is the only NGO in India that is recognized by the nation's construction unions.

Informal Bidi Workers. Unlike its construction organizations, Maharashtra's bidi unions are the same as elsewhere in India – registered unions that are affiliated with left-wing political parties.[51] Despite this affiliation, however, Mumbai's bidi unions focus more on attaining welfare benefits from the state and less on traditional work-based benefits from employers. As in construction, this decision to shift their focus from work to welfare was spurred by the state's growing interest in private-sector growth and commitment to unregulated labor.

Maharashtra's bidi unions began in the 1920s as part of the nationalist movement. As in construction, these unions attempted to organize informal bidi workers during the 1970s by using the power of their labor to disrupt production. In December 1979, for example, Mumbai's bidi workers held a 140-day strike to demand minimum wages and pensions. Employers, however, found non-unionized workers to employ instead, and the state Labor Ministry did not interfere, thereby squashing the bidi union for more than a decade.[52]

---

[51] In Maharashtra, most bidi unions are affiliated with CPI. Interview, general secretary of CPI's union federation (AITUC) in Mumbai, Sukumar Damle (March 25, 2003); Interview, general secretary of CPM's union federation (CITU) in Mumbai, Vivek Montero (March 23, 2003).

[52] Interview, Sukumar Damle, March 25, 2003. The Maharashtra Rajabidi Tobacco and Cigar Workers' Federation emerged in 1985 under the leadership of Ram Ratnar. Its office is in Ahmed Nagar, a small town outside Mumbai. According to Patkar, the head of the revived Mumbai Bidi Union, when the Mumbai union declined in the 1980s, it was the federation that kept the struggle alive. Ratnar recruited "young cadres" and trained them. Patkar spent a lot of time at Ratnar's house, where he would read books on organizing and meet federation members from across the country. Still the mobilization of workers on the ground remained at a lull during this time. Interview, Patkar, March 2, 2003.

The Maharashtrian government made it clear to bidi workers that it would side with employers on issues concerning competitiveness, especially in urban areas. In 1990, bidi workers from Maharashtra joined workers from other states to hold a rally in Delhi demanding a uniform, national-level minimum wage (of Rs. 55) to undermine capital flight across states. In retaliation, the following year, then Finance Minister Manmohan Singh eliminated the tariffs on tobacco imports, causing the price of mini-cigarettes to fall, which threatened bidi sales and ultimately increased pressures on bidi firms to decrease labor costs further.

In 1996, the Mumbai Bidi Union was revived under the leadership of Ramakant Patkar. "We had to start the union again, because the price of inputs [bidi leaves] had jumped, and wages were not changing. The old union leaders were not doing anything, and all the workers were complaining to me!" recalled Patkar.[53] Patkar's union reemerged just as the state and national governments were embarking on economic reforms to privatize industries and increase competition. Having failed to implement a national-level minimum wage, Maharashtra's bidi workers pressured their state officials to increase the state's minimum wage in the mid-1990s. The state government responded by forming a committee that would examine the minimum wages of bidi workers. Rather than increasing minimum wages or even improving enforcement of existing wages, the government retaliated by lowering the minimum wage for bidi workers in 1997 (Staff Reporter 1998). "The employers said they could not afford the minimum wage in the face of the changing situation, so the government revised the min wage slightly down from Rs. 53 to Rs. 48," explained M. A. Sheik, deputy labor commissioner, who was in charge of issues concerning bidi workers.[54]

In 2001, after INC returned to power in the state, Labor Minister Deshmukh revived the minimum wages committee in response to massive statewide demands from bidi unions. At first the Mumbai Bidi Union was not invited to participate in the committee discussions. After holding several demonstrations in front of the Labor Department's offices, it was invited to sit at the table but was unable to influence the committee's decisions. Although the state officially raised the minimum wage, employers in urban areas avoided complying with the law by hiring bidi workers informally and not providing bidi workers with raw materials. This tactic enabled employers to relinquish any responsibility for the workers'

[53] Interview, March 2, 2003.
[54] Interview, June 16, 2003.

reproduction costs by claiming they were merely trading with the "so-called" workers.[55]

In addition to failing to weaken the state's support for employers' needs, the Mumbai Bidi Union has been less successful than Tamil Nadu's in appealing to politicians' interest in attaining votes. During elections, bidi union members have attended campaign rallies to convince politicians to increase benefits to bidi workers. However, Patkar notes, "the problem is when the party changes, we have to start all over again."[56] Moreover, bidi workers in Maharashtra have limited power to make demands on aspiring political leaders, because as detailed earlier, political parties in the state have attained power based not on mass appeal, but on their deeply entrenched patronage networks among rural elites.

Of the workers interviewed for this study, half reported that they voted for INC, despite the party's blatant disregard for welfare spending and programs for the poor. Although some said they had received books for their children, most said that they voted for INC because "they were told to." Women reported being ordered by their husbands, parents, and even directly by their landlords or community leaders. In short, bidi workers in Mumbai, in contrast to those in Tamil Nadu, largely voted based on their patronage ties. Workers older than 50 years also explained their loyalty to INC as an expression of their loyalty to former Prime Minister Indira Gandhi, one of the most populist leaders in INC. They pointed to Indira Gandhi as "a lady who helped other ladies" and "the only leader who listened to our [bidi workers'] fight." They credited her for the gains that bidi workers have made in the state, such as minimum wages and housing. Although the state INC party has not retained Gandhi's populism, it survives off her memory. Some workers even acknowledged, "Congress no longer helps the poor like they used to. Now they just come to our house during elections." Despite this reality, bidi members continue to vote for INC in Mumbai.[57]

As a result of its repeated failures in getting the state to hold employers responsible for the welfare of informal workers, the Mumbai Bidi Union

---

[55] This system is popularly known as the "buying-selling system" and is most dominant in Mumbai.

[56] Interview, March 30, 2003.

[57] Only 3 out of the 20 bidi interviewees voted for Shiv Sena. Nearly all the women who reported voting for Shiv Sena said they did so because their son had gotten involved with the group. Shiv Sena targets unemployed youth in urban areas. The remaining bidi workers said they voted for CPI, although the bidi union does not require membership in CPI.

was forced to shift its strategy away from traditional class warfare against employers. According to Patkar, it found greater success when it appealed to the economic interests of the party in power, which in 2003–04 was the right-wing BJP–Shiv Sena coalition: "BJP cares about employers, even though they are thieves. So we had to stop asking about employers."[58]

Instead of focusing on minimum wages and job security, the Mumbai Bidi Union has focused on attaining identity cards for the welfare board, which in turn entitles workers to health care, education scholarships for their children, housing, and marriage grants. Because Mumbai employers do not provide workers with material inputs for bidis, they can easily deny that they have any employees. Attaining identity cards for the welfare board in Mumbai, therefore, was particularly challenging. On March 13, 1996, the union held a major demonstration in front of the state Legislative Assembly. Patkar said, "We just demanded that the government acknowledge that Mumbai is in India and Mumbai bidi workers should get what all India's bidi workers get – ID cards." The labor minister came out to speak with the workers. "The ladies were so proud that someone came out to listen to them," recalled Patkar.[59] Five months later, on August 6, 1996, the union leaders went to Delhi to demand identity cards for Mumbai workers, despite the unique employer–employee relationship in Mumbai. Gurudas Gupta, the chairman of AITUC, argued before the national labor minister that Mumbai's workers must receive the benefits that other bidi workers in India receive, even if Maharashtra's employers do not recognize them. He explained that if bidi workers did not receive these benefits, "they will fight harder to resist the current 'buying-selling' set up," said Patkar. In other words, the union convinced the labor minister that Mumbai bidi workers would accept their informal employer–employee relationship as long as it did not detract from their receiving welfare benefits and state recognition. From the state's point of view, this was a minimal concession compared to the costs of formal labor regulation. After this meeting, the government ordered that all Mumbai Bidi Union members receive welfare identity cards.

The Mumbai Bidi Union has been instrumental in ensuring that its members attain the cards and the benefits they entail. Indeed, all the bidi workers whom I interviewed for this study stated that they had an identity card. The union has taken on the role of certifying who is and is not a bidi worker (because employers would not do so). In addition, the

[58] Interview, March 25, 2003.
[59] Interview, March 2, 2003.

union helps members attain the necessary documents from the municipal corporation (such as birth certificates) that are required for approval. "It is us [the union] that are making sure the welfare laws reach workers, not the government!" explained Patkar. Since the union has been able to guarantee the identity cards, its membership has increased. Moreover, "now there are much fewer disputes," said Patkar.[60] State Labor Commissioner Sheik agreed, saying, "We get much fewer disputes from bidi workers now that they have the cards."[61]

On one hand, Patkar lamented the shift away from traditional mobilization that sought representation of workers' interests through a leftist political party: "This area [where bidi workers live] used to have votes for CPI. We had a Corporator, an MLA, and in 1957, even an MP. But now no one [in the union] goes house to house to campaign. The members don't even know who the CPI candidate is!"[62] On the other hand, Patkar justified the shift: "But times have changed, and they [the union leaders] need to change their strategies too. In fact, we had the most success under BJP!"[63]

The Mumbai Bidi Union also focuses on raising awareness among its members of the guaranteed benefits of the Bidi Welfare Board, and on organizing workers to pressure the government to deliver the benefits of the Board. The union not only informs bidi workers about education scholarships for their children but also provides members with the applications, helps workers fill them out, and then hand delivers them to the office of the Welfare Commissioner. Thirty-five percent of the interviewees have received education scholarships since joining the union. The union performs a similar service in attempting to connect members with their due health care benefits, especially with regard to kidney failure.[64]

At the time of this study, the union's highest priority campaign was for state provision of housing. Nearly 100 percent of the bidi workers interviewed for this study spoke about their need for a new home, and

---

[60] Interview, March 25, 2003.
[61] Interview, June 16, 2003.
[62] Interview, March 30, 2003. Corporators are at the municipal level.
[63] Ibid.
[64] The Bidi Welfare Board has deemed kidney failure a work-related illness, because of the long, uninterrupted hours bidi workers spend sitting and rolling bidis. Often, workers skip food, water, and bathroom breaks in order to complete more bidis, because they are paid on a piece-rate basis. Interview, Director General Labor Welfare Manohar Lal, June 3, 2003.

70 percent stated a home as their primary demand. On July 13, 2002, the Bidi Union held a rally in front of the state Legislative Assembly, demanding that the housing minister grant homes to bidi workers. One year later, on February 17, 2003, 3,500 workers held another demonstration on the same issue. The women I spoke to were extremely proud of their involvement in these rallies. "We brought our bidis and just sat there doing our work in front of the Ministers' offices," exclaimed Laxmi Pandaye, a Mumbai Bidi Union member. "My husband used to yell whenever I attended union meetings. But then when the housing minister came out to talk to us, and my name was in the paper, he proudly showed the article to all our friends. He never forbids me now."[65]

On the surface, housing does not appear to be the workers' most pressing concern. Nearly all the members of the Mumbai Bidi Union already have a home. Although they are very small (one room) and are usually rentals, they are protected from rent increases and have often remained within the same family for generations. Nevertheless, the union has organized its members to rally hard for new houses. The majority of members claimed they needed a home "to attain respect from their children in their old age." "It is our pension," they explained. "Otherwise we have nothing after all our hard work with bidi, and our children kick us out of our homes when we don't bring in any more money." Others saw the homes as an additional source of direct income. "Once we get the homes, we can rent it out for more money. We will continue to live in our current homes," they explained.

Union leaders framed their demands to government officials as a bargain. "Mumbai is in India, and we should get all the benefits other workers are getting. If we do, then we can accept the buying-selling system. If we don't, we will have to fight to have a proper employer–employee relationship. But we know the government doesn't want to upset employers on this issue," explained Patkar.[66] The housing board, Maharashtra Housing Area and Development Authority (MHADA), which is responsible for building government-allocated homes, has been receptive to these claims because the state government first promised homes as a way to placate rising public criticism of liberalization policies. As Shekhar Channe, secretary of MHADA, candidly remarked, "You must understand MHADA is a political organization, and the tenants are voters. Therefore MHADA ends up paying for things because they need to get the voters."[67]

---

[65] Interview, March 1, 2003.
[66] Interview, March 25, 2003.
[67] Interview, June 18, 2003.

5.5 CONCLUSIONS

Maharashtra lends mixed support for my regime-type framework of informal workers' effectiveness, which predicted medium levels of success in states with no pro-poor electoral competition and with pro-liberalization leaders. Although, the level of benefit provision and state commitment in Maharashtra is less than that in Tamil Nadu, informal workers in Maharashtra have attained some minimal levels of welfare benefits from the state, and the state government expresses some commitment to protecting informal workers. The level of success achieved in Maharashtra was not as far above that of West Bengal as might be expected by the Maharashtrian government's pursuit of liberalization. Still given the state's elite-caste political leadership and pro-business economic agenda, it is surprising that informal workers have attained anything at all. This finding emphasizes the secondary significance of liberalization as an additional way for informal workers to attract state attention for their demands. Liberalization is neither a catalyst to the expansion or politicization of informal workers nor a guaranteed obstacle to informal workers' power.

Maharashtra's political leadership, which has been dominated by intermediate and elite interests, has stifled radical class movements. Moreover, INC's historically entrenched power in the state has undermined informal workers' ability to make demands on the state in return for votes. Finally, the state government's deep commitment to rapid private-sector industrialization has increased its interest in unregulated, informal labor. These factors have forced informal workers' organizations in Maharashtra to pursue a cooperative strategy with the state. In sharp contrast to formal workers' unions, informal workers' organizations have not resisted liberalization policies or the state's pro-business industrialization efforts. Instead they have framed themselves as an essential partner in the state's economic agenda. By not fighting hard for a minimum wage and job security, informal workers in Maharashtra assure state officials that they will not challenge the informal nature of their work. However, in return, the state must assure them their welfare needs. In other words, if the state is not willing to guarantee job security or minimum wages for informal workers, the state must then be held responsible for providing informal workers with their basic needs in-kind.

Maharashtra's political and economic context has forced informal workers to settle for minimal welfare benefits. Moreover, informal workers have not yet succeeded in asserting themselves as a group that the state must contend with in order to maintain its own political interests (i.e., retaining power). However, the state's informal workers have found some success in appealing to the government's economic interests (i.e., to support rapid, private-sector–led economic growth). The limited success of this strategy raises important questions as to whether movements in Maharashtra will be able to build on these early successes by strengthening their voice in the future, or alternatively, have to continue settling for the lowest common denominator of benefits.

6

Conclusion

Dignifying Discontent

For decades, workers in rich and poor countries organized around a model that forced the state to hold employers responsible for ensuring their security and basic needs. In return, workers promised to provide their labor without strife. Although nations varied in the degree of protection promised and provided to workers, the ideal contract remained consistent across nations, and workers enjoyed, at the very least, an ideological and material claim to livelihood rights. Since the 1980s, however, the normative roles of the state and of workers have changed, and the conventional contract between them has begun to sever as a result. State governments are increasingly portraying informal, unprotected workers as the ideal worker, even though they operate outside state regulation. Multilateral institutions and public media are tagging governments that retreat from their welfare functions as modern and efficient. Perhaps most striking for students of development, the percentage of people living in perpetual insecurity – with no guaranteed benefits from either an employer or a state – is increasing.

At the source of these trends lies a new economic and political model of development that is proliferating throughout the world as countries liberalize their economies and integrate with one another. Under this model, states and firms pursue economic growth through competition in a global marketplace. To remain competitive, firms argue that they must reduce labor costs by hiring informal workers who, by definition, are not protected by state law. States are supporting firms in their decision to hire unprotected labor by initiating incentive programs that encourage formally protected workers to leave their jobs, creating free-trade zones where firms are not required to comply with labor laws, and contracting public-sector services to private-sector firms that can hire informally. As opportunities in the formal sector diminish, a growing proportion of household members are forced to engage in informal employment.

These trends raise important questions. What is next for labor? What new types of relationships may emerge between the state and labor? What new development paradigms will follow? Recently, scholars have begun to offer preliminary answers to these questions. Most argue that economic reforms that encourage free trade, increased capital and labor mobility, and global competition have pushed labor movements into a crisis characterized by declining union density and a diminishing ability of workers to influence the state. Some scholars claim that, as a result of these trends, labor is no longer organizing as a class to improve its situation, and state governments are increasingly being relieved of their responsibility for ensuring the welfare of workers. Based on this literature, a consensus is emerging in academic circles that class analytics is losing its significance as a tool with which to explain the differentiation of life chances among interdependent economic actors, as well as the political dynamics that follow from such inequities.

In contrast to this recent literature, I find that in India the recent alterations in structures of production have not undermined all class-based struggles motivated by economic relations. India provides an ideal case to begin addressing these questions on state–labor relations within a liberalization context. After building a relatively closed, state-planned economy for four decades, India began to officially liberalize its economy in 1991. India has had active workers' movement and (in one state) was governed by the longest running, democratically elected communist party (until 2011). Today, however, 93 percent of its labor force (82 percent of its nonagricultural labor force) is informally employed.

Although the number of unprotected, informal workers has grown under liberalization, it is vital to remember that informal workers have always existed as a majority in India (and other developing countries). Conventional labor unions, although laudable, have always only reached a minority of India's and the world's workforce. Therefore, by the 1980s (i.e., before liberalization), parallel labor organizations emerged in India to represent the majority of workers who did not qualify for conventional labor protections. "Informal" workers, in other words, are not equivalent to "unorganized" workers.

Today, these organizations are becoming more salient as formal workers are being fired and then rehired on an informal basis. Moreover, the recent changes in state economic policy have, in fact, strengthened these informal workers' organizations. Therefore, it is these organizations that must form the focus of any analysis seeking to understand the future of labor movements. Although workers are indeed losing their earlier claims to labor protection and security, they are not standing by as passive victims. Rather, the poorest, most insecure informal workers are launching alternative ways to dignify their discontent. To examine the details of these alternative movements, I conducted 340 in-depth interviews with informal workers, government officials, and union leaders in India to analyze (1) exactly how informal employment is reshaping workers' collective action strategies and (2) under what state conditions these collective action strategies succeed or fail.

To explore how the informal nature of employment shapes workers' collective action strategies in India, I examined informal workers' organizations in three Indian states with varying political and economic histories. In each state, I studied movements in two industries – construction and bidi – where conditions of work vary enormously. The findings from this portion of the study illustrate that informal workers, like formal workers, are an integral part of the modern class structure, and they therefore can and do organize along class lines to improve their livelihoods. Unlike for formal workers, however, state-sanctioned alterations in structures of production have not undermined informal workers' movements, but rather forced informal workers to cement new forms of political ties with the state, rather than with footloose employers.

Since the mid-1980s, Indian informal workers in the construction and bidi industries have launched a labor movement that, on the one hand, accommodates unprotected, flexible production structures and, on the other hand, fights for new sources of protection for the working poor. Rather than making demands on employers for workers' rights, such as minimum wages and job security (as formal-sector workers have done in the past), informal workers have focused on appealing to the state for citizen rights by making welfare demands. Moreover, because informal workers frequently change employers, they organize around the neighborhood, rather than the shop floor. Their demands have been instituted through industry-specific welfare boards, designed for informal workers. Employers, governments, and workers fund these boards, and in return for membership, workers are supposed to receive benefits such as education scholarships for their children, housing allowances, health care, pensions, and marriage grants. State governments are responsible for implementing the boards, and informal workers' unions are actively involved in holding these governments accountable.

In addition to making material welfare demands on the state, informal workers are forcing the state to acknowledge their status as legitimate workers, even when employers do not. The state's acknowledgment of informal worker status has been institutionalized through the provision of a state-certified worker identity card to informal workers. Interviewees across the three states and two industries emphasized that the identity card enabled them to be viewed as legitimate and worthy citizens when they made demands at their children's schools, municipal offices, and even against police harassment. Because the identity card is tied to their labor, informal workers are in effect making a new class identity that distinguishes them from formal workers. Unlike formal workers who identify themselves in relation to capital, informal workers identify themselves as connected to the state through their social consumption needs. The informal worker identity does not obviate other political identities (such as caste). Rather, individuals politicize multiple identities concurrently, with each one yielding different group-based benefits.

To attain state attention to their demands for welfare goods, an identity card, and neighborhood provisions, informal workers use the currency of their votes, attracting the attention of incumbent politicians who want to retain power, as well as opposition leaders who want to attain power. In return for state-provided welfare benefits and identity cards, informal workers enter an implicit contract with the state, where they provide the promise of their political support and their low-cost, flexible labor on an unregulated basis. In doing so, they are forcing the state to acknowledge that they simply cannot live on the below-subsistence wages, unstable work, and invisibility that neoliberal policies idealize. These findings confirm that organized labor interacts with the state to constantly alter state–labor relations.

By incorporating these findings into existing models of how workers in a particular class location mobilize to pursue their interests, I offer support for a reformulated labor movement model. Unlike the conventional labor movement models that focused only on the relationship between employers and the minority of workers who have already won formal rights from the state, the reformulated model illuminates forms of class-based resistance in the swelling informal sector, where workers are denied the right to make any legal claims on employers. The reformulated model acknowledges that informal workers occupy their own position in the contemporary class structure. Capitalist accumulation in the modern economy has always relied on the labor of formal and informal workers. Unlike with formal workers, however, informal workers' relationship to capitalists remains tenuous. Employers are not obligated to pay informal workers minimum wages, and they can hire and fire informal labor according to market needs. The reformulated model acknowledges that informal workers' unique class location has led to unique interests around which workers can and do mobilize. Although some informal workers' unions are fighting for minimum wages, the shifting structures of production have undermined their bargaining power vis-à-vis employers. Therefore, they expend more resources and energy on, and have encountered more successes in, fighting for welfare benefits and identity cards from the state. These demands decrease the reproductive costs of labor. In doing so, informal workers are pulling the state into playing an even more direct role in their everyday lives than it did for formal workers.

Drawing from this reformulated labor movement model that reinserts class-based agency among informal workers and highlights the dynamic nature of state–labor relations, I developed a theoretical framework to answer my second question regarding the state conditions under which informal workers' organizations succeed or fail in securing material benefits for their members. Despite differences in the conditions of work and growth patterns in the construction and bidi industries, I found no evidence for industry-specific variation in the effectiveness of informal workers' movements. Rather, I found that the variation in strategy and success in attaining state-supported benefits is determined by regional state characteristics. Therefore I used my state framework to illustrate how electoral contexts (i.e., those that have pro-poor competitive elections vs those that do not) and economic policies (i.e., those that support vs resist liberalization) interact with one another and with informal workers' organizations to determine movement effectiveness. In doing so, I showed how social movement structures have a limited capacity to predict informal worker movement success in the absence of a conducive political and economic framework from above.

To test my framework, I examined the interaction between governments and informal workers' movements in three Indian states. Each case represents a different combination of social bases, electoral contexts, and economic policies and is supported by a historical analysis of each state's political patterns. I found that organizations in Tamil Nadu have been most successful in attaining state protection for informal workers. The state's informal workers enjoy higher wages and more state-provided welfare benefits than in West Bengal or Maharashtra. Tamil Nadu's informal workers were able to secure the provision of state-administered benefits because of (1) the interests of competing political parties in mobilizing mass votes from the poor and (2) the ability of informal workers' movements to frame their members as a large, "poor" vote bank for local politicians. The case of Kerala reiterates the findings from Tamil Nadu that pro-poor, competitive elections hold primary significance for informal workers' success. Unlike Kerala, Tamil Nadu also illustrates that even non-leftist parties can strengthen informal workers' movements in a competitive, pro-poor electoral context. At a secondary level, Tamil Nadu and Maharashtra (unlike Kerala) illustrate how informal workers' ability to attain the state's attention is bolstered by the state's commitment to a liberalization agenda. As the state's commitment increases, so does informal workers' bargaining power with the state, because their flexible, low-cost labor is a recognized, vital peg in the state's economic project.

On the flip side, organizations in West Bengal have failed to attain state protection for informal workers. At first glance, Indian scholars may be surprised by this finding, especially given that the state was ruled by the Communist Party of India-Marxists (CPM) for more than three decades. Nevertheless, my findings show that CPM's hegemonic power, along with its earlier lack of interest in liberalizing, made it difficult for unions to frame informal workers' demands in terms that would appeal to CPM's interest in staying in power. Although CPM espoused a class-based ideology, it constrained urban workers' struggles by enforcing a reformist approach and focusing on rural interests. CPM's entrenched political rule restricted informal workers' ability to make new demands on the state in return for their votes, because the state government had little need to seek additional votes. Moreover, its rhetorical criticism of liberalization policies undermined informal workers' ability to frame themselves as a vital part of the new economy. In recent years, as CPM's political power was threatened by an opposition party and it began to reverse its resistance to liberalization, it also began to reverse its resistance to informal work. In doing so, the West Bengal government has initiated some protections for informal workers' welfare. Depending on how well these initiatives are implemented, West Bengal could become a medium-success case. This shift illustrates how alterations in the state's economic and/or political policies can alter informal workers' movement effectiveness.

Finally, the case of Maharashtra lent mixed support for my state framework, which predicted medium levels of success in the state. On one hand, as predicted, the level of benefit provision in Maharashtra is less than that found in Tamil Nadu. On the other hand, informal workers in Maharashtra have attained minimal levels of welfare benefits, and the state government expresses some commitment to protecting informal workers. However, the level of success achieved in Maharashtra was not as far above that of West Bengal as might be expected by the Maharashtrian government's pursuit of liberalization – thereby indicating liberalization's lesser significance (relative to democratic power) for informal worker effectiveness. The state's leadership has traditionally been led and driven by intermediate and elite interests, which have undermined informal workers' ability to make demands on the state in return for political support. However, the state government's commitment to liberalization and private-sector industrialization has increased its interest in unregulated, informal labor. These factors have forced informal workers' organizations in Maharashtra to pursue a cooperative strategy with the state, in which they frame themselves as an essential partner in the state's economic agenda. By not fighting as hard for a minimum wage and job security, informal workers in Maharashtra assure state officials that they will not resist the unregulated nature of their work. However, in return, they are demanding that the state ensures their welfare in housing, health care, and education.

Despite developmental prescriptions for reduced welfare spending during the neoliberal era, these three case studies show that informal workers' new collective action strategies have led to state concessions that vary according to the state's social base, electoral context, and economic agenda. Informal workers' organizations are finding new opportunity structures both in competitive, pro-poor, populism and in neoliberal rhetoric – thereby highlighting the unintended consequences of both. Mass populist appeals for votes, although economically inefficient, provide opportunities for social movements to deepen Indian democracy. Liberalization policies, while idealizing an eclipsed state, enable informal workers to gain political recognition and to pull states even further into managing their economic insecurities.

These findings do not aim to make a normative argument that the new form of unionism by informal workers is better than the conventional form. In fact, the new movement may even be viewed as inferior to the conventional movement, because its spotty implementation and its non-universalist reach undermine the structural changes necessary to eradicate social injustices. Moreover, welfare demands are not a perfect substitute for worker demands. Rather, worker and welfare demands would ideally be met in conjunction with one another. At the moment, however, India's informal workers are attaining more success by mobilizing members and attaining state attention based on their welfare demands. We must remember that conventional approaches, although more ambitious, had failed to protect the vast majority of informal workers. To this extent, new informal workers' movements warrant our attention.

IMPLICATIONS FOR LABOR, THE STATE, AND STATE–LABOR RELATIONS

Following the three puzzles laid out in the Introduction, we can draw several important implications from this study's findings on informal workers' movements.

Labor

Our first puzzle focused on the structural and political class aspects of informal labor. If informal workers are not part of the modern, capitalist proletariat and, therefore, cannot organize as a class (as is commonly argued), then why are informal workers' organizations emerging across the globe? In the preceding chapters, I illustrated how informal workers are indeed an integral part of the modern-class structure and that the nature of informal work allows for class-based organization. The growing number of informal workers under liberalization and globalization, therefore, does not necessarily undermine labor movement activity.

These findings call for a qualification of the prevailing definition of the informal economy outlined in the Introduction. In particular, this definition should specify that the lack of state regulation and protection of informal workers is limited to the conditions of their work and their employer, and does not apply to their welfare at home or in their family. Informal workers in India continue to be legally unrecognized and unprotected in their work and by their employer. However, they have made themselves visible in the eyes of the state by pushing themselves onto the state's agenda as an identifiable and important vote bank – not as "low-caste members" or as "women," but as workers. They have pushed the state to alter labor force surveys to count informal workers, which in turn has armed informal workers with data on their numbers and their economic contributions. In addition, informal workers have attained some welfare benefits from the state, and they are actively fighting for more. Notably, the provision of benefits through the welfare boards does not extend to the general public, but is limited by law to informal workers. Although these benefits are implemented with varying degrees of success, they are now required and regulated under law and thus provide an important claim for informal workers.

As well, my findings urge scholars to rethink the pessimism about the sustainability of class-based movements that undergirds the recent globalization and "race-to-the-bottom-literature." Informal workers' organizations reassert class as an important analytical tool with which to examine differences in life chances and resistance against exploitation. Class structures, especially those in developing economies undergoing neoliberal reform, are being transformed as economic reforms alter structures of production. Despite claims to the contrary, this study illustrates that these transformations do not undermine class as an organizing rubric under which marginalized populations identify, articulate, and demand a shared set of unique interests (based on their access to resources and relationship with other classes). These interests and the strategies used to attain them merely evolve over time. Labor movements are indeed facing new challenges due to globalization, but it does not follow that workers are compliant in the face of these challenges.

By demanding welfare benefits to reduce their social consumption and reproduction costs, Indian informal workers have in essence launched a Polanyian movement to counter both the failure of formal labor movements to encompass them and the intention of neoliberal policies to avoid them. Informal workers' counter-movement pressures the state, rather than the employer, to "decommodify" their labor power. Capital has always found ways to avoid formal labor's attempts to decommodify labor. Informal workers in India are, therefore, trying to hold the state responsible for meeting their social consumption needs, regardless of their informal labor status. In other words, they argue that, if the state will not ensure a living wage sufficient to meet the costs of labor's reproduction, then the state must directly compensate for the deficiency through welfare benefits that can ensure it. Acknowledging, and understanding, the development of informal workers' unique class interests (ensuring basic subsistence at home and for the family, despite their low, insecure wages) is vital to ensuring an adequate response from policy makers and scholars.

Finally, this study's findings on informal workers' movements in India shed light on the unique role women are playing in contemporary labor movements. Informal women workers in India are focusing their movements on exposing the linkages between the public and private spheres, as well as between productive and reproductive work. Although women workers have long stood at the intersection of the public and private spheres, labor movements in India have traditionally separated the workplace from the home environment. Organization and solidarity have traditionally been built on the shop floor, and most labor benefits tended to directly affect the worker in the workplace. Formal workers' unions rarely entered the privacy of workers' homes. As the structures of production become explicitly flexible and the relationships between employer and employees blur, however, so do the distinctions between the public and private spheres. In India, the home has become the site of production (as in the case of bidi), and the site of production has become the home (as in the case of construction). In both cases reproductive labor, such as child rearing, education, health care, marriage, and home ownership, is intertwined with the conditions of productive work. Women's push for acknowledging the interconnections between the private and public spheres and between productive and reproductive work has suddenly found a new window of opportunity. Informal women workers in India have seized this opportunity and played a key role in demanding the state provide welfare benefits that cover the costs of reproductive labor. These benefits not only indirectly subsidize capitalists' productive work but also directly subsidize the reproductive work for which women are held responsible.

State–Labor Relations

My findings on informal workers' class-based organizations led to a second puzzle, which focused on state–labor relations under liberalization and globalization. If informal workers' movements rely so heavily on the state, how sustainable are these movements in the contemporary era of neoliberalism and reduced state intervention? In this study, I illustrated how workers (informal or formal) constantly interact with the state to alter state–labor relations, which are a vital component of international development: understanding exactly how and when state–labor relations evolve is crucial to our understanding of development constraints and opportunities. Informal workers in India are forging a new contract with the state that offers their political support and flexible, low-cost labor in exchange for state-provided welfare benefits.

These findings warrant rethinking state–labor relations in the modern era. The deepening of Indian democracy in terms of the increased mobilization of vulnerable populations and the increasing density of civil society organizations explains class formation in the informal economy. India's democracy has also enabled informal workers to reshape the consequences of neoliberalism. Although liberalization reforms have taken the state out of the detailed planning and control of the economy, they have also given informal labor the opportunity to pull the state deeper into directly managing and providing for the insecurities in their daily lives. In India, informal workers are capitalizing on political parties' need for mass votes and the state's overt recognition of their role in the insecure, unfettered marketplace where employers are privileged. In doing so, they are forcing the state to participate in micro-level decisions involving their children's education, health care, marriage, funerals, and even personal identity.

That these findings emerge from India lends an important geographic extension to the sociology of state and labor, which has focused on the United States and Latin America, especially on the closed economies implementing import-substitution policies. The lack of attention paid to the structural conditions under which labor is able to articulate its bargaining power vis-à-vis the state in Asia is surprising given the important role that low-cost, flexible labor has played in the region's state-driven economic "miracle." This study begins to address unanswered questions on how organized informal labor is shaping and is being shaped by recent political and economic development processes in India – one of the world's fastest growing economies, largest democracies, and largest informal workforce.

The State

Our third and final puzzle examined the state conditions under which informal workers' organizations succeed or fail. Here I found that informal workers' success in attaining welfare benefits from the state depends on whether they are operating in a context in which political parties are competing for votes from the poor and thus are heavily dependent on a mass vote bank that informal workers can claim. At a secondary level, I found that state commitments to liberalization, and thus state recognition of the importance of low cost, flexible labor, provide informal workers with additional leverage to attain state attention. In these contexts, informal workers can demand state-supported welfare benefits in return for political support and industrial peace.

These findings raise important questions on what impact class structures and class politics in the neoliberal context have on the future of the welfare state. The 1980s gave rise to an extensive body of literature, largely stemming from Scandinavia, that analyzed comparative models of welfare states established during the post–World War II era (Esping-Anderson 1985, 1990). These scholars highlighted the primacy of working-class political power in the development of the welfare state. Such arguments gave rise to a renewed interest, albeit limited to developed Western nations, in the interactions among state policies, workers' movements, and, most notably, the concept of citizenship (Hanagan 1997a; Haney 1996; Hasenfeld, Rafferty, and Zald 1987). The citizenship literature's emphasis on rights and obligations or duties allowed for an examination of state activities from above and below.

T. H. Marshall (1964: 92) defined citizenship as "a status bestowed on those who are full members of a community." Nearly thirty years later, Charles Tilly (1997: 600) added a relational aspect to the definition, writing, "Citizenship designates a set of mutually enforceable claims relating categories of person to agents of governments." This status bestows members with rights and obligations vis-à-vis the state. Marshall detailed three types of citizenship rights that had evolved in Western Europe: civil rights connected to individual freedom, such as freedom of speech and property rights, in the eighteenth century; political rights, such as voting, in the nineteenth century; and social rights, such as the right to a minimum of social and economic welfare, in the twentieth century. It was the guaranteeing of social rights that served as the focal point in the postwar scholarship on welfare states. Scholars viewed social rights as a means of mitigating class inequalities, and the working class was highlighted as a primary "claim-maker" that incorporated demands for social rights into a rhetoric of national citizenship (Hanagan 1997b).

More recently, scholars of ethnic politics have shed light on how minorities in divided societies, who are often denied their citizenship rights due to discrimination by a ruling majority, have reinstated some of their social rights and secured their protection through the power of their votes (Horowitz 1991; Wilkinson 2004). These works focus more on developing-country contexts than did the earlier literature on welfare states and citizenship. This study extends this literature on welfare claims in developing countries to illustrate how informal workers in India are also using the power of their votes to reinstate their social rights through the state. Informal workers are almost never included in identity-based discussions of politics. Although informal workers in India have not yet succeeded in guaranteeing social rights for all citizens (as did formal workers in Western Europe), they have succeeded in becoming potent claim-makers for informal workers' welfare in parts of India.

Moreover, women's involvement in informal workers' movements lends important insight into the feminist critique of welfare states launched during the 1990s (Borchorst 1999; Ferree and Hall 1996; Fraser 1989; Fraser and Gordon 1994). Feminist scholars warned against the sole focus on the state–market nexus in existing welfare-state analyses, arguing that ignoring internal family dynamics, as well as women's unpaid domestic and caregiving work, distorts how the welfare state affects women. By claiming welfare and civic rights from the state in return for their informal work, India's informal workers have made important strides in forcing unions and the Indian state to understand power dynamics in the private sphere and incorporate that knowledge into the delivery of welfare benefits in the current era.

Informal workers' strategies also yield important insights on the nature of the state involved in implementing this version of a welfare state for informal workers. This study indicates that welfare programs in the near future may require a context where political parties must compete for mass-based support to retain power. The strong, left-oriented, programmatic leadership of earlier welfare policies may no longer be enough. In other words, vulnerability at the top may be a necessary ingredient to empowerment at the bottom. This vulnerability may come in the form of electoral competitions (as in India's democracy) or in the form of a threatened coup. The particular regime context does not matter. What matters is that a social base is mobilized, organized, and able to fit its interests into the needs at the top. Indian informal workers have attained state protection and welfare by identifying ways to capitalize on political leaders' electoral vulnerability and their interest in retaining or attaining power.

Neoliberalism may be providing an ideal breeding ground for mass-based populism and, therefore, requires a rethinking of our normative claims on populism. On one hand, populist leaders may become the only hope mass workers have for survival and security. This can be seen in India, as well as in Latin America and the Middle East. On the other hand, populist leaders are not known for their commitment to structural change or economic efficiency, which raises important questions on the limits and constraints of the entitlements gained under the welfare systems emerging for marginalized groups in the neoliberal era.

In West Bengal, CPM, a traditional left-oriented political party that strives to meet workers' needs, was found to be least helpful to informal workers. The experiences in West Bengal stand in sharp contrast to those in Kerala, where informal workers have attained numerous benefits under CPM. The difference between the two states is that CPM in Kerala has had to evolve and be flexible to constantly compete for votes with opposition parties, whereas CPM in West Bengal became hegemonic and thus resistant to changing its tried and tested organizational structure and electoral base. Class structures, conditions of work, and structures of production are rapidly changing for all laborers. If left-oriented parties do not soon start appealing to the growing informal workforce, they may lose their claim as the leaders of class struggle and representatives of workers' interests. If, however, left-oriented parties extend their ideological commitment to social justice to include informal workers' movements, the vast majority of the world's workers may greatly benefit.

This study raises several questions for further research. First, given the impact of state conditions on informal workers' movement effectiveness, why do informal workers not alter their strategies to better fit their particular state conditions? At the moment, informal workers' basic strategy remains consistent across sectors and states, despite the state-level variation in effectiveness. This may, in part, be due to the relative infancy of informal workers' movements and the lack of any systematic study on the reasons for their successes and failures – a gap that this study seeks to begin filling. Informal workers in the 1980s and 1990s did not place adequate weight on the impact that state structures might have on their movement effectiveness and thus fought for national-level welfare laws that did not vary by state. These laws are now in place, and informal workers throughout the country are focused on getting them implemented. Tamil Nadu (and Kerala) serve as inspirations to those in other states, despite the fact that these two states' experiences cannot be readily transplanted to other state contexts. An important area for future research will be to investigate whether greater awareness of the state-level causes of failure can spur informal workers to revise their strategies accordingly.

Second, how prevalent are these trends in the non-Indian context? This study's findings from India should be compared in a cross-national perspective to other informal workers' movements around the world. Recent studies have shown evidence of similar findings in other countries, including Peru, Brazil, South Africa, and the United States. Janice Fine's (2006) study on immigrant organizations, known as workers' centers, in the United States finds that immigrant workers are fighting for welfare rights, rather than worker rights, and they are organizing around neighborhoods and community, rather than workplace. Dan Clawson's (2003) study on social movements among minority workers in the United

States, Gay Seidman's (1994) study of workers in South Africa and Brazil, and Kim Moody's (1997) study of workers in France and Canada also find that workers are instigating new movements, dubbed "social movement unionism," that use union democracy as a source of power and social vision to connect the masses with the state. Their findings clearly resonate with my Indian case study. More such studies focusing on informal workers throughout the world are needed to assert the global reach of these trends

Third, how do informal workers' movements vary by industry? Studies across more industries will provide further insight into how pervasive informal workers' movements are and how they may differ according to conditions of work. This study examines casual labor in the manufacturing sector (specifically in the construction and bidi industries). Future research should examine movements among casual labor in the service industry, which is rapidly growing in both developing and developed countries. In India, domestic servants have recently organized to initiate a welfare board that is similar to that of construction and bidi workers. Ruth Milkman (2006) has documented how janitors in Los Angeles have created alternative organizations to attain protection for immigrant workers employed on a contract basis in the service industry.

Future studies should also examine workers' movements among the self-employed. Indian self-employed workers occupy a slightly larger share of the informal economy than casual workers. Moreover, self-employment is being encouraged by states and multilateral institutions throughout the world. In India, street vendors (who are self-employed) are currently organized into large, politically influential unions, and they too are negotiating for welfare benefits and state recognition. In the United States, home care and day care workers have waged similar campaigns where they organized to elect a representative, who in turn secured them an increase in the rate of pay and benefits. Further study is required to examine the varying strategies used in these movements and the varying conditions for their success.

Finally, future research should investigate how formal workers' labor movements are reacting to the growing informal workers' movements. Formal workers' trade union membership is declining the world over, and they may be open to new strategies for the sake of survival. Indian formal workers' trade unions are indeed turning to informal workers' movements for new ideas and strategies on how to handle a future characterized by blurred employer–employee relationships. At the 2005 annual meeting for CITU, the CPM-affiliated union federation that traditionally shunned informal workers, union leaders made understanding and mobilizing informal workers their top-priority agenda item for the year. In 2008, union leaders wrote in CITU's monthly journal:

The concentration of the trade unions has to be fully focused in an organized and planned manner to unionize the workforce in the unorganized [i.e., informal] sector and bring them under the vortex of struggle along with the organized sector workforce. The fulcrum of our struggle has also to be the informal sector. This is certainly a daunting task, but not impossible at all. (Ganguly 2008: 47)

At the same time, some formal workers' union leaders view informal workers' movements as a threat to conventional class-based movements that focused on guaranteeing workers' rights from the employer. During the 1880s in the United States, the Knights of Labor presented an alternative labor organizing model based on residential communities. However, their efforts were undermined by a direct attack from the established trade unions and indirect sabotage by political parties. Both saw the Knights as competitors. Further research on how political parties and formal unions react to informal workers' movements throughout the world can lend greater insights into the sustainability of informal workers' movements.

Informal workers' movements provide an ideal lens for viewing how the great transformations of the twenty-first century are being played out on the ground. As detailed in this book, informal workers' movements in India are playing a vital role in shaping a new relationship between the state and labor in the current era of liberalization and globalization. These institutional responses to alterations in state policy and market structure by both workers and state leaders are not only changing the social contract between state and society but also reshaping the country's economic and political outcomes. Although recent informal workers' movements are far from perfect, they must not be discounted. For decades, the alternative for informal workers was nothing, except the prospect of one day being formalized. For reasons I have already detailed, the likelihood of that prospect turning into a reality was slim. Today, even that slim hope derived from that prospect is starting to fade. Therefore, we should be concerned about the future growth of informal workers' movements.

On one hand, these movements could grow to shape the state's role in workers' lives across all sectors of the economy. They may also reflect a global trend toward social movement unionism, in which traditional union movements are converging with newer social movements to create a new form of mass politics that straddles people's worker and citizen identities. Social movement unionism has been documented in Brazil, South Africa, and even France, Canada, and the United States (Clawson 2003; Moody 1997; Seidman 1994). This study contributes to this literature by adding evidence from the world's most populous democracy. But more importantly, this study shows that India's social movement unionism is being spearheaded by the nation's most precarious workers. It is intriguing that a modern blend of class politics may now be finding a new echo in, of all places, the informal economy.

On the other hand, informal workers' movements could regress into a scenario in which the state continues to extend its responsibilities to its workers, but in an ad hoc manner that eventually mirrors traditional patron–client relations. In this scenario, the structural changes necessary to improve workers' lives would not be made. Informal workers would express their votes as a superficial exchange for a few basic needs, understanding that daily life would remain as vulnerable and insecure as always. Going forward, the labor movement will need to monitor that informal workers' efforts to decommodify labor are, in fact, implemented. Furthermore, communist parties and trade unions need to find ways to incorporate informal workers' interests into their efforts. If they do not, these alternative movements may nurture the populist tendencies in India's democracy and elsewhere, and what could be a profound movement of inclusive protection could spiral into another patron–client relationship that festers on group-based benefits, interest group politics, and deeply undignified discontent.

Appendix I

Photos of Informal Workers in Construction and Bidi

PHOTO 1: Women in the construction industry are hired to do the lowest paid jobs on the site. The most common job is carrying materials from one end of the site to another.

PHOTO 2: The second most common job for women in construction is cleaning cement by hand.

PHOTO 3: Some construction workers are recruited by sub-contractors to live on a site for an indefinite period of time. Employers provide materials to build a temporary home, a few hours of electricity, and a bucket of water for the day. A group of women construction workers are pictured taking a lunch break in front of their temporary homes. The office building under construction 13 shown in the background.

PHOTO 4: For some construction workers, labor recruitment occurs on a daily basis, as men and women workers wait on a street corner until they are picked up for a job. A group of men and women workers are pictured as they wait for a job; the union leader is standing in the middle.

PHOTO 5: In the case of bidi, women workers first buy the raw materials at a local shop. This is a shop owner who sells the bidi leaves and tobacco in a slum where bidi workers live.

PHOTO 6: Women then return to the confines of their homes to roll the bidis. Children often assist their mothers to maximize the number of rolled bidis. This is a woman sitting in the hallway of her apartment building, rolling bidis with her daughter, while her son sleeps by her side.

PHOTO 7: Women then bring their rolled bidis to the local contractor, who inspects their quality, pays by the piece, and adds a brand label. The union leader is standing in the doorway, as women workers await their turn.

PHOTO 8: Finally, the bidis are taken to the "factory," where formally employed male workers package them for sale.

PHOTO 9: Tamil Nadu's Construction Workers Welfare Board, Chennai.

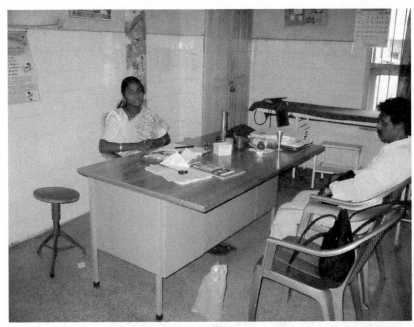

PHOTO 10: An office in one of the health clinics designed for bidi workers and located in the slum where bidi workers reside.

Appendix II

The Evolution of the Count of Informal Workers

This Appendix provides background information for my calculations of the size and characteristics of the informal workforce using the 1999 National Sample Survey on Employment and Unemployment (NSS) (NSSO 2001a).[1] For a more detailed discussion of this issue, see Agarwala (2009). Perhaps the largest obstacle to work on the informal economy to date has been the lack of consensus on how to define, and thus count, informal workers. Recent studies have begun to establish definitions that are becoming consistent, at least within India.

Since the early 1970s, scholars have used a diverse range of methodologies to capture the informal workforce. When Keith Hart first coined the term "the informal sector," there was little agreement about the concept, much less the methodology used to measure it. Almost no national-level data sets collected information on informal workers. As a result, scholars offered different, sometimes even conflicting, conclusions about the causes and effects of informal work.

In 1993, participants in the 15th International Conference of Labor Statisticians (ICLS) agreed that informal workers must be counted in labor force surveys to improve analyses of the modern global economy. To this end, ICLS participants drafted a more precise definition of the informal economy that was subsequently incorporated into the 1993 System of National Accounts (SNA).[2] The ICLS defined the informal

---

[1] The NSS is conducted every five years. It uses three reference periods – yearly, weekly, and daily. For more detailed information on the NSS sample selection, see NSSO (2001a).
[2] SNA sets the international statistical standard for the measurement of the market economy. Most national surveys follow SNA guidelines to maintain international comparability. It is published jointly by the United Nations, the Commission of the European

economy as enterprises that have a low level of organization, little or no division between capital and labor as factors of production, and labor relations consisting of social relationships rather than formal contracts. These enterprises are unregistered and are owned by households that produce goods and services to generate self-employment. Production and household expenditures in these enterprises are usually combined, and financial accounts are rarely maintained (ILO 1993).

In 1998, as part of the Indian government's newfound interest in informal labor, the Department of Statistics incorporated the 1993 ICLS enterprise-based definition of the informal economy into Indian labor surveys, thereby limiting the definition of informal workers to those engaged in small, unregistered enterprises that are run by own-account workers or informal employers.[3] In response, Indian informal workers demanded that the Indian government address the limited nature of ICLS's enterprise-based definition. They argued that it omitted – and thus undermined the ability to empirically examine – a significant subset of informal workers who do not work in small, unregistered enterprises but work as unregulated contractors for formal companies. Because homes or public spaces are not counted as "enterprises," the ICLS definition also excluded the vast numbers of (often women) workers who work alone at home or in multiple locations (such as domestic servants or street vendors) (Satpathy 2004).

To replace the ICLS definition, Indian informal workers advocated an operational definition of informal workers in terms of their employment status (i.e., casual, self-employed, or regular worker) and the characteristics of their enterprises (i.e., the legal status and/or size of the enterprise). This new definition includes informal workers in *both* informal and formal enterprises, as well as regular workers in informal enterprises. It is this broadened definition of the informal economy that I use in this study.

In 1999, the Indian Ministry of Statistics and Program Implementation incorporated this broader definition of the informal economy into the

---

Communities, the International Monetary Fund, the Organization for Economic Cooperation and Development, and the World Bank. The first SNA was established in 1953, and it is periodically updated.

3 "Own-account enterprises" are owned and operated by a single person or in a partnership with members of the same or one additional household. They may employ family members and employees on an occasional basis, but not employees on a continuous basis. "Enterprises of informal employers" may employ one or more employees on a continuous basis. They are distinguished from enterprises of formal employers based on (1) the size of employment and/or (2) the registration status of the enterprise and employees. These limits are defined on a national basis. In India, enterprises with fewer than twelve employees are unregistered and defined as "informal enterprises" (ILO 1993).

NSS. The 1999 NSS conducted a household survey to ensure the inclusion of all home-based and multiple-location workers; for the first time, it included detailed questions on employment status, location of work, and enterprise characteristics. A follow-up survey was then conducted on the enterprises identified as informal to capture the details of output generated.[4]

The NSS is now among the most complete sources of data on Indian labor. First, because it is based on a sample of households, more contract workers and self-employed workers are captured than in enterprise-based surveys. Second, by capturing more informal workers, the NSS provides greater demographic variation (by gender, caste, religion, and region) than the Economic Census or the Population Census. Finally, it includes more details on work type, social conditions, and political organization than the Population Census.[5]

The NSS collects data on employment using the following three approaches:

1. **Usual status,** which asks questions about the 365 days preceding the survey
2. **Current weekly status,** which asks questions about the seven days preceding the survey
3. **Current daily status,** which asks questions about each day of the seven days preceding the survey

The usual status criterion is the most common approach used in employment studies, and I use it here for comparability. In line with common convention, I have included both principal and subsidiary economic activities. Because the new questions included in the 1999 NSS to capture informal workers were only asked of workers in the nonagricultural sector, my analysis does not include agricultural workers. In India, agricultural workers represent 40 percent of the total workforce (NSSO 2001a).

---

[4] The first survey was based on a sample of randomly selected households. The sample design was a stratified multistage one, moving from rural villages or urban blocks to households. The 1991 Census was used as the sampling frame for the selection of villages, and the latest NSSO list of blocks was used as the sampling frame for the selection of blocks. The survey spread across 6,208 villages and 4,176 urban blocks, covering 165,244 households and 819,011 persons. The raw data of the survey covered 819,013 persons; however, two pairs of observations were duplicates. In my analysis, I dropped the duplicates of each pair, thereby totaling 819,011 individual observations (NSSO 2001b).
[5] The NSS still does not capture all seasonal and female workers. Some Indian scholars have advocated time-use surveys as an alternative. For a comparison of the recent NSS to a pilot time-use survey, see Hirway (2002).

TABLE 12. *Informal vs. Formal Workers in India*

	Jobs by Status in Employment				
	Casual workers	Self-employed family workers	Self-employed own-account workers and employers[c]		Regular wage workers
Production Units by Type	Informal	Informal	Informal	Formal	Formal
Formal Economy Enterprises[a]	1	3	5		
Informal Economy Enterprises[b]	2	4	6		7

[a] Formal enterprises include public sector, semi-public, cooperative societies, public limited companies, private limited companies, and other units covered under the Indian Annual Survey of Industries.
[b] Informal enterprises include single proprietaries and partnerships.
[c] Self-employed own-account workers have been grouped with employers because of the small number of employer observations in the NSS.

- Employment in the informal economy: Cells 2, 4, 6, 7.
- Informal employment: Cells 1–6.
- Informal employment outside the informal economy: Cells 1, 3, 5.

Source: ©Emerald Group Publishing; Agarwala (2009).

The broadened definition of informal work suggested by Indian informal workers' movements has reached the international arena. Although this definition has not yet been incorporated into the SNA, in 2003, the 17th ICLS began using the term "informal economy" rather than "informal sector" to capture informal workers in both informal and formal enterprises. In 2001, Ralph Hussmanns (2002) of the International Labor Organisation (ILO) used this definition to present the "Hussmanns Matrix" to distinguish informal from formal workers. In Table 12, I apply an adapted version of the Hussmanns Matrix to the data in the 1999 NSS. As shown, all casual workers and self-employed family workers are categorized as informal, regardless of the type of enterprise for which they work. Whether own-account workers, employers, and regular wage workers are categorized as informal depends on their type of enterprise. Under this schema, all workers in the informal sector fall within the substantive definition laid out in the Introduction – namely, they are not protected and regulated under state law (Portes, Castells, and Benton 1989).

TABLE 13. *Indian Labor Force*

	Male	Female	Total
Total Population	472,784,000	447,858,000	920,642,000
Labor Force (% of total population)	54	26	41
Unemployment Rate (% of labor force)	2.4	1.7	2.2[a]
Nonagricultural Workers (% of total labor force)	44	23.3	37.4
Nonagricultural Workers Employed in Formal Economy (% of nonagricultural workers)	18.6	14.9	17.9
Nonagricultural Workers Employed in Informal Economy (% of nonagricultural workers)	81.4	85.1	82.1
Casual Workers (% of nonagricultural workers in informal economy)	21.4	18.7	20.9
Self-Employed Family Workers (% of nonagricultural workers in informal economy)	7.2	25.7	10.8
Self-Employed, Own-Account, & Informal Employers (% of nonagricultural workers in informal economy)	35.3	27.7	33.8
Regular Workers in Informal Enterprise (% of nonagricultural workers in informal economy)	17.5	13.1	16.7

Note: Calculated by author from NSS 1999–2000.
[a] As in most developing countries, unemployment rates are low in India, because the lack of state support for the unemployed makes it impossible for people to survive without any work.
Source: ©Emerald Group Publishing. See Agarwala (2009).

Using the broadened definition of the informal economy and employing the 1999 NSS, we can count the size of India's informal workforce. In 2001, India became the second demographic billionaire after China, following a 21 percent population increase between 1991 and 2001 (GOI 2001a). Table 13 shows that 41 percent of the Indian population, or nearly 400 million people, are in the labor force.[6] In recent years, scholars, activists, and even government officials have achieved a near consensus on the claim that informal workers comprise 93 percent of the national labor force (Kundu and Sharma 2001; NCL 2002; Oberai and Chadha 2001; Special Correspondent 2002a; Times News Network 2002).[7] This statistic, which was first put forth by informal workers' movements in India that were attempting to increase their salience, includes India's agricultural workers.[8] Even when the analysis is limited to the nonagricultural workforce, however, the numbers remain staggering. More than 37 percent of the labor force, or approximately 141 million people, work in the nonagricultural sectors. Of those, 82 percent are employed in the informal economy. In other words, more than 114 *million non-agricultural workers* in India are unregulated and unprotected by the state.[9]

---

[6] Approximately 15 percent of people not in the labor force are under the age of 5 years or above the age of 85 years.

[7] Of the 8 percent in the formal sector, 6 percent are in the public sector and 2 percent in the private sector (NSSO 2001a).

[8] Some have argued that this figure exaggerates the true situation by including India's massive agricultural workforce, which has never aimed to become formalized (Satnaphy 2004).

[9] I calculated this figure, using the 1999 NSS.

Appendix III

Interview Methodology

For this study, I conducted two sets of interviews. The first set of interviews with government officials and labor leaders served two purposes: they supplemented the dearth of secondary information on India's informal workers' organizations, and they provided qualitative data on the relationship between the state and informal workers from above. Questions to politicians focused on how and why government officials justify their attention to informal workers' needs. These interviews were crucial to testing my hypothesis on the effects of state economic policy and electoral contexts on the success or failure of informal workers' movements.

The second set of interviews included 140 women workers who were members of an informal workers' organization in the construction and bidi industries. These interviews provide insights on how informal workers' view and define their own struggles, as well as information on how they relate to state officials and attempt to gain state attention from below. I analyzed the answers from informal workers alongside answers from government officials to provide a clearer picture of state–worker relations.

The women workers were chosen first from a stratified sample based on locality and then randomly from either the contractor's lists or the membership list (whichever was applicable) in a particular area. Twenty members of one bidi organization and twenty members of one construction organization were interviewed in each city/state. In Kolkata, two construction organizations were included because it is one of the few cities to have both a politically affiliated construction workers' movement and an independent one. Therefore, in Kolkata, I conducted sixty (rather

TABLE 14. *National Sample vs. Study Sample by Industry*

	Construction National Sample	Construction Study Sample	BidiNational Sample	BidiStudy Sample
N	6,268,298	80	1,008,004	60
Average age	33	38	33	49
Caste (%)[a]				
Others	16		4	
Upper caste		8		0
Other Backward Caste	37	15	45	40
Scheduled Caste	27	51	14	0
Scheduled Tribe	7	3	2	0
% Muslim	14	23	49	60
% Illiterate	37	62	49	54
% Migrant		73		60

Note: National sample characteristics are for urban workers, calculated using the 1999 NSS.

[a] Caste is delineated on the basis of the caste-based affirmative action law in India. Castes are listed in order of presumed privilege. Muslims are not categorized by caste. Note the NSS category "other" includes Muslims as well as upper castes.

than forty) interviews. The interviews were supplemented with participant observation and numerous visits to contractor workshops, construction sites, health clinics, slums, and organization rallies and meetings.

The interviews were semi-structured and focused on questions about work, organizational activities, and interactions with government officials. I also obtained background characteristics on family, education levels, and demographics from every interviewee. Each interview ran between one and five hours in length. Although most interviews were held in workers' homes, some were held on the work sites during lunch breaks and in the organization offices. A few of the construction interviews were held at the street corner, while workers were waiting to be picked up for a job. Because of the numerous demands made by family members, neighbors, and contractors on workers' time, some interviews were broken up across several days.

Table 14 summarizes the basic characteristics of the interviewees by industry. All interviewees earn between US$0.25 and US$2.00 per day and are thus considered to be below the poverty line according to the World Bank income-based definition. Although I do not claim that my sample of interviewees is representative of the national data, I include the national figures for urban areas to provide a comparison. Bidi workers in my sample are slightly older than the national average of urban workers in the industry. This may be a reflection of the difference between organized and unorganized bidi workers. Because the bidi industry is in decline, fewer bidi workers are training their children to join the trade or the union, especially in urban areas.

With regard to caste, the bidi interviewees seem to reflect the national picture, in that the majority of the workers categorize themselves as members of Other Backward Classes (OBC) or Muslim. Both these groups are considered to be in the lower and middle socio-economic strata of the population. A large segment of the construction interviewees in the study sample comes from the lowest-caste groups; namely, Scheduled Castes (of Dalits) and some Scheduled Tribes. Although the national data reflect a large number of lower-caste construction workers, they also include a large proportion of OBC construction workers. Finally, although illiteracy rates are high in all categories, the construction workers in my sample exhibit higher rates than that found in the national urban sample. This discrepancy is likely due to the larger percentage of women in my sample, as compared to the national sample. The proportion of women in my sample of bidi workers is closer to that in the national sample, which may explain the smaller literacy gap in those numbers.

References

Agarwala, Rina. 2006. "From Work to Welfare: A New Class Movement in India." *Critical Asian Studies* 38:419–45.

———. 2007. "Resistance and Compliance in the Age of Globalization: Indian Women and Labor Organizations." *Annals of the American Academy of Political and Social Science* 610:143–59.

———. 2008. "Reshaping the Social Contract: Emerging Relations between the State and Informal Labor in India." *Theory and Society* 37:375–408.

———. 2009. "An Economic Sociology of Informal Work: The Case of India." *Research in the Sociology of Work* 18:315–42.

Ahluwalia, Montek S. 2002. *Report of the Task Force on Employment Opportunities*. New Delhi: Planning Commission.

Andrews, Edmund. 2005. "New Zealand Named Best Nation for Business." *New York Times*.

Arandarenko, Mihail. 2001. "Waiting for the Workers: Explaining Labor Quiescence in Serbia." In *Workers after Workers' States: Labor and Politics in Postcommunist Eastern Europe*, edited by Stephen Crowley and David Ost. Lanham: Rowman and Littlefield Publishers.

Bairoch, Paul. 1973. *Urban Unemployment in Developing Countries: The Nature of the Problem and Proposals for Its Solution*. Geneva: ILO.

Balakrishnan, S. 2001. "Success of State Bandh Isolates BJP." *Times of India*. Mumbai.

Bandyopadhyay, Tamal. 1995. "Bengal to Deregister 5000 Unions in Bid to Turn Investor-Friendly." *Business Standard*. Kolkata.

Banerjee, Abhijit, Pranab K. Bardhan, Kaushik Basu, Mrinal Datta Chaudhuri, Maitreesh Ghatak, Ashok Sanjay Guha, Mukul Majumdar, Dilip Mookherjee, and Debraj Ray. 2001. "A Belaboured Economy." *Telegraph*. Kolkata.

Banerjee, Alok. 2000. "Buddhadev's Move Is Seen as Bourgeois Influence in CPM." *Times of India*. Mumbai.

———. 2002. "Buddhadeb Forced to Concede Workers' Right to Strike." *Times of India*. Mumbai.

Banerjee, Nantoo. 1999. "Destination 21st Century." *Telegraph*. Kolkata.

Barnett, Marguerite Ross. 1976a. "Competition, Control, and Dependency: Urban Politics in Madras City." In *The City in Indian Politics*, edited by Donald B. Rosenthal. Faridabad: Thomson Press.

———. 1976b. *The Politics of Cultural Nationalism in South India*. Princeton: Princeton University Press.

Basu, Amrita. 1992. *Two Faces of Protest: Contrasting Modes of Women's Activism in India*. Berkely: University of California Press.

———. Basu, Sajal. 1996. "Left Front Retains Base." *Frontline* 89–90.

———. "Bengal Uses Statistics to Woo Investors." (1997). *Business Standard*. Kolkata.

Benton, Lauren. 1990. *Invisible Factories: The Informal Economy and Industrial Development in Spain*. Albany: State University of New York Press.

Bhattacharya, Malabika. 2000. "CITU Must Play a More Responsible Role." *Hindu*. New Delhi.

Bhattacharya, Dwaipayan. 2004. "The Journey towards a One-Party State." *The Hindu*. Kolkata.

Bhave, Milind S. 2006. *Goods Transport Labour Board, 35th Annual Report, 2005–2006*. Mumbai: A. P. Mulgund and Company, Chartered Accountants.

Bhowmik, Sharit, and Nitin More. 2001. "Coping with Urban Poverty: Ex-Textile Mill Workers in Central Mumbai." *Economic and Political Weekly* 36:4822–35.

Block, Fred. 2001. "Introduction." In *The Great Transformation*, edited by Karl Polanyi. Boston: Beacon Press.

Block, Fred, and Peter Evans. 2005. "The State and the Economy." In *The Handbook of Economic Sociology*, edited by Neil J. Smelser and Richard Swedberg (pp. 505–26). Princeton: Princeton University Press.

Borchorst, Anette. 1999. "Feminist Thinking about the Welfare State." in *Revisioning Gender*, edited by Myra Marx Ferree, Judith Lorber, and Beth B. Hess. Thousand Oaks: Sage.

Breman, Jan. 2002. "An Informalised Labour System: End of Labour Market Dualism." *Economic and Political Weekly* 36:4804–27.

———. 2003. *The Labouring Poor in India: Patterns of Exploitation, Subordination, and Exclusion*. New York: Oxford University Press.

Bromley, Ray, and Chris Gerry. 1979. "Who are the Casual Poor?" In *Casual Work and Poverty in Third World Cities*, edited by Ray Bromley and Chris Gerry. New York: Wiley.

Bunsha, Dionne. 2002. "Maharashtra in the Red." *Frontline*.

Carr, M., M. Chen, and R. Jhabvala (Eds.). 1996. *Speaking Out*. New Delhi: Vistaar Publications.

Castells, Manuel. 1997. *The Information Age, vol. 2: The Power of Identity*. Oxford: Blackwell.

CDC. 2004. "Tobacco Information and Prevention Source (TIPS)." Available at http://www.cdc.gov/tobacco/

Chakrabarti, Debanjan. 1998. *Report on Organisation of Construction Workers Federation of India*. Calcutta: Construction Workers Federation of India.

Chakrabarty, Dipesh. 2000. *Rethinking Working-Class History*. Princeton: Princeton University Press.

Chakrovorty, Aruna. 2001. "Different Parties, Ideologies, but Joint Display of Protest." *Indian Express*. Mumbai.

Chandavarkar, Rajnarayan. 1994. *The Origins of Industrial Capitalism in India: Business Strategies and the Working Classes in Bombay, 1900–40*. Cambridge: Cambridge University Press.

Chatterjee, Partha. 1982. "Caste and Politics in West Bengal." In *Land, Caste, and Politics in Indian States*, edited by Gail Omvedt. Delhi: Authors Guild.

Chaudhuri, Kalyan. 2002. "A Record in West Bengal." *Frontline*:31–35.

Chauhan, Yash. 2001. *History and Struggles of Beedi Workers in India*. New Delhi: AITUC and ILO.

Chibber, Vivek. 2003. *Locked in Place: State-Building and Late Industrialization in India*. Princeton: Princeton University Press.

Chowdhury, Supriya Roy. 2003. "Old Classes and New Spaces: Urban Poverty, Unorganised Labour and New Unions." *Economic and Political Weekly* 50:5277–84.

Chun, Jennifer Jihye. 2009. *Organizing at the Margins: The Symbolic Politics of Labor in South Korea and the United States*. Ithaca: Cornell University Press.

Clawson, Dan. 2003. *The Next Upsurge: Labor and the New Social Movements*. Ithaca: Cornell University Press.

Collier, Ruth Berins, and David Collier. 1991. *Shaping the Political Arena: Critical Junctures, the Labor Movement, and Regime Dynamics in Latin America*. Princeton: Princeton University Press.

"Construction Workers Welfare Board Constituted." (2002). *The Hindu*. Chennai.

CPM. 2009. *CPI(M) Election Manifesto, 15th Lok Sabha 2009*. New Delhi: Hari Singh Kang and Progressive Printers.

Cross, John. 1998. *Informal Politics: Street Vendors and The State in Mexico City*. Stanford: Stanford University Press.

Crowley, Stephen, and David Ost (Eds.). 2001. *Workers after Workers' States: Labor and Politics in Postcommunist Eastern Europe*. Lanham, MD: Rowman & Littlefield.

CSDS. 1999. "West Bengal: Limited Losses for the Left." *Frontline*: 38–39.

Dasgupta, Abhijit. 1999. "Destination Bengal Targets Industry, Basic Education." *The Pioneer*.

Date, Vidyadhar. 2002. "National Renewal Fund Fails to Help Workers." *Times of India*, p. 5. Mumbai.

Deaton, Angus. 2003. "Adjusted Indian Poverty Estimates for 1999–2000." *Economic and Political Weekly*:322–26.

Deaton, Angus, and Valerie Kozel (Eds.). 2005. *The Great Indian Poverty Debate*. New Delhi: Macmillan.

De Janvry, Alain, and Carlos Garramon. 1977. "Laws of Motion of Capital in the Center-Periphery Structure." *Review of Radical Political Economics* 9:29–38.

Deshpande, Rajeshwari, and Nitin Birmal. 2004. "Mild Approval Wins the Day." *The Hindu*, p. 13. Mumbai.

De Soto, Hernando. 1989. *The Other Path: The Informal Revolution.* New York: Harper and Row.

de Wit, Joop W. 1996. *Poverty, Policy and Politics in Madras Slums: Dynamics of Survival, Gender and Leadership.* New Delhi: Sage.

Deyo, Frederic. 1989. "Labor and Development Policy in East Asia." *Annals of the American Academy of Political and Social Scence* 505:152–61.

Dhavan, Prashant. 1999. "Globalisation's Bodyblow Flattens Labour Militancy." *The Hindu.* Madras.

DMK. 2001. *DMK Manifesto: Elections to Tamil Nadu Legislative Assembly.* Chennai: DMK Party.

———. 2004. *DMK Manifesto for the Parliamentary Elections.* Chennai: DMK Party.

———. 2006. *DMK Manifesto: Elections to the Tamil Nadu Legislative Assembly.* Chennai: DMK Party.

Dreze, Jean, and Amartya Sen. 2002. *India: Development and Participation.* Oxford: Oxford University Press.

Dutta, Sujan. 1995. "Giving Labor the Short Shrift." *Deccan Herald.* Bangalore.

Dwaipayan, Bhattacharyya, and Aditya Nigam. 1996. "Advantage Left Front: West Bengal Elections '96." *Frontline:*28–30.

Economist. 2003. "Adapt or Die: Unions Must Start Providing Services Their Members Need," p. 13

Elster, Jon. 1985. *Making Sense of Marx.* Cambridge: Cambridge University Press.

Esping-Anderson, Gosta. 1985. *Politics against Markets: The Social Democratic Road to Power.* Princeton: Princeton University Press.

———. 1990. *The Three Worlds of Welfare Capitalism.* Princeton: Princeton University Press.

Fernandes, Leela. 1997. *Producing Workers: The Politics of Gender, Class, and Culture in the Calcutta Jute Mills.* Philadelphia: University of Pennsylvania Press.

Ferree, Myra Marx, and Elaine J. Hall. 1996. "Rethinking Stratification from a Feminist Perspective: Gender, Race, and Class in Mainstream Textbooks." *American Sociological Review* 61:929–50.

Fine, Janice. 2006. *Worker Centers: Organizing Communities at the Edge of the Dream.* Ithaca: Cornell University Press.

Franda, Marcus F. 1969. "Electoral Politics in West Bengal: The Growth of the United Front." *Pacific Affairs* 42:279–93.

———. 1973. "Radical Politics in West Bengal." In *Radical Politics in South Asia,* edited by Paul R. Brass and Marcus F. Franda. Cambridge: MIT Press.

Fraser, Nancy. 1989. "Women, Welfare, and the Politics of Needs Interpretation." In *Unruly Practices: Power, Discourse and Gender in Comtemporary Social Theory,* edited by Nancy Fraser. Minnesotta: University of Minnesota.

Fraser, Nancy, and Linda Gordon. 1994. "A Genealogy of Dependency: Tracing a Keyword of the US Welfare State." *Signs* 19:309–36.

Frontline. 1999. "No Major Shift in Popular Mood." *Frontline:* 51–52.

———. 2001. "A Spectacular Show: Election Analysis in West Bengal." *Frontline:*121–26.

————. 2002. "Interview with Tamil Scholar from SL, Karthigesu Sivathamby." *Frontline:* 19.

Gangadhar, V. 1995. "Trade Unionism on the Decline." *Sunday Observer.*

Ganguly, P. K. 2008. "Impact of Globalisation on Informal Sector." *The Working Class* 39:40–47.

Geertz, Clifford. 1963. *Peddlers and Princes: Social Change and Economic Modernization in Two Indonesian Towns.* Chicago: University of Chicago Press.

Girija, P. L. T., Geetha Ramakrishnan, and Shyamala Ramakrishnan. 1988. *A Study of Chitals: Women Construction Labour in the City of Madras.* Madras: Institute for the Study of Women.

Government of India. 1929. *Royal Commission Report on the Labour of India.* New Delhi: Royal Commission of Labour.

————. 1952. *Indian Labour Year Book.* New Delhi: Ministry of Labour and Rehabilitation, Government of India.

————. 1960. *Indian Labour Year Book.* New Delhi: Ministry of Labour and Rehabilitation, Government of India.

————. 1970. *Indian Labour Year Book.* New Delhi: Ministry of Labour and Rehabilitation, Government of India.

————. 1980. *Indian Labour Year Book.* New Delhi: Ministry of Labour and Rehabilitation.

————. 1981. *Report on Working and Living Conditions of Workers in the Bidi Industry.* Chandigarh: Labour Bureau, Ministry of Labour Employment and Rehabilitation.

————. 1990. *Indian Labour Year Book.* New Delhi: Ministry of Labour and Rehabilitation.

————. 1991. *Statistical Report on General Election, 1991 to the Legislative Assembly of West Bengal.* New Delhi: Election Commission of India.

————. 1996a. *Statistical Report on General Election, 1996 to the Legislative Assembly of West Bengal.* New Delhi: Election Commission of India.

————. 1996b. *Verification of Membership of Trade Unions Affiliated to Central Trade Union Organisations (CTUOs) as on December 31, 1989.* New Delhi: Ministry of Labour and Employment.

————. 2001a. *Census of India.* New Delhi: Census Bureau.

————. 2001b. *Statistical Report on General Election, 2001 to the Legislative Assembly of West Bengal.* New Delhi: Election Commission of India.

————. 2002a. *Directorate General Labor Welfare Report.* New Delhi: Ministry of Labour and Employment.

————. 2002b. *Minimum Wages in India.* New Delhi: Ministry of Labour and Employment.

————. 2004a. *GDP by Economic Activity, at Current Prices.* New Delhi: Ministry of Statistics and Programme Implementation, National Accounts Division.

————. 2004b. *National Common Minimum Programme of the Government of India.* New Delhi: United Progressive Alliance.

————. 2008a. *Ministry of Labour Annual Report (2007–08).* New Delhi: Ministry of Labour and Employment.

————. 2008b. *Progress Report on the Beedi Workers Welfare Fund.* New Delhi: DGLW Ministry of Labour.

———. 2008c. Verification of Membership of Trade Unions Affiliated to Central Trade Union Organisations (CTUOs), as on December 31, 2002. New Delhi: Ministry of Labour and Employment.

Gokhale, Jayashree B. 1990. "The Evolution of a Counter-Ideology: Dalit Consciousness in Maharashtra." In *Dominance and State Power in Modern India: Decline of a Social Order*, edited by Francine Frankel and M. S. A. Rao. Delhi: Oxford University Press.

Goldstone, Jack A. (Ed.). 2003. *States, Parties, and Social Movements*. Cambridge: Cambridge University Press.

Gooptu, Nandini. 2001. *The Politics of the Urban Poor in Early Twentieth-Century India*. Cambridge: Cambridge University Press.

Gopinath. 1997. "Welfare of Construction Workers: Legal Measures." *The Hindu*, p. H51. Madras.

Gordon, Jennifer. 2007. *Suburban Sweatshops: The Fight for Immigrant Rights*. Cambridge, MA: Belknap Press of Harvard University Press

Grasmuck, S., and R. Espinal. 2000. "Market Success or Female Autonomy? Income, Ideology, and Empowerment among Microentrepreneurs in the Dominican Republic." *Gender and Society* 14:231–55.

Gugler, Josef. 1991. "Political Responses to Poverty." In *Cities, Poverty, and Development: Urbanization in the Third World*, edited by Alan Gilbert and Josef Gugler. Oxford: Oxford University Press.

Gupta, S. P. 2002. *Report of the Special Group on Targeting Ten Million Employment Opportunities per Year over the 10th Plan Period*. New Delhi: Planning Commission.

Hanagan, Michael. 1997a. "Citizenship, Claim-Making, and the Right to Work: Britain, 1884–1911." *Theory and Society: Special Issue on Recasting Citizenship* 26:449–74.

———. 1997b. "Recasting Citizenship: Introduction." *Theory and Society* 26.

Haney, Lynne. 1996. "Homeboys, Babies, and Men in Suits: The State and the Reproduction of Male Dominance." *American Sociological Review* 61:759–78.

Harikrishnan, V., M. Viruthagiri, and P. Jeyasngan. 1997. *Report of Welfare Boards in Kerala, Maharashtra and West Bengal (May 14–27, 2997)*. Tamil Nadu Government: Ministry of Labour and Employment.

Harriss, John. 2000. "Populism, Tamil Style: Is It Really a Success?" *Review of Development and Change* 5.

Hart, Keith. 1973. "Informal Income Opportunities and Urban Employment in Ghana." *Journal of Modern African Studies* 11:61–89.

Harvey, David. 1990. *The Condition of Post-Modernity*. Cambridge: Blackwell.

Hasenfeld, Yeheskel, Jane A. Rafferty, and Mayer N. Zald. 1987. "The Welfare State, Citizenship, and Bureacratic Encounters." *Annual Review of Sociology* 13:387–415.

Held, David, Anthony McGrew, David Goldblatt, and Jonathan Perraton. 1999. *Global Transformations: Politics, Economics and Culture*. Stanford: Stanford University Press.

Heller, Patrick. 1999. *The Labor of Development: Workers and the Transformation of Capitalism in Kerala, India*. Ithaca: Cornell University Press.

Herring, Ronald J. 1989. "Dilemmas of Agrarian Communism: Peasant Differentiation, Sectoral and Village Politics." *Third World Quarterly* 11:89–116.

Herring, Ron J., and Rina Agarwala. 2006. "Introduction: Restoring Agency to Class: Puzzles from the Subcontinent." *Critical Asian Studies* 38:323–57.

Herring, Ron J., and Rex M. Edwards. 1983. "Guaranteeing Employment to the Rural Poor: Social Functions and Class Interests in the Employment Guarantee Scheme in Western India." *World Development* 11:575–92.

Herring, Ronald, and Henry C. Hart. 1977. "Political Conditions of Land Reform: Kerala and Maharashtra." In *Land Tenure and Peasant in South Asia*, edited by Robert E. Frykenberg. New Delhi: Orient Longman.

Hirway, Indira. 2002. "Employment and Unemployment Situation in the 1990s: How Good Are the NSS Data?" *Economic and Political Weekly*:2027–36.

Horowitz, Donald L. 1991. *A Democratic South Africa: Constitutional Engineering in a Divided Society*. Berkeley: University of California Press.

Hussmanns, Ralf. 2002. "A Labour Force Survey Module on Informal Employment: A Tool for Enhancing the International Comparability of Data." Paper presented at the Sixth Meeting of the Expert Group on Informal Sector Statistics (Delhi Group), Rio de Janeiro.

Hyman, Richard. 1992. "Trade Unions and the Disaggregation for the Working Class." In *The Future of Labour Movements*, edited by M. Regini. Newbury Park: Sage.

International Labour Organization. 1993. "Report of the 15th International Conference of Labour Statisticians." *15th International Conference of Labour Statisticians*. Geneva.

———. 1999. *Report of the Director General: Decent Work*. Geneva: ILO.

———. 2008. *World of Work 2008: Income Inequalities in the Age of Financial Globalization*. Geneva: International Institute for Labour Studies and Academic Foundation.

Ionescu, Ghita, and Ernest Gellner (Eds.). 1969. *Populism: Its Meanings and National Characteristics*. London: Weidenfeld and Nicolson.

Isaac, T. M. Thomas, Richard W. Franke, and Pyaralal Raghavan. 1998. *Democracy at Work in an Indian Industrial Cooperative*. Ithaca: Cornell University Press.

Jaffrelot, Christopher. 2003. *India's Silent Revolution: The Rise of the Lower Castes in North India*. London: Hurst & Co.

Joshi, Vasudha. 2000. "Informal Sector: A Review." *Labour and Development* 6.

Katznelson, Ira, and Aristide R. Zolberg (Eds.). 1986. *Working-Class Formation: Nineteenth-Century Patterns in Western Europe and the United States*. Princeton: Princeton University Press.

Kaufman, Robert R., and Barbara Stallings. 1991. "The Political Economy of Latin American Populism." In *The Macroeconomics of Populism in Latin America*, edited by Rudiger Dornbusch and Sebastian Edwards. Chicago: University of Chicago Press.

Kitschelt, Herbert, and Steven Wilkinson. 2007a. "Citizen-Political Linkages: An Introduction." In *Patrons, Clients, and Policies: Patterns of Democratic*

Accountability and Political Competition, edited by Herbert Kitschelt and Steven Wilkinson (pp. 1–49). New York: Cambridge University Press.

———(Eds.). 2007b. *Patrons, Clients, and Policies: Patterns of Democratic Accountability and Political Competition*. New York: Cambridge University Press.

Koba, Mark. 2009. "Freelance Nation: Slump Spurs Growth of Contract Workers." *CNBConline*.

Kohli, Atul. 1987. *The State and Poverty in India: The Politics of Reform*. Cambridge: Cambridge University Press.

———. 1990a. *Democracy and Discontent: India's Growing Crisis of Governability*. Cambridge: Cambridge University Press.

———. 1990b. "From Elite Activism to Democratic Consolidation: The Rise of Reform Communism in West Bengal." In *Dominance and State Power in Modern India: Decline of a Social Order*, edited by Francine Frankel and M. S. A. Rao. Delhi: Oxford University Press.

Koppikar, Smruti. 2001. "United Colours of Politics: Left Finally Met Right and Held and All Party Bandh in Mumbai." *Indian Express*. Mumbai.

Kothari, Rajni. 1989. *Politics and the People: In Search of a Humane India, Vol II*. New York: New Horizons Press.

Kulshreshtha, A. C., and Gulab Singh. 1999. "Gross Domestic Product and Employment in the Informal Sector of the Indian Economy." *Indian Journal of Labour Economics* 42.

Kundu, Amitabh, and Alakh N. Sharma (Eds.). 2001. *Informal Sector in India: Perspectives and Policies*. New Delhi: Institute for Human Development and Institute of Applied Manpower Research.

Lee, Ching Kwan. 1999. "From Organized Dependence to Disorganized Despotism: Changing Labour Regimes in Chinese Factories." *China Quarterly*:44–71.

Lele, Jayant. 1990. "Caste, Class and Dominance: Political Mobilization in Maharashtra." In *Dominance and State Power in Modern India: Decline of a Social Order*, edited by Francine Frankel and M. S. A. Rao. Delhi: Oxford University Press.

Lenin, V. I. 1939. *Imperialism, the Highest Stage of Capitalism*. New York: International Publishers.

Lewis, W. A. 1954. "Economic Development with Unlimited Supplies of Labour." *The Manchester School* 22: 139–91

Luxemburg, Rosa. 1951. *The Accumulation of Capital*. London: Routledge and Kegan Paul Ltd.

Macharia, Kinuthia. 1997. *Social and Political Dynamics of the Informal Economy in African Cities: Nairobi and Harare*. Oxford: Oxford University Press.

Mahadevia, Darshini. 1998. "Informalisation of Employment and Incidence of Poverty in Ahmedabad." *Indian Journal of Labour Economics* 41.

Maharashtra Government. 1993. *Industrial Policy of Maharashtra*. Mumbai.

———. 1995. *Industry, Trade and Commerce Policy*. Mumbai.

———. 2001. *Industrial Policy of Maharashtra 2001*. Mumbai.

———. 2002–03. *Economic Survey of Maharashtra*. Directorate of Economics and Statistics Planning Department. Mumbai.

———. 2007. *Maharashtra State Budget: 2006–07*. Mumbai.

————. 2008. *The Beedi and Cigar Workers (Conditions of Employment) Act Report, 2008*. Commissioner of Labour Labour Department, Rural Desk. Mumbai.

Maharashtra Government, and UNDP. 2002. *Human Development Report of Maharashtra*. Planning Commission. Mumbai: Government Central Press.

Majumdar, Sourav. 1998. "Speeding Up Industrialisation Is Top Priority." *Business Standard*. Kolkata.

Mallick, Ross. 1993. *Development Policy of a Communist Government: West Bengal Since 1977*. Cambridge: Cambridge University Press.

————. 1998. *Development, Ethnicity, and Human Rights in South Asia*. New Delhi: Sage.

Manchanda, Rita. 1993. "Building the Builder's Movement." *Telegraph*, p. H51. Calcutta.

Mandelbaum, D. G. 1970. *Society in India: Change and Continuity*. Berkeley: University of California Press.

Marshall, T. H. 1964. *Class, Citizenship, and Social Development: Essays*. Garden City, NY: Doubleday.

Mazumdar, Dipak. 1976. "The Urban Informal Sector." *World Development* 4,:655–79.

Menon, Parvathi, and Kalyan Chaudhuri. 2001. "Of Continuity and Change: Interview with Buddhadeb Bhattacharjee." *Frontline*:11–13.

MIDS. 1988. *Tamil Nadu Economy, Performance and Issues*. New Delhi: Oxford.

"Militancy Mellowed Down." (2000). *Business Standard*. Kolkata.

Milkman, Ruth. 2006. *L.A. Story: Immigrant Workers and the Future of the U.S. Labor Movement*. New York: Russell Sage Foundation.

Mishra, Ambarish. 2001. "Shiv Sena Woos Working Class." *Times of India*. Mumbai.

Mody, Sujata. 1997. "Tamil Nadu: A Voice and Visibility." *Labour File A3*. Tamil Nadu Government.

Monteiro, Vivek. 2003. "Mumbai's Labor Pains." *Times of India*. Mumbai.

Moody, Kim. 1997. *Workers in a Lean World: Unions in the International Economy*. London: Verso.

Moser, Caroline. 1978. "Informal Sector or Petty Commodity Production: Dualism or Dependence in Urban Development?" *World Development* 6:1041–64.

Mukerjee, Shikha. 1997. "W. Bengal: The Pink Revolution is 20 Years Old." *Times of India*. Mumbai.

Nagaraja, Bhargavi. 1995. "A Long Haul Ahead." *Deccan Herald*, p. D4. Bangalore.

Namboodiri, Udayan. 1998. "War for the Villages." *India Today*, p. 48.

"Nano Wars: Tata Threatens to Make the World's Cheapest Car Somewhere Else." 2008. *The Economist*, p. 63.

NCL. 1969. *Report of the National Commision on Labour (NCL) Employment and Rehabilitation*. Delhi: Ministry of Labour.

————. 2002. *Report of the Second National Commission on Labour*. New Delhi: Ministry of Labour.

NICMAR. 1998. *India Construction Statistics: A Comprehensive Data Book on the Construction Industry and Infrastructre Development Sector in India.* Mumbai: Publication Bureau, National Institute of Construction Management and Research.

NSSO. 2001a. "Employment and Unemployment Situation in India, 1999–2000." Calcutta: National Sample Survey Organisation (NSSO).

———. 2001b. "Informal Sector in India: Salient Features (1999–2000)." Calcutta: National Sample Survey Organisation (NSSO).

Oberai, A.S., and G.K. Chadha (Eds.). 2001. *Job Creation in Urban Informal Sector in India: Issues and Policy Options.* New Delhi: International Labour Organisation.

Padmanabhan, Anil. 1995. "Labouring for a Common Cause." *Business Standard*, p. B5. Calcutta.

Palshikar, Suhas. 1996a. "Maharashtra: A Triangular Contest?" *Frontline.*

———. 1996b. "Pointers to Political Change." *Frontline.*

Palshikar, Suhas, and Rajeshwar Deshpande. 1999. "Electoral Competition and Structures of Domination in Maharashtra." *Economic and Political Weekly* 34.

Palshikar, Suhas, Yogendra Yadav, and Abhay Datar. 2004. "The NCP Emerges in Its Own Right." *The Hindu.* Chennai.

Pandhe, Anil. 2002. "Mass Housing Scheme for Bidi Workers: The Sholapur Experience – The First of Its Kind in Asia." Maharashtra: Maharashtra Economic Development Corporation.

Pandian, MSS. 1991. *The Image Trap: M.G. Ramachandran in Film and Politics.* New Delhi: Sage.

Park, Richard L. 1949. "Labor and Politics in India." *Far Eastern Survey* 18:181–87.

Peattie, Lisa R. 1987. "An Idea in Good Currency and How It Grew: The Informal Sector." *World Development* 15:851–58.

Pederson, Jorgen Dige. 2001. "India's Industrial Dilemmas in West Bengal." *Asian Survey* 41:646–68.

Pereira, Luiz Carlos Bresser, Jose Maria Maravall, and Adam Przeworski. 1993. *Economic Reforms in New Democracies: A Social–Democratic Approach.* Cambridge: Cambridge University Press.

Piven, Frances Fox, and Richard A. Cloward. 1979. *Poor People's Movements: Why They Succeed, How They Fail.* New York: Vintage Books.

Portes, A. 1994. "The Informal Economy and Its Paradoxes." In *Handbook of Economic Sociology*, edited by N. J. Smelser and R. Swedberg (pp. 426–49). Princeton University Press.

Portes, Alejandro, Manuel Castells, and Lauren A. Benton. 1989. *The Informal Economy: Studies in Advanced and Less Developed Countries.* Baltimore: The Johns Hopkins University Press.

Portes, Alejandro, and Kelly Hoffman. 2002. "Latin American Class Structures: Their Compostiion and Change during the Neoliberal Era." Presented at the Annual Meeting of the American Sociological Association. Chicago.

Portes, Alejandro, and Richard Schauffler. 1993. "Competing Perspectives on the Latin American Informal Sector." *Population and Development Review* 19:33–60.

Portes, Alejandro, and John Walton. 1981. *Labor, Class and the International System*. New York: Academic Press.

Prasad, G. Koteshwar, and CSDS Team. 2004. "Alliance Effect, Swing Factor Propelled DPA Victory." *The Hindu*, p. AE-3.

Przeworski, Adam. 1991. *Democracy and the Market: Political and Economic Reforms in Latin America and Eastern Europe*. New York: Cambridge University Press.

Przeworski, Adam, and Michael Wallerstein. 1982. "The Structure of Class Conflict in Democratic Capitalist Societies." *American Political Science Review* 76:215–38.

Ramaswamy, E. A. 1988. *Worker Consciousness and Trade Union Response*. New Delhi: Oxford University Press.

Range, Jackie. 2008. "India's Poor Get Health Care in a Card." *Wall Street Journal*.

Ray, Raka. 2000. *Fields of Protest*. New Delhi: Kali for Women.

Rehman, M. M. 2007. "Operation of Welfare Fund for Beedi Workers in Madhya Pradesh Profile, Problems and Prospect." *NLI Research Studies Series*. Delhi: V.V. Giri National Labor Institute.

Roberts, Kenneth. 1995. "Neoliberalism and the Transformation of Populism in Latin America: The Peruvian Case." *World Politics* 48:82–116.

Rose, Kalima. 1993. *Where Women Are Leaders: The SEWA Movement in India*. London: Zed Books.

Rostow, W.W. 1960. *The Stages of Economic Growth: A Non-Communist Manifesto*. Cambridge: Cambridge University Press.

Rudolph, Lloyd I. 1961. "Urban Life and Populist Radicalism: Dravidian Politics in Madras." *Journal of Asian Studies* 20:283–97.

Rudolph, Lloyd I., and Susanne Hoeber Rudolph. 1987. *In Pursuit of Lakshmi: The Political Economy of the Indian State*. Chicago: University of Chicago Press.

Rudra, Ashok. 1981. "One Step Forward, Two Steps Backward." *Economic and Political Weekly* 15:A61–A68.

Sabel, Charles F., and David Stark. 1982. "Planning, Politics, and Shop-Floor Power: Hidden Forms of Bargaining in Soviet-Imposed State-Socialist Societies." *Politics & Society* 11:397–438.

Samant, S.R. 1998. *Employer's Guide to Labour Laws*. Mumbai: Labour Law Agency.

Sanyal, Bishwapriya. 1991. "Organizing the Self-employed: The Politics of the Urban Informal Sector." *International Labour Review* 130:39–56.

Sassen, Saskia. 1994. "The Informal Economy: Between New Developments and Old Regulations." *Yale Law Journal* 103: 2289–2304.

Satpathy, Anoop. 2004. "Size, Composition and Charaterisitcs of Informal Sector in India." *National Labor Institute Research Studies Series*. New Delhi: V.V. Giri National Labour Institute.

Seidman, Gay W. 1994. *Manufacturing Militance: Workers' Movements in Brazil and South Africa, 1970–1985*. Berkeley: University of California Press.

Sen Gupta, Prasanta. 1989. "Politics in West Bengal: The Left Front versus the Congress (I)." *Asian Survey* 29:883–97.

————. 1997. "The 1995 Municipal Election in West Bengal: The Left Front Is Down." *Asian Survey* 37:905–17.

Sethuraman. 1976. "The Urban Informal Sector: Concepts, Measurement and Policy." *International Labor Review* 114:69–81.

Sharma, Alakh N., and Piush Antony. 2001. *Women Workers in the Unorganised Sector: The More the Merrier?* New Delhi: Institute for Human Development.

Sharma, Kalpana. 2000. *Rediscovering Dharavi.* New Delhi: Penguin Publishers.

Shastri, Padma. 1996. "Bengal Bidi Rollers Working for a Pittance, Says Study." *Pioneer.* Delhi.

Silver, Beverly J. 2003. *Forces of Labor: Workers' Movements and Globalization since 1870.* Cambridge: Cambridge University Press.

Singh, Anil. 2004. "Sholapur Housing Project Was a Big Challenge." *Times News Network*, p. 9. Mumbai

Special Correspondent. 1999. "Beedi Workers Welfare Panel to Be Reconstituted Soon." *The Hindu.* Madras.

————. 2000. "Sops for Unorganised Sector Workers: Chief Minister Launches Welfare Boards." *The Hindu.* Madras.

————. 2000b. "State Announces Task Force for Its 'Vision 2005.'" *Asian Age.* Mumbai.

————. 2001a. "Construction Workers Demand Implementation of Welfare Measures." *The Hindu*, p. H51. Madras.

————. 2001b. "State Amends Labor Laws." *Business Standard.* Calcutta.

————. 2001c. "Welfare Boards for Unorganised Workers: ID Cards Issued." *The Hindu.* Madras.

————. 2002a. "Activate Boards for Unorganised Labour." *The Hindu*, p. H50. Madras.

————. 2002b. "DMK Decision Overturned: All Boards for Unorganised Labour to Be Merged." *The Hindu*, p. H50. Madras.

————. 2002c. "In the Fast Lane: Special Feature on Maharashtra." *Frontline.*

————. 2002d. "MPCC Report Crticises Vilasrao Government." *Times of India.* Mumbai.

————. 2002e. "Unorganised Workers' March Reaches Chennai." *The Hindu*, p. H50. Madras.

————. 2008. "A Smart Approach to Public Health." *The Hindu.* Chennai.

Sreenivas, Janyala. 1998. "Death Merely Added Salt to Their Injuries." *Indian Express.* Bombay.

Staff Reporter. 1994. "Representation for Workers in New Board Sought." *The Hindu*, p. H51. Madras.

————. 1995. "Construction Workers Demand Central Act." *The Hindu*, p. H51. Madras.

————. 1996. "Mandatory Registration of Construction Workers Sought." *The Hindu*, p. H51. Madras.

————. 1998. "Stand off Between Beedi Barons and Workers Ends." *Times of India.* Mumbai.

————. 1999. "A Better Deal for Construction Workers." *The Hindu*, p. H51. Madras.

————. 2001. "Government Should Contribute to Welfare Board." *The Hindu*, p. H50. Madras.

Stark, David, and László Bruszt. 1998. *Postsocialist Pathways: Transforming Politics and Property in East Central Europe*. Cambridge: Cambridge University Press.

Subramanian, Narendra. 1999. *Ethnicity and Populist Mobilization: Political Parties, Citizens, and Democracy in South India*. Delhi: Oxford University Press.

Subramanian, V.K. 1995. "Changing Role of Trade Unions." *The Hindu*, p. H23. Madras.

Sundaram, K. 2001. "The Employment–Unemployment Situation in India in the 1990s: Some Results from the NSS 55th Round Survey (July 99-June 2000)." *Economic and Political Weekly* 34:931–40.

Swami, Praveen. 2002. "A Saffron Triumph." *Frontline*.

Swamy, A. R. 1996a. *The Nation, the People and the Poor: Sandwich Tactics in Party Competition and Policy Formation, India, 1931–1996*. Berkeley: University of California, Berkeley.

————. 1996b. "Sense, Sentiment and Populist Coalitions: The Strange Career of Cultural Nationalism in Tamil Nadu." In *Subnational Movements in South Asia*, edited by S. K. Mitra and R. A. Lewis. Boulder: Westview.

Swenson, Peter A. 2002. *Capitalists against Markets: The Making of Labor Markets and Welfare States in the United States and Sweden*. Oxford: Oxford University Press.

Tamil Nadu Government. 1975. *Report of the Committee to Go into the Living Conditions of Workers in Beedi and Other Unorganised Industries in Tamil Nadu*. Chennai: Office of the Commissioner of Labour.

————. 1998. *Report of the Committees Constituted to Study the Problems and Issues of Unorganised Labour in Tamil Nadu*. Chennai: Office of the Commissioner of Labour.

————. 2000–01. *Government Order, Ms. Nos. 114–116 and 166–167*. Chennai: Department of Labour and Employment.

————. 2003a. *Government Order (2D) No. 23*. Chennai: Department of Labour and Employment.

————. 2003b. *Government Order (2D) No. 37*. Chennai: Department of Labour and Employment.

————. 2004a. *Government Order (2D) No. 75: Integrated Housing Scheme for Bidi Workers*. Chennai: Department of Labour and Employment.

————. 2004b. *Government Order MS 192*. Chennai: Department of Labour and Employment.

————. 2005. *Government Order (D) No. 486: Unorganised Workers-Construction Workers Registered with Tamil Nadu Construction Workers Welfare Board-Pension Scheme*. Chennai: Department of Labour and Employment.

————. 2006a. *Labour and Employment Department Policy Note 2005–06*. Chennai: Department of Labour and Employment.

————. 2006b. *Tamil Nadu Government Orders No. 90, 91, 93 (September 1, 2006)*. Chennai: Department of Labour and Employment.

———. 2007a. *Tamil Nadu Government Order No. 25 (February 8, 2007)*. Chennai: Department of Labour and Employment.

———. 2007b. *Tamil Nadu Government Order No. 200, October 8, 2007*. Chennai: Department of Labour and Employment.

———. 2007c. *Tamil Nadu Government Order No. 492 (June 28, 2007)*. Chennai: Department of Labour and Employment.

———. 2007d. *Tamil Nadu Government Order No. 519 (July 9, 2007)*. Chennai: Department of Labour and Employment.

———. 2008a. *Monitoring Reports on Tamil Nadu Construction Workers Welfare Board*. Chennai: Tamil Nadu Construction Workers Welfare Board.

———. 2008b. *Welfare Boards for Unorganised Workers*. Chennai: Tamil Nadu Construction Workers Welfare Board and Department of Labour and Employment. Chennai.

Tarrow, Sidney. 1988. "National Politics and Collective Action: Recent Theory and Research in Western Europe and the United States." *American Sociological Review* 14:421–40.

Teeple, Gary. 2000. *Globalization and the Decline of Social Reform*. Aurora: Garamond Press.

Teitelbaum, Emmanuel. 2011. *Mobilizing Restraint: Democracy and Industrial Conflict in Post-Reform South Asia*. Ithaca, NY: Cornell University Press.

Tilly, Charles. 1984. "Social Movements and National Politics." In *Statemaking and Social Movements: Essays in History and Theory*, edited by Charles Bright and Susan Harding (pp. 297–317). Ann Arbor: University Michigan Press.

———. 1995. "Globalisation Threatens Labor's Rights." *International Labor and Working-Class History* 47:1–23.

———. 1997. "A Primer on Citizenship." *Theory and Society, Special Issue on Recasting Citizenship* 26:599–602.

Timberg, Thomas A. 1978. *The Marwaris: From Traders to Industrialists*. New Delhi: Vikas.

Times News Network. 2001. The Bandh Wagon." *Times of India*. Mumbai

———. 2002a. "Give Licenses to Hawkers, Suggests Labor Panel." *Times of India*. Mumbai.

———. 2002b. "People's Power Fuels Panel's Plans." *Times of India*. Mumbai.

———. 2003. "Bai-watch: Domestics to Get State Help." *Times of India*. Mumbai.

Uchikawa, Shuji (Ed.). 2002. *Labour Market and Institution in India: 1990s and Beyond*. Chiba: Institute of Developing Economies, Japan External Trade Organization.

UNESCO. 2000. *World Education Report*. Quebec: UNESCO.

UNIDO. 1968. "Standard of Industrial Classification of All Economic Activities (ISIC)." *Statistical Papers*, Series M, No. 4, rev. 2. New York: UNIDO.

Unni, Jeemol. 1999. *Urban Informal Sector: Size and Income Generation Processes in Gujarat*. Ahmedabad: Gujarat Institute of Development Research & Self-Employed Women's Association.

Unni, Jeemol, and Uma Rani. 2000. "Employment and Income in the Informal Sector: Case of a City Economy in Gujarat." *National Seminar on Employment Generation in India*. Gandhinagar, Gujarat, India.

Vaid, K. N. 1997. *Contract Labor in the Construction Industry.* Mumbai: Publication Bureau, National Institute of Construction Management and Research.

———. (Ed.). 1999. *Women in Construction.* Mumbai: NICMAR Publications Bureau.

Venkatesan, Radha. 2003. "Taking the Plunge." *The Hindu*, p. S15. Madras.

Vilas, Carlos. 1992. "Latin American Populism: A Structural Approach." *Science and Society* 56.

Vora, Rajendra. 1996. "Shift of Power from Rural to Urban Sector." *Economic and Political Weekly*: 95–104.

Voss, Kim. 1993. *The Making of American Exceptionalism: The Knights of Labor and Class Formation in the Nineteenth Century.* Ithaca: Cornell University Press.

Washbrook, David. 1989. "Caste, Class, and Dominance in Modern Tamil Nadu: Non-Brahmanism, Dravidianism and Tamil Nationalism." In *Dominance and State Power in Modern India, V. 1*, edited by Francine Frankel and M. S. A. Rao. Delhi: Oxford University Press.

Weeks, John. 1975. "Policies for Expanding Employment in the Informal Sector of Developing Countries." *International Labour Review* 111:1–13.

Weiner, Myron. 1959. "Changing Patterns of Political Leadership in West Bengal." *Pacific Affairs* 32:277–87.

West Bengal Government. 1978. *Statement on Industrial Policy.* Kolkata.

———. 1994. *Policy Statement on Industrial Development.* Kolkata.

———. 2001. *State Assisted Scheme of Provident Fund for Unorganised Workers in West Bengal.* Kolkata: Labour Department: Basumati Corporation Ltd.

———. 2004. *West Bengal Human Development Report.* Kolkata: Development and Planning Department.

———. 2007. *Labour in West Bengal.* Kolkata: Department of Labour.

———. 2009a. *Progress Report under Building and Other Construction Workers' Act.* Kolkata: Department of Labour.

———. 2009b. *Report on Electrification of Houses under West Bengal Beedi Workers' Welfare Scheme.* Kolkata: Department of Labour.

———. 2009c. *Statement Showing the Status of Allotment of Fund and Sub-Allotment thereof for Construction of Houses for Beedi Workers under West Bengal Beedi Workers' Welfare Scheme.* Kolkata: Department of Labour.

Western, Bruce. 1995. "A Comparative Study of Working-Class Disorganization: Union Decline in Eighteen Advanced Capitalist Countries." *American Sociological Review* 60:179–201.

Wiles, Peter. 1969. "A Syndrome, Not a Doctrine: Some Elementary Theses on Populism." In *Populism: Its Meanings and National Characteristics*, edited by Ghita Ionescu and Ernest Gellner. London: Weidenfeld and Nicolson.

Wilkinson, Steven. 2004. *Votes and Violence: Electoral Competition and Ethnic Riots in India.* Cambridge: Cambridge University Press.

World Bank. 1995. *World Development Report 1995: Workers in an Integrating World.* New York: Oxford University Press.

———. 1997. *World Development Report 1997: The State in a Changing World.* New York: Oxford University Press.

———. 2003. *World Development Report 2004: Making Services Work for Poor People*. New York: Oxford University Press.

Worsley, Peter. 2001. "Populism." In *The Oxford Companion to the Politics of the World*, edited by Joel Krieger. Oxford: Oxford University Press.

Wright, Erik Olin. 1997. *Class Counts: Comparative Studies in Class Analysis*. Cambridge: Cambridge University Press.

Wyatt, Andrew. 2008. *Party System Change in South India: Political Entrepreneurs, Patterns and Processes*. London: Routledge.

Yadav, Yogendra. 2004. "Left is Right in West Bengal Once Again." *The Hindu*. Kolkata.

Yashar, Deborah J. 2005. *Contesting Citizenship in Latin America: The Rise of Indigenous Movements and the Postliberal Challenge*. Cambridge: Cambridge University Press.

Zolberg, Aristide R. 1995. "Working-Class Dissolution." *International Labor and Working-Class History*:28–38.

Index